The Empty Church

THE EMPTY CHURCH

CHURCH

Theater, Theology, and
Bodily Hope

SHANNON CRAIGO-SNELL

OXFORD
UNIVERSITY PRESS

OXFORD
UNIVERSITY PRESS

Oxford University Press is a department of the
University of Oxford. It furthers the University's objective
of excellence in research, scholarship, and education
by publishing worldwide.

Oxford   New York
Auckland   Cape Town   Dar es Salaam   Hong Kong   Karachi
Kuala Lumpur   Madrid   Melbourne   Mexico City   Nairobi
New Delhi   Shanghai   Taipei Toronto

With offices in
Argentina   Austria   Brazil   Chile   Czech Republic   France   Greece
Guatemala   Hungary   Italy   Japan   Poland   Portugal   Singapore
South Korea   Switzerland   Thailand   Turkey   Ukraine   Vietnam

Oxford is a registered trade mark of Oxford University Press
in the UK and certain other countries.

Published in the United States of America by
Oxford University Press
198 Madison Avenue, New York, NY 10016

Library of Congress Cataloging-in-Publication Data
Craigo-Snell, Shannon Nichole.
The empty church: theater, theology, and bodily hope / Shannon Craigo-Snell.
pages cm
ISBN 978-0-19-982792-3 (hardback) 978-0-19-063009-6 (paperback)
ISBN 978-0-19-982793-0 (ebook) ISBN 978-0-19-937368-0 (online content)
1. Liturgics.   2. Public worship.   3. Theater—Religious aspects—Christianity.
4. Performing arts—Religious aspects—Christianity.   I. Title.
BV178.C73   2014
261.5'7—dc23   2013043937

For Marilyn

Contents

Acknowledgments

TO ELLEN O'BRIEN, Jack Zerbe, Mark Hopkins, Steve Terrill, Anne Ebersman, Jason Jacobs, Todd Shilhanek, and Cheryl Jividen Barnett, thank you for teaching me about theater.

Thanks to Nick Wolterstorff for encouraging this project in its early stages and to David Kelsey for a book inscription that kept my courage up at the end.

Many colleagues at Yale University and Louisville Presbyterian Theological Seminary have supported this project in various ways for which I am grateful, including: Skip Stout, Siobhán Garrigan, Serene Jones, Emilie Townes, Kristen Leslie, Jan Holton, Dale Martin, Diana Swancutt, Ed Waggoner, David Hester, Amy Plantinga Pauw, Lewis Brogdon, Cláudio Carvalhaes, Sue Garrett, Brandon McCormack, Kathryn Johnson, and Scott Williamson.

The community of Ludger Viefhues-Bailey and Steve Davis has been one of the greatest blessings of my life, without which this book would never have been written.

Marilyn McCord Adams patiently read drafts of every chapter and impatiently demanded that I write more. Although I doubt he knows it, Bob Adams made participating in Presbyterian worship, and the Reformed tradition generally, possible again. There are always enough points and cookies.

Students at both Yale and Louisville Seminary have contributed a great deal to this work and given me more joy than I can tell on these pages. Thanks especially to Deb Trevino, whose comment on another matter sparked chapter 4, and to Traci Simmons.

The Constructive Theology Workgroup was a vital part of the community in which this text was written. Thanks to the group as a whole and especially to Paul Lakeland, John Thiel, Laurel Schneider, Don Schweitzer, Peter Heltzel, Shelly Rambo and Susan Abraham and Jim Perkinson.

Thanks also to colleagues J. Kameron Carter, Willie James Jennings, Amy Laura Hall, Joshua Edelman, Blake Beattie, Aimee Light, and Madhuri Yadlapati. And thanks to the late John Jones, whom I dearly miss.

I have presented some of the ideas in this text in various settings and am grateful for the conversation and community this has fostered. In particular, I note the Institute of Theology, Imagination, and the Arts. The 2012 conference "Theatrical Theology" gathered many of my favorite scholars, and I thank Trevor Hart and Wes Vander Lugt for the opportunity to join them. Thanks also to the International Society for Religion, Literature, and Culture; the Karl Rahner Society; and the Prolix pastors group. I have learned from conversation with each of these communities.

First Presbyterian Church of New Haven deserves special mention, as the insightful questions of the adult education class vastly improved this manuscript. Thanks also to Crescent Hill Presbyterian Church in Louisville. At least a chapter of this text was drafted in the margins of church bulletins.

Kalbyrn McLean's editorial eye improved the manuscript considerably. Ann Phelps and Rachel Heath were fabulous research assistants and conversation partners. Tom Zoellner untangled several linguistic knots. Amanda Hayes and Elana Levy are women of valor; let their works bring them praise at the city gates.

I cannot express my gratitude for the community of women that sustains me and gives me hope on a daily basis: Shawnthea Monroe, Leslie Callahan, Susannah Mozley, Edita Tamulionyte, Jen Ho, Cyndi Hess, Jill Bracksieck, Camille Lizarribar, Anna Parr, Karen Seto, and Terri Boustead.

I thank the people at Oxford University Press who brought this project to completion. Cynthia Read, editor extraordinaire, knows both theater and theology well. She understood what I was up to and offered expertise, patience, and humor. Stuart Roberts, Gwen Colvin, Charlotte Steinhardt, and Alyssa Bender were skillful and kind.

Many thanks to my extended family—Craigos, Snells, and Haslackers alike—for the numerous ways in which they supported the writing of this book. The fact that my cousin Dennis Craigo read my first book convinced me I could write this one.

I thank my children—Jacob, Elias, and Lucy—for asking "why church?" every Sunday, thereby keeping me focused on my goal. Truly, they are blessing and joy.

My gratitude to Seth Craigo-Snell simply overflows.

The Empty Church

Introduction

Why Church?

My first memory having anything to do with church is of not wanting to go. I sulked in the basement on Sunday morning when I was six, refusing the indignity of having to wear white woolly tights. Such a boring venue as church, in my young mind, was not worth this uncomfortable clothing. My parents relented, and the question "to go or not to go?" was left for me to decide. I have been pondering it for decades now.

The real question underlying this has always been: Why go to church? What happens there that merits the effort?

There are a number of easy and not-particularly theological answers to these questions. Church provides a community, a ready-made social network, and an opportunity to meet people and make friends. Church offers ethical instruction for children, a structure of meaning making for families. There is music, a calm hour in a busy week, engaging reflections from the pastor, and—on occasion—free food.

There are also a number of theological answers to these questions. One should go to church because it is part of the discipleship to which Jesus calls his followers. One must go to church to partake of the sacraments and be part of the body of Christ. The august tradition of doctrinal ecclesiology describes the church in many distinctive ways: the church is one, holy, catholic, apostolic; the people of God, a sacrament in the world, a mystical communion.

Each of these descriptions tries to answer (at least implicitly) the questions of why Christians ought to go to church, what happens there, and why church is vital to Christian identity. But I confess that none of these different answers settles the question "why church?" for me.

Church has no monopoly on social life, for one thing. The benefits of community can be found in many kinds of organizations, most of which meet at an easier time of day. And the theological answers—discipleship, sacraments, etc.—seem awfully abstract at 10 a.m. These answers have the power to make me feel guilty when I don't go to church, but not the power to get me out of bed. On Sunday mornings, I want a different kind of answer. I want an answer to the question "why church?" for my own life.

Why Theater?

One resource for grappling with this question came to me when I was studying theater at Guilford College years ago. I read classic texts in Western theater in which directors such as Peter Brook, Jerzy Grotowski, and Bertolt Brecht describe what theater is, what theater ought to be, and what role theater should play in society. Working in theater and not church, these directors had neither the resources nor the restrictions of traditional dogmatic theology to guide them. They attempted to analyze and communicate their own concrete experiences of communal and embodied meaning making. They worked to account for mystery and miracle in straightforward ways. However, at times their subject matter requires religious language. In describing theater, some directors end up relying on language from church, using terms such as inspiration, incarnation, and even crucifixion.

This is quite evocative. If church language is useful in describing how theater works, perhaps theatrical language could be useful in describing how church works. Perhaps it might be worthwhile to step away from traditional language regarding the doctrine of ecclesiology, just temporarily, and take up a different lens and lexicon. If there are similarities between church and theater, then perhaps the descriptions of how theater works could be useful in understanding how church works.

Why Performance?

Many Christians perceive links between church and theater. In any adult Sunday school class, there is bound to be at least one former actor or one avid theatergoer, eager to explain connections between church and theater. People offer thoughtful metaphors about life as theater, faith as drama, God as director, Jesus as actor, acting as spiritual journey, and so forth. Countless theologians also have touched upon the subject, employing analogies between theater and Christianity in ways that are complex, subtle, and wonderfully illuminating.

As often as analogies between theater and Christianity are employed, there are also connections that are not thoroughly articulated. Some overlaps between the two fields have been simultaneously obvious and overlooked. For example, in a 1955 Harvard lecture called "How to Do Things with Words," J. L. Austin argued that when people say specific things in the right times and places, the uttering of those words *does* something. Austin's example is a marriage vow. In the context of a marriage ceremony, saying "I do" performs the act of getting married.[1] To say can be to do. Austin's work has been widely read and used by theologians.

Austin's thesis is remarkably similar to a common theatrical practice, in which actors note what action each line in a play is to perform. They answer the question, "what will saying this line do?" Actors have been identifying such performative actions since Constantin Stanislavski developed his System for acting, long before Austin delivered his lecture. Both Austin and Stanislavski were writing about how words do things, but their separate works were read by different audiences. Theologians, theorists, and philosophers read Austin. Actors and directors read Stanislavski.

I needed conversation partners who had read them both. I found these conversation partners in the emerging field of performance studies, and with them I found the theoretical approach that could help me bring theologians and directors into dialogue.

Answering Questions

This book is my long-delayed answer to the question "why church?" In the following pages, I offer my own understanding of what happens at church and why church is vital to Christian identity. To formulate these answers, I bring together a unique and eclectic set of conversation partners. I do not engage the abundant theological texts on the doctrine of ecclesiology. Instead, I bring together authors from Christian traditions, performance theory, and theater.

From this perspective, I see church not as a building, nor an institution, nor a group of people, but rather as a performance. Specifically, I view church as a disciplined performance of relationship with God in Jesus Christ, mediated by Scripture, in hope of the Holy Spirit. This leads me to see church as something that happens throughout the lives of Christian communities. This does not negate the importance of Sunday morning worship. Such worship is the central performance that trains and rehearses us for the rest of our lives. I argue that Christian worship shapes us—intellectually, emotionally, physically, and volitionally—into fit players in the ongoing drama of God's salvation. Church forms us around the story of Jesus Christ, preparing us not just to hear the story or to tell it, but to perform it in lives filled with faith, hope, and love.

Coming Chapters

Building upon the strand of theological tradition that connects theater and church, I draw together theater studies, performance studies, and theology in order to construct an ecclesiology that attends to the performative qualities of Christian life. From the theoretical resources of theater studies and performance studies, I argue for particularly performative views of epistemology, theological anthropology, and biblical hermeneutics. In each of the middle four chapters of the book, I bring a Christian theologian and a theater director into conversation. These chapters have both descriptive and prescriptive force, analyzing how church functions and how it might—given a fuller understanding of its performative nature—function better.

On one level, these chapters follow a pattern that begins with how Christian worship shapes persons in relationship with biblical narratives, moves to explore how church both reinforces social hierarchies and has countercultural resources, argues for the importance of interrupting the familiarity and repetition upon which both church and theater rely, and calls for a performative emptiness that hopes and expects new experiences of inspiration. On another level, given that my performative understanding of church emphasizes biblical narrative, the chapters follow a Christological pattern of incarnation, life and ministry, Cross, and empty tomb.

In chapter 1: "Setting the Stage," I introduce the concept of performance and describe its three elements of event, interaction, and doubleness. Exploring how Christians interpret Scripture in communal and embodied ways, I develop the outlines of performative anthropology, epistemology, and hermeneutics.

In chapter 2: "Training the Actors," I argue that Christian formation involves being shaped by the biblical narrative as it is interpreted communally, in ways that are profoundly embodied and performative. To develop this, I explore the use of emotion and bodily gestures in the Ignatian Exercises and the acting techniques of Constantine Stanislavski. As a director, Stanislavski trained actors to cultivate a wide array of experiences, which would be distilled over time into strong emotional memories. Through bodily disciplines, these emotions could be recalled on stage to perform a variety of theatrical roles. Stanislavski's terminology is useful in identifying the ways that the Ignatian Exercises—as well as church liturgy—cultivate a storehouse of affections grounded in the Christian narrative of redemption, affections that can be accessed through a repertoire of associated bodily gestures. While Stanislavski's exercises train the actor to play a multitude of characters, Christian worship forms the person to enact a character congruent with the Christian story.

Yet the formation of the person through social practices does not happen only in church and it is not necessarily a good thing. We are socially constructed in a sinful and broken world, shaped to continue patterns of oppression and domination. The church is not immune to any of this; indeed it is an active participant in shaping a sinful world.

In chapter 3: "Changing Roles," I turn to liberation theologian Letty Russell and director Augusto Boal to address the dangers and possibilities of being formed within the institutional church. Like theater, church has the consistent potential to become a support to the status quo. These authors highlight the ways in which church and theater can engender new perspectives and move toward justice. For Russell, struggling in solidarity with the poor creates new understandings of the love of God. For Boal, acting exercises that demand the performer to take up multiple roles create a sense of empowerment to choose and challenge the roles one plays in life. Both authors identify ways in which communal and embodied actions—when they involve work for justice and engaging multiple roles—open doors to previously inaccessible kinds of knowledge. Applying these insights to church, Christians are trained to identify with multiple characters in the drama: worshippers stand in the place of the prodigal son, the faithless disciples, the lame man who walks, and the blind man who sees. Through worship, we are trained to enact ourselves as repentant sinners, forgiven children, and cocreators with God. The story—and the performance of it in worship—demands a concrete kind of care for those who suffer, a stance of solidarity with the poor and oppressed. Thus for reasons both epistemological and theological, the content of the drama has the power to shape Christians in countercultural modes that resist oppression and domination.

Chapter 4: "Changing Scenes" continues exploring the importance of multiple roles in Christian liturgical formation, beginning with womanist theologian Delores Williams's reflections on Sarah and Hagar. Williams notes that it is easy for Christians to fall into a pattern of identifying primarily with one person in a given biblical story. She challenges this by demonstrating the powerful shifts of perspective that can happen when a story is seen through the eyes of a different character. She thus frames her theological reading of the crucifixion by identifying with Hagar, rather than Sarah, in the story of Ishmael and Isaac. This prompts Williams to note the implicit endorsement of surrogacy in Christian claims that Jesus suffered and died on behalf of others. Williams traces the complex ways in which Christian views of Jesus as surrogate intertwine with cultural forces of oppression to condone social systems in which the flourishing of some is based on the suffering of others. She states boldly that the cross is in no way salvific.

I use the work of director Bertolt Brecht to interpret Williams's intervention into contemporary theology. Brecht finds easy emotional identification with characters on stage to be one way that theater promotes complacency. He uses different techniques to alienate the audience from the characters, reminding theatergoers that they are watching a play and prompting them to think critically about the performance. Similarly, Williams's prophetic voice alienates Christians from familiar readings of biblical texts and highlights how particular interpretations become culturally ingrained to the point of invisibility. Her work demonstrates the potential for seeing situations anew through biblical stories, a potential also evident in the narrative structure of parables and several New Testament stories. Drawing on Williams and Brecht, I argue that the prophetic voices of theologians and pastors are needed to critique church performances and the employment of Christian affections. Such voices enact a holy alienation and reengage the intellectual and volitional challenges of Christian faith.

The primary content of the Christian narrative, I contend, is that God is with us. This is the source of our hope. While social construction is real and sin is ubiquitous, there is more than human striving and brokenness. In chapter 5: "Striking the Set," I bring together director Peter Brook's typology of four kinds of theater with Karl Barth's early writing about religion. In a book called *The Empty Space*, Brook grapples with the question of how theater—an embodiment of tradition and repetition—can remain open to inspiration. Using incarnational language, he offers insights about how theater productions can aim for the holy, tell the truth about the rough realities of human life, and create spaces in which the invisible can become visible. Brook's language resonates with that of Barth's early writings, where he rails against human strivings toward God and demands that the church always remain an empty crater where the bomb of Jesus has detonated. Similarly struggling with the importance of tradition and the need for openness, both Brook and Barth call for disciplined engagement with tradition that cultivates ongoing emptiness. Brook's work lends restraint and practical considerations to Barth's prophetic voice, while Barth makes clear that the emptiness Brook describes is a hope for God. Writing in postwar Europe, both men appreciate what is today called social construction, yet in their separate communities they call for the enactment of hope that there is more: the active expectation of the presence of God.

Hope involves openness to what is new and what is beyond our calculation and control. Fidelity to the heart of the tradition of Christian worship—a communal performance of hope in the presence of the Spirit of God—may well require loosening our grip on particular traditions that no longer serve this end.

My conclusion is a description of church as a performance of disciplined relationship with God in Jesus, mediated through the Bible, in hope of the Spirit. This means that church happens not just in formal worship, but whenever Christians perform such relationship. While this expands church well beyond the sanctuary, it also emphasizes the importance of liturgical worship in forming Christians as characters crafted by the texts of the Bible, as these texts are interpreted in community. This formation includes shaping how Christians know themselves and the world around them in ways that involve the intellect, emotions, body, and will. Through worship, Christians develop a repertoire of whole-personed knowledge, or affections.

Both history and theology demonstrate that Christian churches often perform in ways that do serious harm in the world. Yet there are Christian traditions that can actively work against this. Liturgical worship requires Christians to imaginatively inhabit multiple roles within the biblical texts. This multiplicity disrupts simplistic identity formation and easy identification with any one character in a given circumstance. The command to act in solidarity with the poor takes this further, requiring Christians to see the world through their neighbors' eyes and to place themselves in new situations. Both imaginatively and concretely, Christians step into multiple roles and begin to see the stage from various perspectives.

Through liturgical worship, Christians can be formed as people who hope, and therefore as people who live in expectation of the presence and

grace of God. This hope, like all Christian affections, is emotional, intellectual, volitional, and bodily. It is something to be lived into and out of, in
the sanctuary and outside it. Living in hope means cultivating a discipline
of emptiness that awaits and appreciates the presence of God. This
requires a self-critical stance within the church, such that the performance
is always provisional, ongoing, and open to further inspiration.

I

Setting the Stage*

THERE ARE TWO distinct ways to connect church and theater: one *analogical* and one *analytical*. First, church and theater are analogous in some respects, such that careful attention to the similarities and differences between the two can be illuminating. Second, contemporary concepts of performance and performativity, which are used in many disciplines as analytical tools, provide apt and insightful descriptions of what happens in church worship. These two different ways of connecting church and theater—analogical and analytical—provide the backdrop for this project and therefore warrant some exploration.

Analogy

The analogy between church and theater functions on several levels, beginning with how we use the words "church" and "theater." Both terms can refer to a specific building, a particular event, a broad tradition spanning centuries and continents, a specific group of people, a type of activity, and so forth. Each term holds room for a measure of difference (William Shakespeare and Neil Simon, Southern Baptist and Roman Catholic) while claiming recognizable continuity between various churches and theaters. This can be both useful (allowing broad-scale analysis) and dangerous (masking difference and projecting uniformity). Referring to "the church" can imply a singularity among the vast multiplicity of churches, which vary wildly in each space and time and still more so across geographical and historical distance. The same is true for references to "the theater." Such implications are patently false and contribute to the marginalization of distinctive traditions. Yet while neither church nor theater is singular and uniform, we share a loose and culturally negotiated understanding of what constitutes both church and theater. It is often extremely useful to discuss what happens in churches or theaters in a generalized way that is not exhaustive but still meaningful. I believe that the content of the following pages will make clear that I do not imagine either church or theater in a singular way, but rather maintain a constant awareness and appreciation for the multiplicity of both. While I do use the terms "church" and "theater" in a generalized way, I avoid using articles (the church, the theater) in order grammatically to mark multiplicity while attempting simple prose.

Some of the similarities between church and theater are obvious and often noted. Church can be seen as a theatrical event where actors perform a ritualized drama on a stage in front of an audience, complete with props and costumes. Many authors draw upon this kind of analogy to explore different elements of the Christian tradition.

Several theologians use general metaphors of theater and drama in their depictions of the relationship between God and creation. John Calvin and Karl Barth portray the cosmos as the theater of God's glory.[1] Hans Urs von Balthasar uses the overarching metaphor of drama to describe the interaction between God and humanity in history, an idea picked up by several contemporary theologians, such as Francesca Murphy, who draw upon his work.[2] Here the church is not drawn into specific analogy with the theater, yet the background sense of their similarity bolsters the metaphor.[3] Nicholas Lash and Frances Young use analogy between church and theater to address biblical interpretation by communities and preachers, respectively.[4] Other authors make implicit use of analogy between theater and church to generate more specific interventions into theological conversations. One example of this is T. J. Gorringe, who offers a theology of providence that envisions God as a theater director.[5] Another is Max Harris, whose vivid engagement with theater studies provides a fresh discussion of the Incarnation.[6]

Some more recent authors, such as Samuel Wells and Kevin J. Vanhoozer, use analogies between church and theater to respond to contemporary theological trends. Vanhoozer (who also draws upon von Balthasar) describes the congregation as a theater company, the pastor as director, and Scripture as script. He thus aims to retain recent emphasis on the lived realities of Christian practices while reasserting the importance of Scripture and doctrine.[7] In a different vein, Wells uses the analogy between church and theater to support a theological movement away from narrative, which has been influential in the past fifty years, toward drama in order to describe Christian ethics as improvisation.[8] The concept of drama retains the importance of story and text, while also emphasizing embodiment, community, time, and interpretation of the story.[9]

Analogies between theater and church abound and contribute to a number of different theological projects. The second way of connecting theater and church—analytical—has been used by a different set of scholars, who undertake analysis of performance and performativity.

Analysis

The concept of "performance" functions as an analytical tool in many disciplines. Genealogies of the current use of "performance" as an intellectual concept vary significantly, in part because it has arisen in several different academic fields. Marvin Carlson charts the development of performance studies within anthropology, psychology, theater studies, and linguistics.[10] Each discipline has a particular story to tell about how the term operates, and each includes a number of scholars who use "performance" in different ways.

One strand of the development of performance studies includes the ethnographer Milton Singer.[11] Investigating the "cultural pattern of India," in the middle of the twentieth century, Singer was advised by Indian friends to observe festivals, theater, rites, and rituals. Singer discovered that "cultural themes and values" were manifest and transmitted in such performances.[12] Ronald Grimes notes, "[Singer] assumed rather than argued that such performances display what is central for a culture, that they more revealingly expose deeply held values than do other, non-performative aspects of the same culture."[13]

For Singer, the defining characteristics of a performance are a "limited time span, a beginning and an end, an organized program of activity, a set of performers, an audience, and a place and occasion of performance."[14] While Singer's view includes a number of events not typically considered to be performances, it is easy to see the similar patterns among them. It is not difficult to think of a wedding as a performance. However, other thinkers have stretched the category of performance much further. Erving Goffman applies terms of performance to interactions in everyday life, including greetings, manners, and table service.[15] In Goffman's work, "actions are deemed performances when they are not only done but done to be seen."[16] Goffman looks closely at the effort to manipulate how the "audience" of people around us interprets our actions.[17] While this view of performance is far broader than Singer's, it is still easy to follow the analogy—we are actors in our own lives, playing different roles for the people we interact with day to day.

These two authors are the tip of an iceberg of differing definitions of performance.[18] One could imagine that the multiplicity of meanings of the term ultimately renders it useless. However, I, along with many others, think that is not the case. In fact, the arguments about what the term means are an important part of its meaning. Performance has been famously described as "an essentially contested concept" by Mary Strine, Beverly Long, and Mary Hopkins.[19] They claim, "the disagreement over its essence is itself a part of its essence."[20]

This means the concept of performance brings baggage into any discussion it enters. Each scholar who attempts to chart her own use of the term also invokes—explicitly or implicitly—the work of other authors who use the term differently. It gestures toward a variety of views, even when it is nailed down to a specific usage.

This would not be productive if the various discourses about performance were purely contentious, without any common ground. There is some general sense of what the term means—not a consensus, but a starting point. My understanding of performance focuses on three characteristics: event, interaction, and doubleness.[21]

First, a performance is an *event* that takes place in a specific time, place, and community. Performances are neither permanent nor eternal; they are temporal and transitory.[22] As theorist Peggy Phelan writes, "Performance's only life is in the present."[23] Each reading of a book and showing of a movie can be seen as a performance.[24] Because it is an event, instead of a static entity, interpreting and analyzing a performance requires paying attention to its context. While a performance is fleeting, it can have long-lasting effects. An artistic performance can change people's viewpoints; a political performance can influence social structures. Each performance has a beginning and end, a before and after.

Second, a performance is an *interaction*. It is deeply relational. There are many relations at play in any given performance. One kind of relation is between the performer and the audience. The audience may be a group of theatergoers in red-upholstered seats, a few coworkers that one is trying to impress, or even one's own self. Another relation at work in performance is between the performance, the performer, and the larger culture that surrounds them. A performance is both a manifestation of and a response to the culture in which it is produced.[25]

A third element of performance is *doubleness*. The word "doubleness" indicates there is not an undifferentiated unity between the performer and the role or action she is performing. It denotes tension that takes place in performance. One type of tension is repetition. A performance is an event happening in the present that is also a reenactment of past events. The most influential definition of performance is that of theorist Richard Schechner, who identifies it as "restored behavior."[26] This is any action that has been done before, prepared, or rehearsed. Restored behavior includes not only acting scenes onstage with memorized lines and choreographed movements, but also small patterns and gestures that we use every day. When we shake hands, hail a taxi, or say grace before a meal, we are repeating "strips of behavior" that we have learned.[27] Each of these mundane actions is "twice-behaved behavior."[28] Indeed, much of daily life consists of repeating pieces of behavior that we have seen before, done before, or been taught. Thus performance theorist Richard Schechner writes, "the everydayness of everyday life is precisely its familiarity, its being built from known bits of behavior rearranged and shaped in order to suit specific circumstances."[29]

Note that this description of behavior emphasizes both repetition and innovation—we take learned bits and reshape them. No performance is a pure repetition of the past, since contexts and relationships are always changing. Therefore, in our repetition there is room for improvisation, innovation, and resistance.[30] Performance is thus always linked to both the past that it repeats and the future it rehearses.[31]

Another tension is illustrated in the relationship between an actor and the role he plays. Schechner states that when Lawrence Olivier performed the role of Hamlet, Olivier was both "not Hamlet" and "not not Hamlet."[32] There was a productive, dialectical tension between Olivier and Hamlet within the performance.[33] Performance takes place in the liminal space "between the negative and the double negative."[34]

A third type of tension is between a person and the ideal she is aiming to enact. Imagine an athlete, practicing sprints in an effort to improve her best time. She is running toward a faster version of herself. Something similar can be seen in the performance of social roles. For example, a newly married woman might clean her apartment and set out cookies before her mother-in-law arrives for a visit. She is performing the social role of a daughter-in-law, a role that is new for her and yet she has seen it performed by others in the past. In both cases, there is not an undifferentiated unity between the person performing and the role she performs.

There is tension in performance: between then and now, between negative and double negative, between current action and ideal. Thus Carlson describes performance as an action that is "placed in mental comparison with a potential, an ideal, or a remembered original model of that action."[35] While I have described three different types of tension, they are all related, blurred, and intertwined. All three tensions are present in performance. This is what the word "doubleness" denotes. Carlson refers to the tensions in performance as "the peculiar doubling that comes with consciousness and with the elusive *other* that performance is not but which it constantly struggles in vain to embody."[36]

Doubleness can resonate with understandings of performance that center on the play between actual and imaginary, and between the real and the mimetic. In colloquial terms, performance often means doing something for show or pretending to be something (or someone) you are not. In performance theory, doubleness does not necessarily suggest pretense in this way. As noted above, the doubleness of performance can be seen in our most routine behaviors, such as waving to a neighbor or greeting a colleague. Viewing such actions as performances does not imply that they are deceptive or inauthentic. It does, however, highlight that we are not the sole inventors of our own actions. Our behavior is not entirely our own. Schechner writes, "restored behavior is 'out there,' separate from 'me.' To put it in more personal terms, restored behavior is 'me behaving as if I were someone else,' or 'as I am told to do,' or 'as I have learned.' Even if I feel myself wholly to be myself, acting independently, only a little investigating reveals that the units of behavior that comprise 'me' were not invented by 'me.' "[37]

The idea of doubleness is different from pretense in another, related way. The concept of performance does not necessarily support a static view of identity in which there is one clear, prior self that then pretends to be something different than it naturally or originally is. Indeed, the idea of performance often indicates the ways in which our actions in the world constitute who we are on a deep level. Our performances shape us. To some degree, Olivier is influenced by playing Hamlet, the athlete becomes a faster runner, and the newlywed learns to be a daughter-in-law. To many scholars who write about performance, including Judith Butler, the doubleness of performance points toward the fluidity, multiplicity, and plasticity of human identity, as well as to possibilities for social and political change.[38]

This broad stroke description of performance—an interactive event of restored behavior—might lead to a sense that everything is a performance. If everything *is* a performance, then clearly the term "performance" loses delineating value. However, the growing use of performance studies in academia is not about defining things as much as it is about focusing questions. The determination of what IS a performance is made according to cultural standards.³⁹ In the West we agree that a production of Hamlet IS a performance. What the field of performance studies invites us to do is to interpret or analyze a much broader spectrum of events AS performance.⁴⁰ This simply means analyzing them in a particular way. It encourages attention to the things I have just mentioned in my description of performance——to event, interaction, and doubleness; to the relationship with culture and the formation of identity.

For example, consider the painting *Jimson Weed*, by Georgia O'Keefe. This artwork could be analyzed in many different ways—as an artifact, an object, a text, etc. If it is analyzed AS a performance, certain things will come into focus, while others will fall from view. Someone analyzing *Jimson Weed* as a performance could be interested in when it was painted. The painting of *Jimson Weed* was a performance. It was an event, it was an interaction between O'Keefe and the culture she inhabited, and it was characterized by doubleness (between what O'Keefe had in mind and what emerged on the canvas, between what she was taught and how she innovated, and so forth).

One could also analyze a contemporary viewing of *Jimson Weed* as a performance. It is an event. It is an interaction between the artist and the viewer as well as the viewer and the contemporary art world. And there is an aspect of doubleness in each viewing of the painting (between what the viewer learned in school about O'Keefe and the emotional reaction to seeing one of her paintings up close, etc.). The analysis of *Jimson Weed* as a performance will pay special attention to event, interaction, and doubleness.

At the same time, such a performance analysis of the painting would be uninterested in the painting as such, hanging on the wall in a museum in New Mexico, at 2:00 a.m. when the halls are empty. The painting as object, by itself, abstracted from the events, relationships, and contexts in which it was painted and in which it is viewed, cannot be analyzed from a performance perspective. One would need a different conceptual tool to see the painting in such a way.

Performance and Performativity

A related conceptual tool will also prove useful here. For many scholars, the doubleness and restored character of performance highlight the plasticity of human identity and the ways in which human persons are socially constructed, meaning that we come to be who we are over time, in relation to other people and the culture around us. These ideas have been explored more fully by theorists such as Judith Butler, under the concept of "performativity." Butler draws on postmodern theories and linguistics, particularly the work of J. L. Austin, to describe performativity.[41] For Butler, performativity refers to the ways in which the repetition of culturally normative gestures and performances generates a sense of an abiding self, characterized by a particular sex and gender. In the same way that shaking hands and hailing taxis are strips of restored behaviors, it is also a performance of restored behavior to walk with a masculine swagger or to hold a coffee cup with a feminine curve of the hand. Someone who consistently performs patterns that are associated with heterosexual femininity will appear to be a straight woman. What is new in Butler's account is that she flips traditional understandings of causality. It is not the case, she claims, that a human being first exists with the stable identity of a straight woman and then her actions in the world naturally fall into patterns that indicate this. Instead, actions in the world—patterns of restored behavior—generate the appearance of a stable, heterosexual, female identity. Butler overturns the assumption that a stable gender generates certain behaviors, and instead asserts that the repetitive performance of these behaviors generates the appearance of a stable gender. Butler claims, "There is no gender identity behind the expressions of gender; that identity is performatively constituted by the very 'expressions' that are said to be its results."[42]

This position is best understood in its polemical context. Begin with a more conventional, modern view of the human person. This view assumes the individual has a specific stable identity that expresses itself outward in particular behaviors and desires, which then fall into patterns recognized and acknowledged as natural by the larger culture. For example, a man expresses himself in masculine postures and a deep vocal pitch, a penchant for blue and green, and a desire to have sex with women. These outward characteristics of a man accurately express his inner reality, make perfect sense to the surrounding culture, and afford him a known location within the social structure. Butler contends that this view is false. Instead, she proposes that the individual is taught, trained, and disciplined to behave in certain ways—from posture to pitch to sex partners—in order to be understood and accepted within existing societal norms. The repetition of these behaviors over time produces the illusion that there is a stable self behind them. Put much too simply, while more conventional views claim that identity generates behaviors, Butler argues that behaviors generate identity.

As mentioned above, while the term "performance" can easily bring to mind a person with a definite and stable identity who is pretending to be someone else, the theoretical concepts of performance and performativity actually move in a very different direction.[43] Authors who analyze much of life as performance point out that what might feel like an authentic and unique expression of a stable self is actually a repetition, albeit with some innovative alterations, of behaviors we have seen before. A poem echoes Audre Lorde, uses iambic pentameter like Shakespeare, draws on conventions of rhythm and rhyme. A painting is reminiscent of Frida Kahlo, shows the influence of Mark Rothko, follows in the traditions of modern realism. Even our expressions of individuality are repeated and learned behaviors. For example, a teenager chooses an outfit to express her identity, layering clothes and colors in a way that is both distinctly hers and culturally predictable, a repetition of current styles that will be easy to date in photographs. Her individual choices incorporate markers of identity (masculine, feminine, heterosexual, homosexual, bisexual, white, black, Hispanic, middle class, upper class, working class, and so forth) that make sense to her peers and are recognizable precisely because they are repeated and learned. In this way self-expressions are attempts to fully embody an imagined or idealized version of the self, a performance of one's own self. This does not mean that such expressions are inauthentic. Rather, it suggests that the whole notion of a stable self who expresses her identity in words, movements, art, relationships, and so forth might be overly simplistic.

In an expressivist model of the self, actions, words, and bodily gestures are understood to be outward expressions of a stable, abiding internal self. Imagined spatially, the movement is from inside to outside. One could imagine an anti-expressivist model of the self as a simple reversal of this movement. The movement is still unidirectional, but moves from outside to inside. The actions, words, and bodily gestures of a person create the appearance of a stable inner self.

Yet both of these models are inadequate to the complexity of human life and the multiplicity of influences that contribute to human identity. We do not come into the world as blank slates awaiting the inscribing hand of culture to determine our identities. Neither do we enter as fully formed, a priori identities eager to express themselves to the waiting world. We perform in patterns that are learned from our surrounding culture, so that nothing is quite as unique and innovative as we might imagine. At the same time, our behaviors are never pure repeats of prior events. The contextual and fleeting nature of performance means there is room for resistance and change. For all of these reasons, simplistic expressivist and anti-expressivist views fail. The strength of a performative model of the self is that it can be multidirectional. Actions, words, and gestures shape, generate, and cocreate who we are at the deepest levels (outside to inside), while at the same time, who we are at the deepest levels is expressed in our actions, words, and gestures (inside to outside). All of this takes place within cultural and social contexts that also have roles to play in the performance. These societal contexts regulate our performances, set conventions for stock characters, delineate interpretive lenses, and offer constant feedback—positive and negative—as we perform ourselves. Such a performative view cannot be easily imagined with simple linear models; the ideas of "inside" and "outside" falter as lines of relationality curve and multiply. This multidirectional sense of performativity offers a rich appreciation for the social construction of the self without generating ontological claims that make it difficult to account for aspects of identity such as agency, heredity, and biology. This sense of the human person as performatively constituted—this performative anthropology—is one of the analytical tools rooted in the concept of performance that I bring to this ecclesiological exploration.

Performing Church

To understand church as performance means viewing it through the lenses of event, interaction, and doubleness.[44] It means seeing church as an event rather than as a static entity. The continuation of the church across time and space is a matter of ongoing performances. Church exists in overlapping sequence or lineage of historical events rather than in a static, eternal reality safe outside the tumult of time. Such a view highlights the historicity of the church, while it also makes it more difficult to view the church primarily as an institution. This raises many questions. What happens in church? What are the boundaries of this multiform and ongoing event? Is the performance of church limited to congregational worship, or does it pop up in other times and places?

Likewise, understanding church as interaction immediately raises questions about who is involved. Who are the persons involved in this event? How do they interact with each other? With the world around them? With God? In what ways is this performance of church a manifestation of, reaction against, and/or challenge to the broader culture in which it takes place?

The term "doubleness" is less familiar than the terms "event" and "interaction," yet perhaps it is easiest to recognize this characteristic of performance in church. Church involves a great deal of restored behavior, as worshippers repeat words and gestures handed down over centuries. The tension between current action and ideal is also present and has been described by many theologians. Theologian Serene Jones uses the terms "empirical" and "normative" to distinguish between church as it is and church as it ought to be.[45] Other theologians have drawn distinctions between the visible and invisible church, as well as between the hidden and revealed church.[46] These phrases can be used to point to a doubleness, comparing church as it is enacted with a potential or ideal performance of church that we are aiming for but do not fully inhabit. In this context doubleness takes on a particular theological meaning that it does not have elsewhere. Part of the reason that any specific performance of church does not fully become the ideal for which it strives is the reality of sin. We are not what we are called to be. Actual churches are communities of fallen people, performing badly in a broken world. Across centuries and continents, Christian churches have perpetrated enormous harm.

Christian communities have visions of what church should be, visions that vary but carry many common themes of faith, hope, love, hospitality, and service. We fall far short of these visions, often enacting pride, fear, hate, exclusion, and domination. Because of this, it would be inaccurate to describe church simply as a place of welcome and care, a community of faith and hope. At the same time, it would be theologically inaccurate to define church by giving an exact accounting of all churches. The vision of what church ought to be is part of its identity, constitutive of church in a very real way. There is a productive, dialectical tension here that is generative of the performance of church. Part of the tragedy of Christian communities causing harm—part of what demands a response of lament, repentance, and justice—is that this is not what church is supposed to be. When we perform in these ways we are not being true to ourselves. The idea of doubleness keeps this discrepancy between what church is called to be and what it is in view, while also raising questions about identity. What is the congregation aiming for in church? What comprises their vision of what church ought to be? What pieces of behavior are they repeating, and does this help them embody their aim?

Even the tension of the negative and double negative is present in church. On any given Sunday, the performance of a specific congregation does not embody all that Scripture and tradition tell us that church is. At best, we are lackluster performers making a schoolchildren's attempt at something that is supposed to be truly important and meaningful. We fidget and lose focus. We sing of triumph and glory with dirge-like tempo and obvious disaffection. We are comically incompetent at our liturgical task of worshipping almighty God. Clearly, our performance is not the in-breaking of the New Creation. And yet...it is also not not a moment of the Kingdom in our midst. So how do we hold that tension well?

The concept of performance is a useful analytical tool that raises certain types of questions when applied to Christian church. These questions shape the coming pages and generate a new perspective on the event, interaction, and doubleness of Christian worship.[47]

Performing Scripture

With these conceptual tools in hand—analogy between church and theater and analysis of performance and performativity—I now turn to an examination of church. While there are many ways to develop connections between church and theater, my approach is governed by my conviction that what distinguishes church is its relationship to Jesus Christ, a relationship mediated by the Bible. The biblical text functions very differently in different traditions, denominations, and congregations, yet Christian communities continue to return to this text. Indeed, it would be very difficult for me to understand a contemporary performance with no relationship to the Bible at all as church. This serves as both guide and safeguard for me. While in the pages that follow I develop a very broad understanding of church, I am wary of applying that name to performances by persons of other religious traditions or no religious tradition. I believe Scripture is central to the performance that is church. It is, theatrically speaking, our script. In a very real way, both church and theater are events of interpretation, where groups of people attempt to fully understand a shared text.[48]

For the most part, Christian interpretation of Scripture happens in community: not only within a tradition, but also within a present community of believers.[49] Similarly, theatrical interpretation is a communal endeavor. A theater company is a group of people striving together toward an experience of the sublime.[50] The individuals have different roles and functions, yet each is a part of the communal process of interpretation. This, too, seems similar to Christian communal interpretation, which involves people in varied functions: as teachers, prophets, ministers, and lay leaders.[51]

This interpretation within a community is not shut off from the rest of the world. If a theater company fails to address the larger society, it will have to close its doors. The same is true of a Christian community. To ignore the issues of the broader world, the challenges to interpretation, is to forfeit the role of interpreter. So both churches and theaters must balance between internal community and external connection, between integrity and pertinence.

Within a theatrical setting, the interpretive process itself is varied—there are sets, costumes, music, and lights. In a similar manner, Christians shape their understanding of Scripture through many different means. We choose our sacred spaces carefully, adorn them with artwork, light them with sun spilling through stained glass, fill them with the scent of incense, make them ring with song. We also come in costume, be it some liturgical garb or our own "Sunday best." The fact that we engage all of our senses in Christian worship underlines the fact that it is an embodied experience. We don't just think about praising God: we do it, with our arms and legs and eyes and noses and voices all together.

When a company interprets a script, there are many rehearsals where the lines of the text are repeated often and committed to memory. The performers try to understand the intentions behind the lines, the relations between the characters, the import of a scene. The community attempts to discern what the author was getting at as well as what this script can say to this time and place. The actors place themselves in the characters; stand as ones commanded, insulted, promised, betrayed. An entire community employs a full spectrum of means and media to interpret the script. They create an event that was latent in the text.

On one hand, a script is complete on its own. Otherwise we would not be able to evaluate scripts and decide which ones to perform. On the other hand, a script is incomplete, inherently moving toward greater fulfillment in the event of performance. Much like a theater building or set, a script contains an empty space, open for the cast. In the very nature of its being a script, it asks to be performed. One can study a script as a piece of literature, but to do so is, to some degree, to miss the point. It is meant to become an event.[52]

Furthermore, the interpretation of the script is a vital part of that event. A script is not a set of guidelines in the same way as a list of instructions for assembling a child's toy. Both require interpretation, but the assembly instructions increase in quality as the amount of interpretation needed decreases. Thus the best instructions would require the least interpretation.

The same is not true for scripts. Consider Shakespeare's *Measure for Measure*. In the final scene, the Duke proposes marriage to Isabel, a young woman planning to become a nun. Does she say yes or no? Shakespeare does not tell us, forcing every company that produces the play to make its own decision. This perfect play is incomplete alone. The need for interpretation in a script is not a shortcoming. Rather, the very structure of a script contains an incompleteness that offers an invitation for our embodied and active interpretation, an invitation to create an event that is more than a script alone can be.[53]

I believe that Scripture, like script, is both complete and incomplete.[54] It witnesses to the incarnation, ministry, death, and resurrection of Jesus of Nazareth and also moves toward further completion in the continuing life of the Christian community and the coming of the Kingdom of God. Outside of Christian community, seen alone as merely literature, is the Bible complete? Or does it, like a script, provide the framework for the words, movement, and speech of a community? Does it move toward events of proclamation and conversion? Does it hearken the coming of an event that is the new creation? Does it call out for the cast?

This is an important point because if the Bible, like a script, does in some sense command performance and create event, then this says something about the nature of biblical interpretation. In church, as in theater, interpretation is neither an individual nor an exclusively mental matter. Indeed, it involves the entire person—intellect, body, emotion, and will—and the entire community. Acting out of their relationship with Scripture, Christian communities shout and dance, they get happy and they mourn together, they bake casseroles and sing hymns and comfort one another and open soup kitchens and raise money for the homeless. If Christian interpretation is really like theatrical performance interpretation, then these events and activities are not merely the results of an understanding that comes from interpretation: they are part of the interpretive process. We do not interpret, understand, and then act on our understanding; but rather our actions are part of our interpreting, constitutive of our understanding.

The emphasis on ritual and community found in the church underlines the fact that the connection between comprehension and behavior runs both ways. We teach our children to sing "Jesus Loves Me" not only as an affirmation of something they know, but as a way for them to know it. We bow our heads, bend our knees, lift our arms and raise our voices, not merely to express an understanding previously gained, but in order to comprehend more fully the reality and meaning of the Word of God.

In academic terms, what I am describing here is a performative epistemology.[55] We know in performing. This is not a new insight in Christian
theology. Specifically in regard to liturgy, Christians have traditionally
affirmed that the practice of prayer and liturgy governs understandings of
doctrine. *Lex orandi, lex credendi.* I am offering one explication of this traditional wisdom, using the concept of performance and the context of
performative anthropology.[56]

Theatrical interpretation happens when a cast and crew—working
within the specifications of the script and the guidelines of a tradition—
create the event called for by the script. I believe Christian communities
interpret by acting out, embodying, creating the events called for by
Scripture. Our understanding of Scripture comes to fullness within our
performance of it.

The rituals of Christian worship appear quite similar to theatrical performance. A small group of actors/clergy performs on a kind of stage in
front of an audience/congregation, often speaking memorized lines and
using distinctive props. Yet I suggest that all Christians are performers,
and the entire Christian life is a performance in which we attempt to enact
and create the events called for by the script/Scripture. Those who sit in
the rear pew on Sunday mornings are no less actors than the clergy up
front. We need only think of *Hamlet* to fit the performance of the liturgy
by the clergy into the theatrical tradition of a play-within-a-play.

This point in the analogy holds the most tension, for here I am explicitly suggesting that Christians perform Scripture both in worship and in
life. Clearly this is untrue if taken in the most literal sense. My life is too
surprising to be scripted, the plot line looks decidedly unbiblical, and the
characters that walk the boards with me are not named Melchizedek or
Jeroboam. Indeed, some of the most theatrical sections of Scripture, which
describe a setting in detail and give minute stage directions for dramatic
sacrifices and rituals, are the parts of the Bible that seem most remote
from my own experience.

However, I think if we explore this analogy in a more playful and less
literal manner, the idea of performance will resonate. We perform the
Scripture in several ways. When we read or sing the psalms together, we
perform them. When we enact scenes from the life of Jesus, breaking
bread and washing feet, we are performing. When we obey a direct commandment, we are, in some sense, performing that commandment. And
perhaps most important, we ourselves are characters who have been crafted
by this text. While the present performances of our lives are undeniably

extemporaneous, Christians enter each scene and engage in each dialogue as characters delineated and delimited by this text. The words of Scripture shape our words, and our thoughts and lives as well. As Christians we claim that the story of Scripture is our story. Our lives are shaped by and lived within the Christian narrative.

This claim that Christians perform—and, in performing, interpret—Scripture throughout our lives is actually rather pedestrian. It indicates that while we can know something of God when we read that we should turn the other cheek, we will know more fully when we feel the blow. I see something of God in the commandment to rest every seventh day; my vision is clearer in the grace of actually resting. I may encounter God in the story of Jesus ministering to the poor and outcast, yet my encounter is far more intimate if I place myself in that story and struggle in solidarity with the oppressed. In theatrical performance interpretation, the place where the fullness of meaning is located—where it abundantly over-flows—is in performance.[57]

Theatrical performance, like Christian practice, has a script, is communal, is done in dialogue with society, employs a variety of methods and of media, and is embodied. Unlike academic interpretation that leads to an article or assertions of the meaning or sense of a text, the interpretation that happens in and among Christian communities leads to and is continued in an embodied performance: the event of worship and of life.[58]

Here I am parsing both a performative epistemology and a performative hermeneutic. It is not just that we know in performing, it is also that we interpret the Scripture in our performance. Theologian Bruce T. Morrill writes, "The mercy at the heart of the gospel which Christians receive...is only genuinely *known* by those who themselves *act* mercifully in history and society."[59] It is in our performance—both within and outside the sanctuary walls—that we interpret Scripture. Furthermore, the result of our interpreting is not a set of static assertions, but rather our ongoing performance.

Performance Interpretation in Scholarly Context

My view of biblical hermeneutics—that Christian communities interpret Scripture through embodied, communal performance of worship and life—has been formed in conversation with the work of theologian Hans Frei and philosopher Nicholas Wolterstorff. From Frei, I garner an appreciation for the importance of both the text of Scripture and the community in which it is interpreted. The particularity of the biblical narrative matters; our story is irreplaceable. At the same time, how we understand this story is guided by communal traditions of interpretation. These traditions rule out some interpretation, but allow for several, which are then evaluated on the basis of fruitful use for the community.[60] I learn much from Frei's emphasis on the ways that Christian communities are shaped by the interpretive traditions they create and embody.[61] Thus my depiction of Christian communal interpretation looks a good bit like Frei's. A performance is a form of storytelling, in which a community interprets the story according to its own traditions. One of the norms upon which such an interpretation is evaluated is whether or not it is valuable for the community itself. Or, in my own terms, a group of people creates the event called for by the script, imagining what it might say to a specific community, and yet always and only retells the story.

At the same time, in my portrayal of Christian performance interpretation, I part ways with Frei on a number of issues. First, for all of his value on the interpretive community, at times Frei implies that the meaning of the text rests within the text alone.[62] While one could disagree with this idea from a number of perspectives, it is completely incompatible with performance analysis. This idea, in effect, attempts to say that the meaning of *Jimson Weed* resides in the paint and canvas, the image hanging on a wall in a darkened gallery at 2:00 a.m. In contrast, I am interested in the Bible as it is performed in church, as event, interaction, and doubleness. The event of church is a performance of interaction between people and God. While it is not yet the consummation of that relationship, it is (in this doubleness) an approximation of that intimacy we hope to live into and be gifted with by God. This is what is fascinating and powerful about the Bible: as script, it mediates the disciplined performance of relationship with God. To abstract this text from event and interaction is to miss the point completely.

The implication that the meaning of the Bible rests within the text alone is also incompatible with my contention that both script and Scripture call out for further completion in action. In Christian performance interpretation as I understand it, the fullness of meaning is located at the point where the narrative of the script and the life of the community become one story in the event of performance.

Second, I reject the primary form of scriptural interpretation that Frei advocates, which he calls the "sensus literalis" or "literal reading." He describes this as "the (largely but not wholly) informal set of rules under which [Scripture] has customarily been read in the community," and says this tradition is "the closest one can come to a consensus reading of the Bible as the sacred text in the Christian church."[63] Reading the Bible "literally" is often taken to mean that the interpreter plays no role in determining the meaning of the text. If this is what it means, there is no such thing as a literal reading of the Bible, since all texts require interpretation. Frei's description of literal reading offers a more nuanced view of what communities who claim they are reading "literally" are actually doing: they are interpreting the texts according to the traditions of the community, which are so familiar and well learned that members of the community are often unaware that they are applying any traditions of interpretation at all. While I think this generous analysis is insightful, Frei's approbation of the term can mask the fallacy upon which the colloquial understanding of "literal" is founded: that there is one right meaning of the text, residing in the text and clear to view. Furthermore, this, in turn, can camouflage the theological, social, and political conservativism that both influences, and is influenced by, the idea that there is a literal reading of the Bible. These problems are exacerbated by Frei's description of the sensus literalis as being nearly a "consensus reading" of the Bible.[64] That any one reading of the Bible nears consensus within Christian communities is patently false, and such a misrepresentation is only possible if the prolific diversity of Christian communities falls from view.

Wolterstorff understands Frei to be advocating a kind of performance interpretation, largely because in Frei's hermeneutics the community provides rules for interpreting Scripture and valid interpretations are evaluated as good or bad on the basis of their practical use for the community.[65] This emphasis on community, particularly in evaluating the results of interpretation, is problematic for Wolterstorff. He advocates "authorial-discourse" interpretation, in which the final issue regarding the results is not about practical use for the community, but rather is "whether one's conclusions are correct, whether they are true—whether the discourser did in fact, by authoring or presenting this text, say what one claims he said."[66] Convinced that God speaks in the Bible, Wolterstorff wants to find out what God said. In contrast, states Wolterstorff, "the performance interpreter doesn't claim to have *found out* what the author said."[67]

I find this challenge to performance interpretation illuminating in two ways. First, it reminds me how very much work goes into finding out what the author said in many theatrical productions. Dramaturges and text coaches, directors and designers find things out about scripts in the theater, and what they find out profoundly shapes the production. In the church, these roles are played by historians and biblical scholars, theologians, preachers, and studious laypeople.[68] Thus I agree with Wolterstorff that church has both room and need for authorial-discourse interpretation, for truth claims and arguments, discussion and debate about what God really says when God speaks. Second, I find Wolterstorff's complaint about performance interpretation—that it doesn't result in defending a truth claim about the speech of God—to be fairly accurate for both good and ill. Christians cannot claim definitive accuracy in our comprehension of the text by any other means than our own performance. I can say that God, in and through Scripture, did not say that violence is a preferred mode of treatment among individuals. But ultimately, I cannot claim accuracy in my belief that God abhors violence by any other means than acting nonviolently. I cannot prove I have found out that God says violence is not acceptable, or even argue for it in a way that is not susceptible to countless counterarguments, proof texts, and pitfalls. I can, however, act on the basis of my understanding of what I have found out about God. It is not so much a matter of asserting the accuracy of my discernment as witnessing to my belief. Furthermore, a commitment to act nonviolently may well help me to understand the fierce gentleness of God in a more vivid and subtle way.

While Wolterstorff, a Christian philosopher, argues against performance interpretation as an appropriate model for how churches interpret Scripture because of the limited ability of a performance to assert what an author said, Samuel Wells, a Christian ethicist, offers other concerns. The analogy between theater and church is compelling to Wells, yet he resists describing what happens in Christian life (not merely in worship) as performance for four specific reasons. Performance suggests enacting a written script, for Wells, and this is inadequate as a metaphor for the profoundly extemporaneous realities of Christian life. First, Scripture does not provide "a comprehensive version of life."[69] Events occur that are not mentioned, let alone scripted, in the Bible. Second, the Bible does not encompass "the whole of the church's narrative," as it does not cover the last two thousand years of Christian life.[70] Third, within the ongoing historical reality of the church,

> the idea of [the Bible as] a script suggests the recreation of a golden era. It suggests that there was a time when the characters did get it right, when Israel was holy and faithful to God, when the disciples

heard Jesus' words and straightaway put them into action—and that the task of the church is to reenact that righteousness, to conjure up once more the glorious days of intimate fellowship.[71]

In this regard, argues Wells, the notion of performing Scripture can be backward looking, rather than appropriately placing the drama of the present within the broader setting that begins with creation and is consummated in the eschaton. Fourth, and finally, Wells asserts, "the notion of a script can militate against genuine engagement with the world."[72] To view Christian life as performing a complete story of a past, golden era does not necessarily lead to contemporary social involvement.

For all of these reasons, Wells moves from the base metaphor of performance to a particular analysis of Christian ethics as improvisation.[73] He analyzes Christian moral formation through the lens of improvisation, drawing connections between how improvisers rehearse and Christians worship, between how improvisers perform and how Christians make moral decisions. In doing so, Wells demonstrates the clear usefulness of the category of improvisation for understanding Christian ethics.[74] However, I am less persuaded by his critique of the use of performance in understanding how Christians interpret and live out Scripture.

The problems Wells raises all depend upon a notion of performance as reenacting a set script. While this is a logical and straightforward way of understanding the claim that Christians perform Scripture, it is not what I intend to convey. When I say that Christians perform Scripture, I do not mean that they enact a set script by reciting memorized lines. Metaphors and analogies are illuminating precisely because they compare two things that are both similar and different. If Christians were simply enacting memorized lines, the tension in the metaphor would be lost and it would cease to be helpful. It is because there is dissimilarity between Christian life and theater that the comparison of the two can prove insightful. Furthermore, my understanding of performance includes the broader meanings of the term derived from performance studies.

How do Christians perform Scripture? When a Christian community enacts the Last Supper in a communion service, they create the event called for by Scripture in a sense analogous to theatrical performance. This is stretched a bit further when the community gathers to feed the hungry at the local homeless shelter. They are, in a sense, reenacting the feeding of the multitudes, but the congregation is serving macaroni and cheese, not loaves and fishes, and they brought the provisions themselves.

This can be taken a step further. A child in the congregation dies and the people of the community deliver homemade meals to the grieving family for two months. This performance does not happen at the front of a stage or a church or a shelter. Instead, it takes place in quiet drop-offs on the porch. Here the congregation is not reenacting a scene from the Bible: they are not performing Scripture in that way, wherein performance is understood as analogous to theatrical performance. However, they are still performing in a number of other ways. Each of these three examples shows a congregation performing the commandments of Scripture. "Do this in remembrance of me" (Luke 22). "Feed my sheep" (John 21). "Comfort, comfort my people, says your God" (Isa 40). The congregations in each example are also performing the Scripture, I contend, in acting as characters crafted by this text. They are performing the role of Christian communities, as this role has been created—through study, ritual, tradition, and so forth—in response to Scripture.

The astute reader will realize that at this point I am exploiting a certain amount of slippage between meanings of the word "performance," and in so doing am moving between an analogical approach that compares theater and church and an analytical approach that describes what Christians do as performance. Earlier I claimed that Christians are performing Scripture both in church worship services and in lives shaped by Scripture. The concept of performativity addresses just how this is so. When someone bakes a casserole for a grieving family, they are not enacting a specific script within the Bible, and they probably are not directly following a commandment within the text. Instead, they are acting as good Christians should; as they saw their mothers do; as other members of the congregation do; as another Christian once did for them. It is an event, an interaction, and it has an element of doubleness. The impulse to bake a casserole can be an expression of an inner feeling of compassion, a response to external expectations, a habit formed by baking many casseroles, and probably a few other things besides, all at the same time. Our behaviors in the world do express our identities, but they also shape our identities, and all within complex cultural contexts that apply various pressures on who we are and who we aim to be.

The concept of performativity relates to more traditional theological terms such as habit, virtue, and formation. While some of the specifics of contemporary theories of performativity are new, Christian communities have long recognized—at least implicitly—that what we do shapes who we are.

One of the reasons Wells turns to improvisation as an analog for Christian ethics is his interest in formation. As Wells describes it, improvisation is largely about formation, as it involves performers being "schooled in a tradition so thoroughly that they learn to act from habit in ways appropriate to the circumstance."[75] This is similar, he contends, to Christian ethics, the heart of which "lies in the formation of character."[76] A person's character is formed over time into patterns, instincts, and habits. When a moment of moral decision arises, such a person responds instinctively, in keeping with her moral formation. Thus Wells uses improvisation as a way to argue against focusing on moral decision making in tricky situations. Instead, he draws attention away from the decision and toward the moral formation that shapes the person who decides.[77] Wells brings the idea of improvisation into play to get a clearer view of the workings and importance of moral formation.

There is a clear difference between improvisation (as Wells employs it) and performance (as I employ it). Wells intervenes into the discourse of contemporary Christian ethics by observing a distinction between formation and the moral dilemma and then saying formation should be the focus of Christian ethics. He divides "the time of moral effort" (formation) from "the time of moral habit" (dilemma).[78] He uses strong metaphors that underline the importance of this distinction in his thought. Thus he makes clear divisions between Eton (where the character of British upperclass men was formed) and Waterloo (where these men took part in winning the battle), between the lecture room (where a doctor learns medicine well or badly), and the operating room (where he saves or kills the patient).[79]

While Wells's distinction between formation and dilemma is useful in his challenge to contemporary ethics, it is quite different from both theater and the concept of performativity I have developed in this chapter. In theater, interpretation of the script cannot be separated from the performance of the play. A theater company interprets a script all through the rehearsal process and on stage on opening night and in every performance until the show closes. Interpretation is not just part of the rehearsal, during which a particular understanding of the script is developed, which is then performed on stage.[80]

Interpretation continues in the performance, in at least two ways. First, a theater company's understanding of the script changes over the run of the performance. Performing itself—and doing so with different audiences, on different days, within different contexts—continues to influence and alter the company's view of the play, and how the company performs.[81] The opening night audience laughs in unexpected places. The lead brings more anger into act 3 after he is mugged on the subway. The audience is more alive when they have come into the theater from a springtime rain, and bits of intensity are found in previously neglected scenes. Each performance contributes to the formation of the actor, the company, and the communal understanding of the script. Second, the fullness of the meaning of the script does not lie in the understanding of the text arrived at by the theater company. It resides in the event of performance—embodied, relational, contextual, and so forth.

Playwright Tom Stoppard challenges us to "look on every exit as being an entrance somewhere else."[82] If the playing fields of Eton prepared British boys for Waterloo, for what did Waterloo prepare British men? That experience, too, was formative. The lines between rehearsal and performance cannot be so neatly drawn.

My understanding of the interpretation in performance also marks a clear distinction between my sense of how Christians perform Scripture and that proposed by Vanhoozer. He wants to affirm a post-critical form of authorial-discourse interpretation of the Bible, without neglecting the lived practices of Christian communities emphasized by Frei and George Lindbeck.[83] Thus Vanhoozer writes, "The church is a company of players gathered together to stage scenes of the kingdom of God for the sake of a watching world. The direction of doctrine thus enables us, as individuals and as a church, to render the gospel public by leading lives in creative imitation of Christ."[84] In describing the Bible, he states, "The remembered past is rendered through a plot, which in turn renders a proposition: a possible way of viewing and living in the world. The reader, thus propositioned, becomes a player in the ongoing drama of creation and redemption."[85] The meaning of the Bible—God's communicative act in authorizing the canonical text—is first to be understood and then to be "rendered" dramatically by Christian communities.[86]

What does the term "render" mean in this context? Perhaps Vanhoozer is drawing upon the writing of Nicholas Lash, whose work on performance interpretation of Scripture has become canonical. Lash claims that Christian communities, through worship and life that is constituted by performance interpretation of Scripture, render or bear witness to the story of God's grace in Jesus Christ. He writes, "Christian practice, as interpretative action, consists in the *performance* of texts which are construed as 'rendering', bearing witness to, one whose words and deeds, discourse and suffering, 'rendered' the truth of God in human history."[87]

Lash uses the term "render" to emphasize the value of Christian communal life and de-center the prestige of academic interpretations of the text. He also clearly rejects the notion that a text has a single, stable meaning in and of itself, outside of human interpretation.[88] While Vanhoozer might take up the term "render" from Lash, he uses it differently. Vanhoozer does not argue that the text itself, as text, has such a singular and stable meaning. Yet he is committed to the idea that the text of the Bible has a theology apart from its use in Christian communities,[89] that is, "not Scripture as used by the church but Scripture as used by God."[90] He does not fully explain how Christian communities gain access to this meaning of the text, and by this omission seems to indicate that the text itself "renders" such meaning. The text renders a meaning—God's meaning—that we understand and then perform.

This contrasts with my own view of performance interpretation of the Bible. I claim that performance does not begin where interpretation ends, but rather that performance is part of interpretation. Furthermore, I argue that the Bible itself commands performance and that the fullness of the meaning of the text resides within the ongoing, complex, performative interactions between Scripture and Christian communities.[91] Both of these claims involve the epistemological contention—absent in Vanhoozer's text—that Christians know the Bible in ways that are profoundly communal and embodied.

These points are vital to my understanding of performance, Christian interpretation of Scripture, and church. The interpretation of the Bible is not a view gained through embodied processes (such as rehearsal), which then congeals into a static or even merely intellectual thing. It is embodied, communal, and ongoing. It is event, interaction, and doubleness. As Christians, we keep coming back to this text, looking for meaning. We are not hoping to be reminded of what we already know, but eager for new insight.[92] We come to the text different each time—with new troubles and queries, new wrinkles in our lives and ourselves. And each time the text continues to change and shape and form us, such that our performance of our own identity is always related to the words and stories here. Using the concept of performativity to describe Christian worship and Christian life helps emphasize that when we are performing Scripture in worship and ritual, we are also performing ourselves as Christians, and performatively shaping ourselves as Christians.

There is another clear distinction between my view and Vanhoozer's. Drawing on rich theological traditions regarding witness and mission, Vanhoozer identifies the audience of Christian performance as the "watching world."[93] In sharp contrast, I do not assign the role of audience to any set group of people. While the concept of audience is included in my description of interaction as an element of performance, I do not specify who functions as audience to performances of church.

Almost any talk of theater requires acknowledging the role and importance of audience. Therefore analogies between theater and church invite assigning roles. Who is the director? Who are the actors? Who is the audience? I have done some of this in the preceding pages, naming Scripture as script and Christians as actors. Also, many theorists define performance in ways that make the audience central. For example, Goffman defines performance as "all the activity of a given participant on a given occasion which serves to influence in any way any of the other participants."[94] Carlson writes, "Performance is always performance *for* someone, some audience that recognizes and validates it as performance even when, as is occasionally the case, that audience is the self."[95] Thus the existence of an audience is implied in both analogical and analytical approaches. However, both approaches also offer reasons why the role of audience should not be firmly or exclusively assigned to any specific group of people. Several twentieth-century theater directors, particularly Augusto Boal, challenge conventional notions regarding the division of actors and audience. Likewise, several theorists emphasize that the audience for any given performance might be multiple and fluid. Goffman acknowledges that in the performance of social roles, each actor is also audience for the performances of others.[96] The audience for performances of church is multiform. It might include persons that Christians intend to see the show (as Vanhoozer asserts), fellow Christians who are also performing (following Goffman), our own selves (per Carlson's suggestion), and perhaps God. The audience of a Christian performance might be any and all of these.

Why Church?

I have chosen to view and describe church as performance. What is being performed in church? While answering this question will take up many of the pages that follow, a provisional answer is that the Bible functions as script for Christian communities. We perform the Bible in several different senses, from performing a set script to performing a commandment to performing ourselves as people shaped by this text. All of these different kinds of performance are ways in which the community interprets the Bible. This leads me to the claim, both pedestrian and novel, that Christians are performing and interpreting the Bible in their everyday lives. Thus church, as I have described it so far, happens not just on Sunday mornings, but throughout the lives of Christian communities.

Have I finally arrived at the conclusion that I can sleep in on Sunday morning? Alas, no. Oddly, realizing that church happens in many different times and places does not make the set worship of Christian liturgy less important, but rather underlines its formative and vital place in the lives of Christians. This is the central performance, the performance that rehearses us for all else, the actors' workshop where our performances train us in our craft, and the focal drama that makes explicit what all of our performances are about.[97] While my vision of church is temporally and geographically expansive, it emphasizes the importance of the worship hour in the church building.

Drawing on both analogy and analysis, I find the concept of performance wonderfully suggestive for ecclesiology. It does not offer clear and immediate answers to my question "why church?" It does not immediately explain what happens at church, why church is vital to Christian identity, and why it is worth getting up early on Sunday morning. Instead, the concept of performance serves to shape questions about ecclesiology, to focus attention on certain aspects of church, and to suggest conversation partners.

2

Training the Actors

Introduction

In the previous chapter, I described church as performance. This view of church is expansive, in the sense that Christians perform church throughout their lives when they act as characters crafted by the biblical texts. Sunday morning worship is vital to this performance view of church because it is the central, focal performance that rehearses us for all other performances. Christian liturgy is the performance that forms us as fit players in the ongoing drama of salvation. It is the actors' workshop, rehearsal space, and drama school that shapes us as people who perform a story about Jesus, as known in the texts of Scripture.

How does this happen? What happens in Christian worship that forms us in this way? This is the question I ask in this chapter. Because my view of church emphasizes embodied performance, I am looking for an account of Christian liturgical formation that includes the whole person. I claim that church forms us not only to think as Christians, but also to feel and act as Christians. Therefore, I need an account of Christian formation that attends to how we are shaped to think, feel, will, and act in patterns congruent with the Christian story.

To arrive at such an account, I draw upon the work of four authors who offer distinctive insights: Don Saliers, Ignatius of Loyola, G. Simon Harak, and Constantin Stanislavski. The discussion that follows takes the form of a kind of ideal dinner party, to which I have invited an eclectic set of guests who each have unique perspectives on the topic at hand. In conversation with these men, I develop a view of liturgy as a performance that forms us emotionally, intellectually, volitionally, and bodily. I argue that in worship we develop a storehouse of belief-laden emotions that are congruent with the Christian story of salvation and relationship with Jesus Christ. At the same time, we learn a repertoire of physical gestures that can be used to access these belief-laden emotions. Thus our whole selves are formed and reformed through the performance of Scripture in church. Furthermore, this performance is ultimately one of relationship with Jesus Christ, steeped in the Scriptures through which we know him.

Passional Knowing

Theologian Don Saliers is one of the most influential voices concerning the liturgical formation of the person. Saliers uses a number of theatrical metaphors. He writes of Christians being "taken into the dramatic narrative of Jesus Christ" in worship,[1] of prayer and liturgy as rehearsal,[2] and of "the world of human affairs [as] the theater of God's activity."[3] More important than his choice of metaphors, however, is his exploration of the formation of affections as an account of how worship shapes the self.[4]

Although "affection" refers to a friendly sentiment or emotion in colloquial English, as a theological term it means something more. It refers to a kind of knowing that is not simply intellectual, but is also emotional and volitional. For roughly the past four hundred years, scholarship in the West has focused on the goal of empirical, objective, universal knowledge, on the model of scientific experimentation or Euclidean geometry. From Descartes onward, dominant academic practices have involved abstracting oneself from embodiment, community, and ethical commitments. However, Christian communities have continued liturgical practices—including interpretive practices described in chapter 1—that involve a much richer vision of knowledge. Saliers's account of Christian formation in worship attempts to honor and explicate this rich knowledge. Part of how he does this is by retrieving and developing the term affection, as it was used by Jonathan Edwards.

Christian affections are emotions that also involve the intellect and require concepts, as the emotions and beliefs of Christian faith are intertwined.[5] The emotion of being grateful to God for creation is bound to particular beliefs: God is creator, creation is good, the act of creation is gracious. Likewise, the emotion of remorse over sin is bound to particular concepts: nature, sin, the goodness of God. These emotions require beliefs. At the same time, having particular religious beliefs requires emotion, although such emotions can be felt in many different ways. To believe that one is sinful requires, in some form or another, an emotion of remorse.[6] In Saliers's words, "in matters of religion (and morals as well) the having of certain emotions is *part* of what it means to hold certain beliefs."[7] Furthermore, these emotions and beliefs are profoundly connected to how the person wills herself to be in the world. For example, the affection of gratitude for creation shapes how one interprets and interacts with the natural world. Thus in Saliers's view, knowledge of God "must be a passional knowing—a process of being formed in specific affections and dispositions in the way we live that manifest what is known about God."[8]

Affections are "belief-laden emotions" that also involve the will, as they are part of the person's intentions toward the world.[9] Saliers writes, "the concept of affection designates a basic attunement which lies at the heart of a person's way of being and acting."[10] In Saliers's terminology, affections are "deep emotions" and "abiding motives" that shape how we understand the world and how we act within it.[11]

Saliers contends that Christian faith is, among other things, a "pattern of deep emotions" and Christian life is constituted and governed by this "pattern of particular affections."[12] Christian worship both expresses and shapes this pattern of affections, and it does so in relation to Scripture.[13] Biblical texts "arouse, sustain, and articulate deep emotions" in such a way that worship steeped in these texts educates our capacities for certain emotions that are vital to the Christian story.[14] Christian worship "involves a kind of formation and shaping of our human passions by the Word,"[15] Affections such as "gratitude, joy, and patterns of repentance, compassion and forgiveness" are vital to Christian faith and life.[16]

Saliers argues that Christian worship, particularly prayer, trains the person in a distinctively Christian pattern of affections. He asserts that Christian liturgy forms the person to know, feel, and will in ways that are shaped by the Christian story of salvation, known in Scripture.

This does not mean that Christian narratives relentlessly create strong feelings of gratitude, joy, and the rest. In fact, Saliers uses the concept of affections to counter both rationalist avoidance of religious experience and enthusiastic overemphasis on strong feelings in worship.[17] He is not focusing on momentary emotional states, but rather on the life-shaping effects of deep emotions formed through the sustained discipline of worship over time. If we routinely thank God for creation, this will influence how we view the world and how we respond to it. The discipline of expressing gratitude for creation, Saliers argues, helps us to retain a disposition of thankfulness even when things are going badly.[18] The repeated participation in the Christian drama of repentance and forgiveness helps us to become people who view ourselves with an awareness of our own sinfulness, and (we hope) to view all others with the compassion of people who ourselves have been forgiven. At the same time, Saliers claims, emotions such as "bitterness, despair, and hopelessness" are not aroused and inculcated in worshippers by the Scriptures.[19] Prayer and liturgy do not nurture these as deep emotions. While Christians experience these feelings, such emotions "are not integral to this form of life."[20] Thus Saliers argues that prayer "forms and critiques" the emotional life of the Christian, encouraging a pattern of deep emotions that are shaped by the particular narratives of Scripture.[21]

In worship we learn the stories of Scripture and we are formed in the affections attendant to these texts, such that our knowledge is passional knowing—intellectual, emotional, and volitional bound together.[22] In her ongoing practices of worship, including prayer, the Christian rehearses affections in community, and this rehearsing "forms the person's very character."[23]

Saliers also appreciates the importance of physical senses, embodied activities, and ritual gestures in the kind of passional knowing he describes. In a book titled *Worship Come to Its Senses*, Saliers mentions the importance of "the non-verbal languages of worship: gesture, music, the visual, the interpersonal interaction."[24] Elsewhere Saliers asserts, "ritual action, language, music, and symbol are ways of knowing."[25] Yet he chooses not to fully explore how bodily knowing contributes to liturgical formation for two reasons that are important cautionary notes. First, Saliers knows physical gestures and bodily sensations have different meanings in different cultural settings. Given the incredible diversity of Christian traditions, it is difficult to say anything about how ritual gestures function theologically without privileging one cultural location over another.[26] Second, Saliers is concerned that church will become a performance (in a more traditional sense of the word) designed to stimulate bodily sensations and strong feeling states.[27] He writes:

> [One] factor that prevents worship from becoming a corporate act of hope is when effort is expended largely on entertaining or dramatically manipulating the congregation. All authentic worship has a dramatic element. One cannot read the Bible over time, or enact the feast of Christmas, Easter, or Pentecost without being taken into the dramatic narrative of Jesus Christ. But when the aim is concentrated solely on eliciting a response from the pews, something intrinsic to worship is lost...When worship is viewed and practiced primarily as a means to an end—whether conversion or aesthetic enjoyment—it loses its character as the hope-filled offering of praise and thanksgiving to God.[28]

When worship becomes a performance in this sense, then strong feelings—both physical and emotional—become a goal to be achieved (for the worship leaders) and a good to be expected (for the parishioners).[29] This is a far cry from the religious affections that Saliers believes worship should both express and form.

With these cautions in mind, I want to explore further the liturgical formation of affections that Saliers discusses. He portrays the person as being shaped in a distinctively Christian pattern of affections that are formed in relation to the scriptural texts. To see in more detail how these affections are produced, I turn now to a kind of case study, a text that pays explicit attention to how affections are produced.

A Case Study of Christian Formation

St. Ignatius of Loyola, founder of the Jesuit order, completed the text of *The Spiritual Exercises* in 1535.[30] This slim volume is a guidebook for a particular form of spiritual retreat and is the product of more than a decade of Ignatius's work, prayer, and experience.[31] The form of retreat he describes in the *Exercises* has been practiced by countless Christians in the past four centuries. It is the basis of spiritual training for members of the Society of Jesus and continues to be popular among clergy, avowed religious persons, and laypeople. The Exercises are focused on making an important decision in one's life, such as whether or not to join a religious order. However, over the centuries many Christians have performed the Exercises repeatedly, even annually.[32] For people who perform them once, in order to determine a life-shaping decision, and for people who perform them repeatedly, the Exercises can be profoundly formative, deeply influencing personal identity and relationship with God. Thus I am looking to this text as a case study in Christian formation.[33]

With this lens in place, I find the Exercises to be a training manual for precisely the kind of Christian affections Saliers discusses. The Exercises set out a program for intensive training in belief-laden emotions congruent with the Christian narrative, as it is known in biblical texts and particularly in relationship with Jesus Christ. Furthermore, the Exercises offer a picture of Christian formation that includes and integrates intellect, emotion, will, and body. In short, they are a pedagogical program for the whole person, aimed at knowledge of God that results not merely in statements of belief but in a whole-personed way of being in the world.

During the exercises, a director guides the person performing the exercises through a prolonged period of silence, meditation, contemplation, and prayer. The Exercises are divided into four weeks, with an understanding that any given "week" might take more or less than seven days.[34] The first week of the Exercises focuses on awareness of one's own sinfulness and moves toward repentance and amendment (the purgative way). The meditations in this week review the entire history of sin, place the Christian's own sin within that broader view, and aim toward severing sinful attachments. The second week draws meditations from the life of Christ and emphasizes imitation of Christ and commitment to service (the illuminative way). Here the focus is on making an important life decision. The third and fourth weeks center, respectively, on the passion of Christ and the resurrection (the unitive way).

The movement of the Exercises is based upon the redemption of humanity wrought in Jesus Christ, beginning with the epic sweep and tragedy of sin, moving toward the incarnation and ministry of Jesus, through the passion, to the resurrection. The retreat is shaped by contemplations upon this Christian narrative and engagement with biblical scenes in this drama. The form of the Exercises guides the Christian who performs them to understand the arc of her own narrative in ways that fit it to that shape, to bend her own life story into alignment with the story of redemption in Christ.

Within this broader pattern there is another pattern of five exercises followed within each day.[35] These exercises likewise follow patterns, such that the same steps are involved in the first exercise of each day, and so forth. Thus the Exercises present nested patterns in repetition: the overarching pattern of redemption in Christ, into which the Christian's own narrative is embedded; the pattern of daily exercises; and the pattern of the steps of each exercise.

Looking closely at some of the elements of these patterns highlights Ignatius's use of emotion and the body in the formation of Christian affections. A typical exercise starts with a prayer and then has a number of steps called "preludes." In one prelude, the Christian is to locate the specific subject of the meditation or contemplation within a broader historical frame: either within the vast drama of redemption or within the particular context of the life of Jesus.[36] In another prelude, the Christian creates "a mental image of the place."[37] If the contemplation is to be about an event in the life of Christ, then the Christian should imagine the temple, road, or shore where the event takes place. If the exercise is a meditation on something abstract, more imaginative depictions of place are employed. For example, when meditating on sin, Ignatius suggests that "the mental image will consist of imagining, and considering my soul imprisoned in its corruptible body, and my entire being in this vale of tears as an exile among brute beasts."[38]

The next prelude is to ask God for what is desired, which is determined by the subject matter of the particular meditation or contemplation. Note that what is desired here is emotional. In the first week, Ignatius asks for "shame and confusion" in awareness of his own sin. He writes, "if the contemplation is on the Resurrection I shall ask for joy with Christ rejoicing; if it is on the passion, I shall ask for pain, tears and suffering with Christ suffering."[39] In the second week, focused on making a decision, the prelude asks "for an intimate knowledge of our Lord…that I may love and follow Him better."[40]

The Christian then meditates on or contemplates a particular point, a topic derived from the biblical text. The topics of the meditations and contemplations follow the pattern described above, moving from the subject of sin and repentance in the first week to events in Jesus' life in the second week, the passion in the third, and the resurrection in the fourth week. After the meditation or contemplation on the topic at hand, the Christian then performs a "colloquy," in which she imagines that she is part of the scene she has just pictured mentally, and there converses with the other members of the cast. For example, she might pray directly to Jesus as he hangs on the cross,[41] or to Mary, or God the creator.

Each day has two meditations or contemplations that follow this pattern: prayer, preludes, principal points, and colloquies. These two exercises are then repeated to form the third and fourth exercises of the day. Yet Ignatius is aiming for something more than mere repetition.[42] In the third exercise, the Christian is to "dwell upon the points in which [she has] felt the greatest consolation or desolation, or the greatest spiritual relish."[43] There is a particularly emotional flavor to this repetition. Specific instructions are only given for the first instance of this third exercise, which is on sin. In the colloquies for this exercise, Ignatius asks for "abhorrence" for his sins and "horror" of the world (that is, worldly and vain things).[44] The second repetition (the fourth exercise of the day) is to be an intellectual "résumé" of the third exercise, incorporating an intellectual element into the emotional dynamics of the previous exercise.

The fifth exercise of the day is often called the Application of the Senses.[45] It follows the same patterns as the other exercises—prayer, preludes, points, colloquies—but the central points in the meditation involve directed use of the senses and imagination. There are five points, correlating to the five senses. In the first week, when the senses are applied within exercises focused on sin and repentance, the Christian is to use her five senses to imaginatively experience hell. An excerpt from this exercise follows:

> *First point:* To see in imagination the great fires, and the souls enveloped, as it were, in bodies of fire.
>
> *Second point:* To hear the wailing, the screaming, cries, and blasphemies against Christ our Lord and all His saints.
>
> *Third point:* To smell the smoke, the brimstone, the corruption, and rottenness.
>
> *Fourth point:* To taste bitter things, as tears, sadness, and remorse of conscience.
>
> *Fifth point:* With the sense of touch to feel how the flames surround and burn souls.[46]

Throughout the Exercises and most clearly in the Application of the Senses, Ignatius employs the imagination to engage the senses and evoke emotions.[47] The Christian is to both pray and strive for strong emotions. She should ask God for emotions (joy, pain, shame, confusion, and so forth) and use her understanding to "move more deeply [her] affections through the use of the will."[48] She is to "desire" and "beg" for emotions appropriate to the topic of the meditation, the scene in the salvation story with which she is engaged in a given exercise.[49]

Ignatius is not cultivating emotions just for the sensation of having strong feelings. Rather, this evocation of emotions is part of how the Exercises help the Christian shape her own life into conformity with the arc of the redemption story that is the pattern of the Exercises as a whole. Emotions are part of how the Christian is formed in congruence with the drama of salvation. The manipulation of emotions in the Exercises works to imbue the particularly Christian pattern of affections in the Christian. As Saliers notes, there is a pattern of deep emotions that shapes Christian life. While Saliers writes about how these are formed in worship and prayer, in the Exercises we have a dense version of this process. Over the course of a month, the Christian is steeped in the salvation narrative of Christianity, studying biblical texts, praying, meditating, and intentionally experiencing the emotions concomitant with acceptance of this narrative. As Saliers argues, Christian affections are "belief-laden emotions," bound with intellectual commitments and worldviews.[50] The kind of sorrow and shame that the Exercises inculcate in the first week are only possible if the Christian accepts a worldview in which God is good and humanity is sinful. The emotions that the Exercises cultivate are intertwined with the intellect and the will of the Christian; they are "affections" in Saliers's sense, ways of knowing and intending the world.[51] One way of viewing the Exercises, then, is as an intensive course in the passional knowing that Saliers describes.

Importantly, Ignatius also brings the body intentionally and explicitly into the process of formation. For the first week, Ignatius writes,

> I will not think of pleasant and joyful things as heaven, the Resurrection, etc., for such consideration of joy and delight will hinder the feeling of pain, sorrow, and tears that I should have for my sins. It would be better for me to keep in mind that I want to feel sorrow and pain, remembering death and the judgment.
>
> For the same reason I will deprive myself of all light, closing the shutters and doors when I am in my room.[52]

Here the Christian is to use her will to guide her thoughts toward sorrow-inducing ideas, and is likewise to manipulate her bodily sensations in order to generate an appropriately sad emotional state. Similarly, in the fourth week, the Christian is to use both mental discipline and bodily sensations to generate joyful emotions. Ignatius writes:

> I will strive to feel joy and gladness at the great joy and gladness of Christ our Lord. [I will] occupy my mind and thoughts with things that cause pleasure, happiness, and spiritual joy, for example, the thought of heaven.
>
> [I will] take advantage of the light and the comforts of the season, for example, the refreshing breezes of spring and summer, and the warmth of the sun and of a fire in winter, in so far as the soul thinks or can presume that these things may help it to rejoice in its Creator and Redeemer.[53]

Ignatius is aiming for a form of knowledge that incorporates intellect, will, and emotion. Part of his pedagogy includes the manipulation of bodily sensation. This strongly suggests that the knowing Ignatius desires for the Christian is a bodily knowing, as well. In describing passional knowing,

Saliers claims that one cannot really feel repentance without holding beliefs about sin, self, and God. Conversely, one cannot truly hold these beliefs without experiencing any form of the emotion of repentance. Ignatius's use of bodily sensations adds a further dimension to this view of passional knowing. In response to his text, I argue that Christian affections are known in the body as well as the mind, emotions, and will. Posed as a question: can one really feel repentance and believe in one's own sinfulness before God without any concomitant bodily sensation? Ignatius prayed for tears and wept. For another person repentance might not arrive with tears, but with a lump in the throat, slumped shoulders, or a sinking feeling in the pit of the stomach. One can repent without tears, or without any one particular embodiment of grief, but can one truly repent without any such embodiment?[54] I think not.

Perhaps the part of the Exercises that most clearly addresses manipulating bodily sensations concerns penance. Here Ignatius addresses limiting food and sleep as well as "chastising the flesh" by causing oneself physical pain. Ignatius recommends moderation in such practices, but also assumes their usefulness. Again, Ignatius is not interested in using the body to simply create sensations or emotions. Rather, he suggests using the body to further the passional knowing that is Christian faith. In this context, bodily sensations are bound to emotions and to theological beliefs.

Ignatius asserts that "exterior penance is the fruit of interior penance," which is to say that "sorrow for one's sins" is what initiates exterior penance.[55] At the same time, "a deep sorrow for our sins" can be one of the effects of exterior penance. I believe this reflects the complex intertwining of bodily sensation, emotion, and intellectual beliefs. Knowledge of oneself as sinner includes sorrow. Without this knowledge and concomitant emotion, causing oneself bodily pain is not penance at all. Yet when such passional knowing is present, exterior penance can contribute to it, can deepen both intellectual knowledge and emotional sorrow. The multidirectional lines of influence between intellect, will, emotion, and bodily sensation resonate with a performative anthropology as discussed in the previous chapter. Interior penance is expressed in exterior penance; exterior penance deepens interior penance; the entire process involves bodily sensation, intellect, emotion, and will.

There is one further use of the body in the Exercises that should be mentioned here, which will be taken up in greater detail later. Near the beginning of the retreat, the Christian is instructed to make a "particular examination of conscience," aimed at removing a "particular sin or defect."[56] Ignatius writes, "Each time that one falls into the particular sin or defect, he should place his hand on his breast, repenting that he has fallen. This can be done even in the presence of many people without their noticing it."[57] This is not an obvious example of manipulating bodily sensations to further passional knowing, as a discreet placing of a hand on one's breast does not so clearly align with repentance as light and laughter align with joy. It appears to be, at the very least, a physical gesture of attention and acknowledgment.

Looking at the Spiritual Exercises as a case study in Christian formation affirms much of Saliers's account. The Christian is formed in a pattern of affections that conform to the story of redemption as known through the Bible. These affections involve intellect, emotion, and will. Ignatius uses the body in this formation process, indicating that affections are bodily, as well.

Bodily Affections

Given the importance of embodiment in my performance view of church, I want to know more about how liturgical formation happens in the body. For this, I first turn to the work of G. Simon Harak, who writes about formation, the body, and the Spiritual Exercises in a book titled *Virtuous Passions: The Formation of Christian Character*. His primary subject is passion, that is, "being moved," and the role of passions in Christian ethics.[58] While he describes them somewhat differently, Harak's "passions" align with Saliers's "affections" in many ways.[59] Harak brings to the conversation an appreciation for the ways the body is involved in passions on a biophysical level, as well as a sense of the centrality of relationships in forming a pattern of passions that disposes the person to understand the world in a particular way.

Harak contends against a modern view that sees emotion as a hindrance to objective knowledge. His vision of passion incorporates rationality, emotions, and embodiment.[60] He begins by addressing connections between the body and knowing, drawing on scientific studies of "the biochemical foundation of habit."[61] In habitual actions, animals respond to situations before the stimulating signals "reached the processing center (visual cortex) of the brain."[62] He states, "In habituation, the higher functions of discrimination and intention become features not just of the brain, but *of the body as well*."[63] He uses the phrase "*organic nature* of affectivity" to refer to the "profound, systemic unity between higher, cognitive functions of the brain and the perceptions and movements of the body."[64] The body participates in knowing; it "shares in rationality."[65] This is both profound and familiar. Many daily, habitual activities—such as driving a car—involve ways of knowing and interacting in the world that are cognitive and physical. My hands turn the wheel without conscious thought; my foot hits the brake far faster than I could cognitively decide stopping was necessary.

Harak engages further scientific studies regarding emotions, noting that when researchers measure such things "as heart rate, respiration, skin conductance levels and sweating, gastrointestinal and urinary activity, secretory functions, pupillary response, hormonal changes, and electrocortical changes…it becomes clear that each individual passion does have its own specific bodily signature."[66] He concludes that emotions are embodied, as well. Passions, or affections, are bodily, emotional, and intellectual.

Further, affections involve the will, as they are vital to developing Christian virtue. Harak's interests are primarily ethical, regarding the formation of proper Christian passions. He argues that learning virtue is "learning how to be moved (angered, shamed, delighted, drawn) by the right persons and things, to the right extent, for the right reasons, in the right way, at the right time."[67] Given his research into the biophysical aspects of passions, the learning of virtue is physical as well as intellectual, emotional, and volitional.

Exploring further how passions are developed, Harak argues that interactions shape an individual's human nature over time.[68] It is primarily through embodied relationships that the human person builds up a "dossier" of passions that shapes how she understands the world. "*Passions*, then, *are learned* from early embodied interactions between infants and caregivers. The organism's "dossier" is first assembled in those interactions. And those learned, embodied passions then continue to *dispose* the organism to take its subsequent interactions with the other in a certain way."[69] The human person is shaped through interaction such that she knows and experiences the world (is moved) in particular ways—intellectually, physically, emotionally, volitionally. Over time, she develops a disposition, a "dossier"[70] of habits, passions, and expectations for what interactions will be like. Thus Harak writes, "passions have a causal history [and] we can understand passions as experiences of the past coming into interaction with the present."[71] What Harak theorizes here is also something we can observe: a child raised in a loving family learns affections of trust, passions of joyful exploration. Having always been treated with kindness by the people in her life, she expects kindness, interprets people as fundamentally good, and offers kindness to others.

Appreciation for how passions are learned over time is part of why Harak emphasizes the interactive and fundamentally interpersonal nature of being moved. For Harak, virtue is learning to be moved appropriately in and through meaningful interpersonal relationships.[72] A person's dossier of passions, formed through relationships, shapes how she understands or "takes" the meaning of every other relationship in her life.[73] While this can happen wonderfully for a child raised by a loving family, it can also happen terribly for persons who are treated with cruelty or neglect. Furthermore, even in the best instances, the passions of a child are inadequate for the harsh and disparate realities of adult life. A person's dossier can be changed; there is ample room for ethical growth. The means of changing a person's disposition is immersion in right relationships, which form a new dossier of passions.[74] Both growth and healing are fostered by appropriate relationships.

When Harak turns to the Spiritual Exercises, he says their purpose is to *"train the passions."*[75] In particular, they train the passions in relationship with Jesus. Through the use of the imagination to evoke emotions and an emphasis on the body, the Exercises help the Christian engage in an embodied relationship with the incarnate Christ that reforms the person's dossier.[76] The Exercises train the Christian to "feel with Jesus," "struggle with Christ," "labor with Christ," and "be moved as Jesus was moved."[77] As Jesus is paradigmatic of Christian ethics, learning Christian virtue involves learning passions that resonate with "the experience of union and mission with Jesus."[78] Such passions contribute to a person's disposition and dossier, and form the basis of discernment regarding experiences of passions in the future.[79]

While Saliers emphasizes the ways in which worship forms Christian affections in congruence with the biblical texts, Harak highlights the importance of interpersonal relationship in Christian formation. The difference between them on this point is a matter of degrees of emphasis rather than conflicting content. Relationship with God is clearly vital for Saliers, as is the Bible for Harak. Yet the distinction between them highlights the reality that Christian affections are formed in congruence with the story of salvation and in relationship with Jesus Christ. These two contexts of formation are mutually implicated, as to be shaped by the Christian story is to be in relation with Jesus, and to be in relation with Jesus is to take one's place within the Christian story. The Bible is central in both regards. Indeed, performing Scripture in Christian community is performing relationship with Jesus Christ, mediated by Scripture.

Harak's understanding of the biophysical aspects of passional knowing is also helpful as I aim to account for the formation of the whole person in Christian worship. He turns to science to support his view of embodied knowledge, and there has been significant advancement in scientific study of this sort since Harak published *Virtuous Passions*. There is growing interest in the emerging field of embodied cognition, wherein scientists use various methodologies to study how the body participates in human knowing.[80] Yet given my view of church as performance, another resource presents itself: the work of Constantin Stanislavski. Like Ignatius, Stanislavski offers a pedagogical program for the formation of whole persons, although the context is very different.[81] Ignatius offers a guide for retreat; Stanislavski offers a plan for rehearsal. Stanislavski is not interested in forming Christians, but actors. His text on training actors offers two vital concepts regarding formation: emotion memory and the method of physical action.

Formation for Performance

Stanislavski was a Russian actor and theater director who developed an enormously influential program for training actors. Concerned by the mechanical and artificial style of acting prevalent in the Russian theater at the beginning of his career, Stanislavski sought to bring natural emotion onto the stage. His System is a complex process of formation for actors as well as an intricate approach to the development of any given character and theatrical production. Often confused with "Method" acting, a related technique developed by Stanislavski's student, Lee Strasberg, Stanislavki's System uses a wide range of imaginative, physical, psychological, and intellectual techniques to achieve characters on stage that appear profoundly natural and true to life.[82]

Such true characters are, for Stanislavski, part and parcel of the central work of interpreting the play. Commentator Joshua Logan writes that Stanislavski "was first and foremost the interpreter of the author's play."[83] The work of interpretation involved the entire theater company in discerning the main idea of the play, which Stanislavski called the "super-objective."[84] While the play includes many smaller scenes, events, and interactions, each of these must be guided by the main idea of the play. Each actor analyzes her role—in collaboration with the rest of the company—in order to understand the smaller aims that motivate her character in each bit of the play. Thus Stanislavski taught actors to identify the "objective" of each small bit of action onstage—to label, with an active verb, precisely what the character is trying to do with every bit of dialogue or movement onstage.[85] In a good performance, each actor's objectives will move logically and consecutively toward the communal communication of the super-objective.[86] Thus the interpretive process of Stanislavski's System identifies a single dramatic arc to the play and multiple, nesting intentions among characters within that framework. This consecutive unfolding of a coherent logic to the play is important to the naturalism in performance Stanislavski sought.

In terms of emotion, such naturalism happens best through inspiration, when a performer feels the emotions of the character in an immediate and insightful way, living them truly on the stage. However, inspiration is beyond our control. For Stanislavski, inspiration was a gift of the subconscious and could not be controlled through conscious intent or effort. He writes, "we are supposed to create under inspiration; only our subconscious gives us inspiration; yet we apparently can use this subconscious only through our consciousness, which kills it."[87] In many ways, the System is a way out of this predicament, a process of intentional and conscious work that cultivates the possibility of inspiration. It aims at arousing the subconscious obliquely, by indirect means.[88]

Stanislavski's work has much to recommend it as a resource for understanding the role of the embodied worship in formation of Christian identity. In a text that depicts an actor studying his craft, *An Actor Prepares*, Stanislavski introduces several elements of his System that could bear theological fruit, including the use of the imagination, faith, communion, attention, and objectives.[89] However, here I am going to focus on only two pieces of Stanislavski's work that I think are most pertinent to the issue of how embodied worship forms Christian identity.[90] The first of these is emotion memory; the second is physical gesture.

Emotion Memory

Stanislavski asserts that just as our memories can bring back ideas and images, they can also bring back emotions, such that we experience an emotion again. He describes emotion memory as "that type of memory, which makes you relive the sensations you once felt... Just as your visual memory can reconstruct an inner image of some forgotten thing, place or person, your emotion memory can bring back feelings you have already experienced."[91] Stanislavski distinguishes between sensation memory (remembering a taste, smell, sight, etc.) and emotion memory, but also says the two run "parallel to one another" such that sensation memory can evoke and influence emotion memory.[92]

However, emotion memory is not an exact recording of the precise emotions felt in a particular situation that is then played back later. Instead, emotions are distilled, simplified, and changed in memory. The emotions of one event can mingle with those of another event that is connected in some way. Distinct emotional experiences can coalesce in memory to form a unique emotion memory associated with the connecting element. For example, a person might experience the death of a pet as a child, the predictable loss of a grandparent as an adolescent, and the sudden death of a friend in adulthood, and from all of these form an emotion memory of grief. In this way, emotion memories can change over time as distance or new experiences alter our perspectives.

In *An Actor Prepares*, Stanislavski conveys his System by narrating the experiences of a fictional acting class. He describes emotion memory through the eyes of the student Kostya Nazvanov, who develops particular emotion memories through events that happen on the way home from class. Walking home on a crowded street, Kostya sees an old man who has been run over by a streetcar. He stumbles into a ghastly scene with a dismembered corpse, a weeping woman, an apothecary trying vainly to help, indifferent bystanders, and small children playing near spilled blood. At first Kostya is depressed by this. He then wakes in the night, terrified.[93] A few days later he passes the same street corner and reflects on the accident.

> As I thought, my memory of the catastrophe seemed to become transformed. At first it had been raw and naturalistic, with all the ghastly physical details, the crushed jaw, the severed arms, the children playing with the stream of blood. Now I was shaken as much by my memory of it all, but in a different way. I was suddenly filled with indignation against human cruelty, injustice and indifference.[94]

Kostya's responses to the accident continue to change. On a clear, snowy day, the scene of the accident evokes thoughts of life, death, and eternity, and the terrifying picture of the tragedy becomes "majestic, stern."[95] The memory of the accident also begins to mingle with other memories. He remembers the weight of a streetcar that ran off the tracks months before, which Kostya and other passengers pushed back on the rails. He remembers an Italian man bending over a dead monkey, tending to it the way the apothecary had tended to the dead man. Kostya is surprised to find that the memory of the dead monkey evokes stronger emotions in him than the recent streetcar accident. He reflects, "I think that if I had to stage the street accident I would search for emotional material for my part in my memory of the scene of the Italian with the dead monkey rather than in the tragedy itself."[96]

When Kostya describes all of this to his teacher, (both of whom are alter egos of Stanislavski[97]), the director is not surprised. He says:

Each one of us has seen many accidents. We retain the memories of them, but only outstanding characteristics that impressed us and not their details. Out of these impressions one large, condensed, deeper and broader sensation memory of related experience is formed. It is a kind of synthesis of memory on a large scale. It is purer, more condensed, compact, substantial and sharper than the actual happenings.

'Time is a splendid filter for our remembered feelings—besides it is a great artist. It not only purifies, it also transmutes even painfully realistic memories into poetry.'[98]

Each actor has a storehouse of emotion memories. While it would be wonderful to have an infusion of subconscious feeling appropriate to the character every time one is on stage, this doesn't happen. Thus the actor cultivates "repeated feelings drawn from emotion memory," which are "the only means by which you can, to any degree, influence inspiration."[99] Therefore, the actor should live a life that is "full, interesting, beautiful, exciting, and inspiring," in order to develop her store of emotion memories.[100] Then she must learn to access them, using the indirect and oblique means that will not strangle subconscious feelings. One of the primary ways of accessing such memories is through external stimuli, through bodily sensation and sensation memories.

To demonstrate this, the director arranges an exercise for the students in Kostya's class. While they are gathered onstage, the sound effects and lighting change.

First we had the light of a sunny day, and we felt very cheerful. Off stage there was a symphony of noises, automobile horns, streetcar bells, factory whistles, and the far-away sound of an engine—all the audible evidence of a day in a city.

Gradually the lights were dimmed. It was pleasant, calm, but slightly sad. We were inclined to be thoughtful, our lids grew heavy. A strong wind came up, then a storm. The windows rattled in their frames, the gale howled, and whistled. Was it rain or snow beating on the panes? It was a depressing sound. The street noises had died away. A clock ticked loudly in the next room. Somebody began to play the piano, fortissimo at first and then more softly and sadly. The noises in the chimney increased the sense of melancholy. With the coming of evening lights were turned on, the piano playing ceased. At some distance a clock struck twelve. Midnight. Silence reigned. A mouse gnawed on the floor. We could hear an occasional automobile horn or railroad whistle. Finally all sounds stopped and the calm and darkness was absolute. In a little while grey shadows heralded the dawn. As the first rays of sunlight fell into the room, I felt a great relief.[101]

Stanislavski's narrative, reminiscent of Ignatius's instructions regarding light and darkness, raises questions. Does sunshine make us cheerful through a biological trigger, whereby humans simply respond to sunlight with positive emotion? Or is the process more complex, such that many of us have happy memories of sunlit days and the sensation memory aroused by sunshine evokes emotion memories of happiness? Given our exploration of embodied and passional knowing thus far, we can speculate that there are several factors in play. Bright sunlight triggers the production of serotonin, a chemical associated with happiness, in the brain. The bright lights onstage—not true sunlight—might not stimulate serotonin production. However, this physical response to sunlight increases the likelihood that a person will have happy memories of sunny days. Many people take vacations during summer months, generating associations between leisure and sunlight. Such connections can be reinforced by cultural images of happiness on sunny beaches and the pleasures of summertime. All of these factors, and quite possibly more, could be involved in the students' response to the sunny lighting onstage.[102]

Of course there is also the possibility that an actor might respond quite differently to such an experiment with light and sound. There are a number of illnesses—such as lupus—that are exacerbated by exposure to sunlight. Similarly, several common medications make the skin burn easily in even moderate sunshine. I can imagine a person who has such an illness, or has taken such a medication for a long period of time, responding to bright lighting with wariness rather than happiness. There might even be differences in communal responses to sunlight. Imagine, for instance, a group of people from Seattle, Washington, for whom sunlight is a rare treat, side by side with a group from Albuquerque, New Mexico, who routinely cross the street to the shady side to avoid the intense heat of the sun.

Lighting and sound are only two of the stimuli that Stanislavski describes as evoking emotion memory. The setting is important to him, and much of his work assumes a well-funded theater in which naturalistic sets and props are readily available. Even more than these, however, he wants the actor to rely on the logic of the play and of the interactions with other actors onstage to trigger appropriate emotional memories, thus generating the repeated feelings that actors rely on. These are all things that can be worked on by the theater company in order to "lure" emotion and inspiration to the actors.[103] Another way actors can attempt to obliquely access emotion and inspiration is through physical action.

The Method of Physical Action

From the early stages of his development of the System, Stanislavski urged actors to use appropriate physical actions to access emotion memory and enter a creative state. He once described the physical action that will arouse the desired emotion as "the bait" to which "the feeling will rise."[104] Yet while physical action was always part of the System, it came at a relatively late stage in the rehearsal process in Stanislavski's early work and was less influential than the idea of emotion memory among theater companies that drew on his techniques. One of the problems with a strong emphasis on emotion memory was that acting often took a heavy psychological toll on the actors who were remembering past experiences in order to feel strong emotions on stage.[105] To avoid some of these issues and to underline the unity of the System as a whole, Stanislavski shifted the emphasis of his teaching toward physical actions in his later years.[106]

Stanislavski's use of physical action to lure emotion, creativity, and inspiration is based on his view of knowledge as embodied. As theater scholar Jean Benedetti writes, Stanislavski believed "[t]here is a physical aspect to thought and a mental aspect to action."[107] Stanislavski exploits these connections by using physical actions in two complementary ways.

First, the logic of a play and the objectives of the actor suggest emotions. The actor can search for the physical gestures that are connected to the desired emotion. Performing these gestures can then stir the emotions.[108] By this technique, the actor can consciously move her body in order to indirectly access the subconscious and obliquely evoke emotions. In Stanislavski's words:

> An actor on the stage need only sense the smallest modicum of organic physical truth in his action or general state and instantly his emotions will respond to his inner faith in the genuineness of what his body is doing. In our case it is incomparably easier to call forth real truth and faith within the region of our physical than of our spiritual nature. An actor need only believe in himself and his soul will open up to receive all the inner objectives and emotions of his role.[109]

Second, because physical action and thought are intertwined and bound with emotion, Stanislavski asserts that improvising physical actions is part of analyzing a play, part of interpreting the author's work and understanding the super-objective. The analysis of the role, according to Stanislavski scholar Sonia Moore, involves the actor's entire person. She writes, "The search for the logic and consecutiveness of actions is the most subtle analysis of the role, in which the actor's mind, his senses, his intuition, the muscles of his body—his whole spiritual and physical nature—participate."[110]

Consider the example raised in the previous chapter, Shakespeare's *Measure for Measure*. At the end of the play, the Duke proposes to Isabel. Does he do this as an arrogant ruler, without any doubt that she will be his wife? Or does he do this as a man humbled by his appreciation of Isabel's true worth, uncertain of her response? These two options (among many others) would correspond to very different physical gestures on the part of the Duke. Does he stand and proclaim the impending nuptials to all? Does he kneel before Isabel? These options would also fit within very different understandings of the play as a whole, very different super-objectives. Earlier in his career, Stanislavski might have advised the company performing *Measure for Measure* to read through the play and discuss all options, come to an understanding of the super-objective, break each scene into smaller units and identify objectives, and eventually get on their feet and work on the physical actions of the performance. Later in his career, when Stanislavski emphasized the method of physical actions, he might have advised the same company to get up from the table much sooner. Trying out different physical actions would then be part of the interpretive process by which the company comes to understand the superobjective of the play and the motivations of each character. The Duke declaims from a balcony that Isabel will be his bride; he drops to one knee to implore her—one option makes sense to the cast and influences their understanding of the Duke's character as a whole. Trying out different physical gestures helps the company to understand the play and the characters in this scenario.[111] In this way, physical actions are part of the analysis and interpretation of the play. This happens most markedly in rehearsal; it also continues throughout the run of any production.

While Stanislavski shifts emphasis from emotion memory in the early part of his career to physical action in the later part, the two are deeply connected in his work. Each actor has a storehouse of emotion memories, which are useful in luring repeated feelings on stage. To access these emotion memories, actors use a variety of stimuli, including light, sound, sensation memory, and—perhaps most importantly—physical action.[112] Stanislavski states, "Carrying out the logic of a physical action will bring you to the logic of emotions, and this is everything for an actor."[113]

Stanislavski relies on the principle that body, intellect, emotion, and will are intertwined and develops the practical implications of this for actors.[114] At least one commentator claims that the basis of using physical action to stimulate emotion is biophysical, such that a particular physical gesture will evoke a specific emotion through biophysical responses. Moore asserts, "Science established that every nuance of emotion is connected with a particular physical action. Therefore, that action must be carefully selected on the basis of the play's circumstances. It must be the indispensable physical action connected with the emotion which the actor must bring out."[115] This resonates with some of the scientific research that Harak relies upon, which suggests that certain bodily signatures of certain passions hold cross-culturally. For example, particular facial expressions correspond to happiness in multiple cultures around the world.[116]

Yet given Stanislavski's description of emotion memory, it is easy to imagine that the connections between physical actions and emotions could run in multiple directions. Perhaps a smile both expresses and stimulates[117] happiness around the globe due to biophysical connections. There might also be deep connections between physical actions and emotions that are created through individual experience or cultural repetition. For example, the action of saluting might stimulate emotions in someone who has been in the military. Another example: I am teaching my sons to remove their baseball caps at church as a gesture of respect. The gesture comes first in this teaching, and my 8-year-old finds it to be meaningless. But from years of repetition it means something to my 12-year-old. I can watch him swipe that cap off his head and begin, ever so subtly, to inhabit a more respectful emotional space when he walks into the sanctuary.

Sometimes the lines between biophysical and historical influence are quite fluid. After sitting to eat a turkey dinner, I feel content and sleepy. This is partially due to the tryptophan in warm turkey meat, which causes drowsiness, and partially due to memories of many Thanksgivings, when supper was followed by an afternoon nap.

In all of this, context matters. The feelings associated with pouring tea might be quite different for someone in England than for someone in China, for a waitress in a tea shop, or a woman in her own home. Far from imagining that physical gestures or external stimuli could evoke particular emotions in any circumstance, Stanislavski constantly invokes the importance of the logic of the play and the coherence of the characters in his use of super-objective and objectives.

In the previous chapter, I discussed understandings of the self that focus on the outward expression of inward realities and understandings of the self that focus on outward gestures creating the sense of an abiding inward reality. I argued that performative views of the self can offer a more nuanced perspective, in which influence runs in multiple directions and delineations between inner and outer falter. With the help of Stanislavski's work on emotion memory and physical action, I am suggesting something similar here regarding the relationship between emotions and actions. Sometimes an emotion is expressed with a bodily signature through biophysical processes that appear cross-culturally. Sometimes a bodily gesture becomes linked to an emotion through repeated association, such that the gesture itself can trigger the emotion through memory and habituation. Most often, I suspect, the relationship between a given physical gesture and specific emotion flows in multiple directions.

Revisiting Ignatius

Inquiring into the formation of Christian persons through worship, I began with the work of Don Saliers. He describes Christian faith as a pattern of deep emotions, or affections, which are shaped in congruence with

the Christian narrative of redemption. These affections are a kind of passional knowing, in which emotions, intellect, and volition intertwine. To
this picture of passional knowing, G. Simon Harak adds further dimensions. He argues that the body is involved in this knowing, and that each
person develops a dossier of passions through relationships with others
over time. This dossier, or disposition, shapes how the world is perceived,
understood, and lived into. Discussing the Ignatian Exercises as an intensive course in the formation of Christian passions, Harak focuses on the
individual's relationship with Jesus. The Exercises contribute to this relationship in many ways, including inviting the Christian to imagine herself
in the scenes of the story and thereby learn to feel in relationship with
Jesus in the pattern of his life.

Stanislavski adds still more to this conversation, specifically the concept of emotion memory and the method of physical action. Emotion
memory refers to a storehouse of emotions distilled from experiences
over time. These emotion memories can be evoked to generate feelings in
the actor onstage. Stanislavski discusses different ways of triggering emotion memories, including the stimulation of bodily sensation and the use
of physical actions. With these tools from the world of theater in hand,
I want to turn again to Ignatius to see if we can further our understanding
of Christian formation.

In this light, the Exercises can be seen as a crash course in Christian
affections, interactively instilling a pattern of passions that are congruent
with the larger Christian narrative precisely because they are learned in
relationship with Jesus, as he is known in this story. This is the intentional
cultivation of a particularly Christian store of emotion memories. Or,
more fully, it is the cultivation of a storehouse of Christian affections.
These are emotion memories, but also more, since they are belief-laden
emotions that shape our intentions in the world.

As noted above, Ignatius employs the body in two distinct ways in the
Exercises. First and most prominently, he enjoins the Christian to manipulate bodily sensations in order to evoke the emotions desired in a given
exercise. Bodily manipulation is a pedagogical tool in the service of a form
of knowing that includes emotion, intellect, and will. Thus in the first
week of the Exercises, the knowledge of oneself as sinner—which incorporates emotions of sorrow and grief, intellectual beliefs regarding the
human person in relation to God, and will to amend—can be enhanced by
depriving oneself of light and pleasure. Indeed, Ignatius's instructions
regarding how to use light and darkness to encourage emotions of joy and

sorrow resonate deeply with Stanislavski's experiment with lighting and sound effects onstage. Each author perceives and exploits connections between bodily sensation and emotions. Further, there is room in both of their work to understand this connection as multidirectional. Stanislavski uses lighting to stimulate emotion that then generates gesture, as well as using gesture to stimulate emotion, analyze a play, and possibly influence choices about lighting. Ignatius says that exterior penance must stem from interior penance, which can also be one of the benefits of exterior penance.

For Stanislavski, the goal in the manipulation of bodily senses is to evoke emotions in the actor appropriate to a particular character, in keeping with the logic of the play and the objectives of the character. For Ignatius, the goal is somewhat different. He aims to ignite particular emotions in the Christian that do not change from role to role, but rather from week to week as she follows the arc of the Christian story. These emotions are not performed onstage, but rather cultivated as emotion memories that are in some sense normative for the Christian, in that resonance with emotions appropriate to union with Jesus is then a means of discernment for passions throughout the rest of life.[118] Harak refers to a dossier of passions that forms a disposition in the person, shaping what she expects of the world and how she takes its meaning. The Exercises are the shaping of such a dossier, or more precisely, the re-shaping of the person's existing dossier, in relationship with Jesus as known in the Christian narrative. Ignatius uses the manipulation of bodily sensation in crafting this dossier within the person.

The second way that Ignatius uses the body in the Exercises, mentioned briefly earlier, is to encourage the Christian performing the retreat to touch her hand to her breast in a gesture of repentance whenever she realizes she is sinning. Seen through the lens of Stanislavski's writing, it can be understood as a physical gesture associated with the affection or passion of repentance. As discussed above, while some external stimuli and physical gestures can be connected to particular emotions on a bio-physical level, they can also be connected through association and emotion memory. This part of the Exercises could exploit any existing connections between the gesture of touching one's breast and repentance for any given Christian. It could also forge such connections. In that first week, when the Exercises use multiple techniques to induce the passion of repentance, this gesture could be an intentional response to the emotion of repentance. Three intense weeks later, the same gesture could well evoke the emotion of repentance. Further, this emotion is not isolated, but belief-laden and volitional, an affection. If this is the case, then Ignatius uses the body not only to build a storehouse of Christian affections, but also to craft physical gestures associated with these affections.

Performing Church

This chapter explores how Christians are formed by worship, particularly in church as embodied performance. Responding to Saliers's concern that Christian worship practices are too diverse and culturally specific to interpret meaningfully, I have used the Spiritual Exercises of Ignatius of Loyola as a textual cipher for worship, a case study to consider. I now want to apply the insights gained to Christian worship, to see if the general account given could apply in diverse circumstances and persuasively explain some of the ways embodied performance forms Christians. I offer this account of Christian Sunday morning church services.

In church, we learn a pattern of deep emotions that is particular to Christianity. By hearing the words of the Bible, imagining the various scenes of this multilayered tale, and enacting bits of the story, we are trained in a pattern of affections that is particular to Christian faith and known in relation to Jesus. Various physical stimuli are employed in this training. Visual art, music, incense, dancing, food, embracing one another—all evoke emotions and teach us passional knowing congruent with the Christian story. The emotions experienced in worship become part of our storehouse of emotion memories, mingled, distilled, and poetically rendered over time. Furthermore, the physical actions of worship are associated with these emotion memories and the passions of which they are a part. The acts of kneeling, bowing, clasping hands, singing, and so forth become connected with the emotion memories as they are formed. These physical acts then have the power to stimulate the connected emotions and affections. Drawing on Saliers and Harak, I affirm that worship teaches Christians a pattern of affection and a dossier of passions. Employing the wisdom of Stanislavski, I would also say liturgy cultivates in Christians a storehouse of affections that are part of passional knowing, and trains us in a repertoire of physical actions that can stimulate these affections.[119]

This process varies according to community, context, and individual. Different congregations will use different gestures, fostering affections that differ in many ways even while they share roots in the same story.

Each person will bring to worship a storehouse already filled with emotion memories from other contexts and events. Thus while the pattern—the formation of affections and a repertoire of physical gestures with which to access them—is broadly applicable, it will play out in wildly diverse (and sometime divergent) ways.

For example, when I tear a piece of bread in the ritual of the Eucharist, it stirs in me an emotion memory that combines a church in West Virginia that was a safe haven for a confused adolescent, a campesina mass in Nicaragua that met my guilt with profound hospitality, a service—place and time forgotten—when sharing in my child's first communion opened new intimacy, and the sturdy comfort of fresh-baked biscuits. Each time I take communion, some portion of this emotion memory arises, and it is also added to. When I come to church distracted, perhaps little emotion is felt and therefore little is added to the storehouse of emotion memory. But over time, over years of worship, when I have eaten the bread of life in fear, in anger, in joy, and in reverence, I have formed an emotion memory that is rich and deep. It is part of how I know God and it shapes how I hope to be in the world. This emotion memory and the affection of which it is part are evoked by the physical gestures of the ritual of the Eucharist.

The particularities of how this pattern plays out are important. Church communities attend to them in various ways, without the conceptual language of "emotion memory." For example, in many congregations there are women and men who have been abused by their fathers, for whom the language and imagery of fatherhood stirs emotion memories of fear, pain, or anger. Responding to these issues, some church communities avoid parental language for God or temper the images of God as father with other metaphors that highlight the provisional nature of human language for God. Visual images, music, and gestures can all stir very different emotion memories for different people. What brings hope to one can bring fear to another, and communities are already engaged in the hard work of negotiating this multiplicity.

Christian worship forms us as whole persons, shaping how we know ourselves, God, and the world in ways that interweave emotions, intellect, will, and body. Through our embodied performance of worship, we cultivate a relationship with Jesus, known through Scripture, and develop a disposition that resonates with this relationship and this story. As worship engages us emotionally, we acquire a storehouse of affections that are particularly Christian in their connections to the story of Jesus Christ. Although these emotions differ from person to person, they include elements common among and distinctive to Christians, including the hope that the despair of crucifixion will be met with the joy of resurrection. The same embodied performances that build this storehouse of affections also train us in a repertoire of physical gestures that provide access to them. We kneel because we feel reverence for God; we kneel in order to feel reverence for God. Thus the formation of Christians through worship is an ongoing, dynamic process that continues every Sunday, and which we carry out of the sanctuary and into the world.

As I have gathered insights to construct this view of liturgical formation, I have also garnered support for three related concepts developed in the previous chapters. The first of these is performative anthropology. The human person is formed over time through complex interplays of structures and processes that include the biophysical, cultural, social, and more. We act out our being, act our way into being, and act within a broader company and context. Lines of influence move in multiple directions and cannot be neatly untangled.

The second concept is performative epistemology: a claim that knowledge is intellectual, emotional, volitional, and bodily. This has not been the dominant view of knowledge in academic circles in recent centuries. The intellectual pursuits of Europe and America have sought objective, universal knowledge to such an extent that embodied, communal knowledge has been overlooked or denied. Dwight Conquergood contrasts "propositional knowledge" that is "anchored in paradigm and secured in print" from knowledge that is "anchored in practice and circulated within a performance community."[120] He writes:

> Since the enlightenment project of modernity, the first way of knowing has been pre-eminent. Marching under the banner of science and reason, it has disqualified and repressed other ways of knowing that are rooted in embodied experience, orality, and local contingencies. Between objective knowledge that is consolidated in text, and local know-how that circulates on the ground within a community of memory and practice, there is no contest.[121]

This privileging of text-based, propositional knowledge has taken place within political and social contexts in which it has been used to garner power.

Theorist Diana Taylor locates the elevation of written knowledge over performance knowledge within the context of colonization. Taylor argues that colonial conquest legitimized writing over other forms of knowledge and memory, precisely because "[t]he space of written culture then, as now, seemed easier to control than embodied culture."[122] Written texts can be censored and the capacity to write constrained to a chosen few.[123] It was in the interests of the colonizers to elevate the importance of text-based knowledge and de-value performance-based forms of knowledge. Conquergood notes that the continued privileging of texts over embodied, communal ways of knowing supports hierarchies of class, race, and gender, as well as the presumed dominance of the West. He argues that the "hegemony of textualism" upholds "the supremacy of Western knowledge systems by erasing the vast realm of human knowledge and meaningful action that is unlettered."[124]

One of the primary contributions of performance studies has been to highlight performance-based knowing. Taylor argues persuasively that knowledge can be learned, stored, and transferred through embodied performance.[125] She distinguishes between the *archive* of written texts and the *repertoire* of performances.[126] Taylor argues that precisely because repertoires of social memory are hard to critique and control, they can provide spaces of resistance for oppressed cultures. Conquergood finds the discipline of performance studies itself to be a radical act, since it resists the hierarchy of archive over repertoire and values multiple forms of knowledge together.[127]

This shift toward recognizing and valuing performance-based knowledge is particularly useful for Christian theology, which is deeply liturgical and incarnational. It helps articulate the kind of whole-personed, communal knowing that has been happening in Christian worship for millennia. Within Taylor's paradigm, Christian liturgy is a repertoire of embodied knowledge and cultural memory.

The third concept I am developing is a performative hermeneutic: an understanding of Christian biblical interpretation that sees the performance of Christians in worship and in life as not merely the results of interpretation, but part of the interpretive process. The physical gestures of worship and Christian life are part of how we analyze the story of salvation. Washing the feet of a neighbor—or choosing not to enact this bit of biblical text—is not simply the result of how we understand the story; it shapes our understanding as well.

This leads to a final reflection on the story that I claim is central to Christian liturgical formation. Unlike a company of players who perform first one script and then another, Christians perform the Bible, through which our story is known. Throughout this chapter, I have referred to the

Christian story in the singular, which could be understood as implying there is only one and we all know what it is. Yet I use this language within a larger project where I say the Bible is like a script, and within this analogy I claim that the biblical text is in some sense incomplete, calling out for performance. In this context, the phrase "the Christian story" refers to the biblical texts themselves and it notes that I am interested in these texts as they are known to Christians, that is, to people who see these writings as pertaining to redemption or salvation.

There are numerous and diverse performances of this story. Communities and individuals understand and enact this story in ways too multiple and divergent to name. Each of these ways will form Christians in a somewhat different set of affections, passions, emotion memories, and physical actions that are understood as congruent with the Christian story. Also, the Bible as script is more like Shakespeare's *Measure for Measure*— where we have different written accounts of original performances and the script itself leaves much underdetermined—than Beckett's *Waiting for Godot*—where the author copyrighted particular set designs and stage directions.[128] The clear difference is that the Bible is exponentially more multifaceted and complex than any play, in terms of its literary components, its authorship and authority, and its reception and performance.

Thus I use phrases such as "the Christian story," not to gesture toward a unified and textually grounded singularity of Christianity, but rather, within the broader framework of my performance perspective on church, to focus attention on the reality of this text as it is performed in diverse, particular, and multiple ways. These performances, where the bare bones of the words on paper come to life in embodied communities, are church as I understand it. Stanislavski states, "Theater and dramaturgy are one whole…Only as a result of two arts—that of the dramatist and that of the theatrical group—will the new value, the performance, be born."[129]

3

Changing Roles

Introduction

In the previous chapter, I brought together resources from both theater and theology in order to give a concrete account of how the narratives and rituals of church performance shape all aspects of the human person: intellectual, emotional, bodily, and volitional. This is a description of the process that liturgical theologian Siobhán Garrigan calls the "liturgical construction of the self."[1] My efforts to describe how social construction happens within church practices immediately raise two related observations. First, the self is not formed by liturgy alone. Persons are formed in multiple contexts, of which church is only one. Second, social construction works for both good and ill, in ways that promote flourishing and ways that cause great harm.

Multiple Contexts of Construction

The same mechanisms of emotion memory and bodily gesture that operate within church worship also function in other contexts to support the shaping of the self in accord with distinct communities, such as sports teams, family systems, and schools. Indeed, the self is formed within a matrix of interrelated contexts and communities, each of which contributes to the shaping of the person in intellectual, bodily, volitional, and emotional ways. The liturgical construction of the self is always one way, among many, in which the self is formed. Furthermore, these various communities of formation often have different, even conflicting, goals and norms.

Imagine a Christian who learns on Sunday morning to eschew love of mammon and embrace love of God, to store up her treasure in heaven and share her possessions with the poor. She places money in a collection plate, ritually signifying her loyalty to God over wealth and her commitment to care for those in need. But come Monday morning, this same person goes to work in a financial office, giving time and attention to the accumulation of wealth for her clients. In this context she participates fully in rituals of corporate and capitalist hierarchy, wearing a tailored suit, having a business meeting over an elegant lunch, and driving past the crowded bus stop on her way home to a safe neighborhood. This is a stark example of one person inhabiting two contrasting worldviews. In reality, each of us inhabits several, and the conflicts are more complicated. A Christian receives the Eucharist on Sunday morning, partaking in a shared meal of sacramental presence within a liturgy that invokes gratitude for grace abundant, awareness of those who hunger, and a communal sense of equality before God. On Monday evening, after work, she attends a Weight Watcher's meeting that is its own liturgy, with words of encouragement and challenge, affirmation of shared values, and a ritual weigh-in. This meeting is part of her care for herself, attending to health issues regarding weight, and therefore is deeply in keeping with her sense of herself as a child of God who is worthy of care. There is not necessarily significant conflict between the rituals of Sunday morning and Monday night. However, what happens on Tuesday at noon, when a waiter places bread before her on the table? Does she break it in reverence and thanksgiving, or does she tally points, apportioning herself an acceptable allowance for this meal? Quite possibly she does both, overlaying distinct ways of being in the world.

What I am pointing to here is more than a model of dual citizenship, where the Christian is shaped both by church and by the "secular" world. Rather, we each occupy multiple worldviews, are shaped by distinct and sometimes competing narratives, and engage in diverse ritual performances of ourselves. For this reason, comparative theologian John Thatamanil says that in many ways contemporary Americans have syncretic belief systems.[2] This is less likely to mean incorporating aspects of multiple religious traditions than incorporating Christianity with such things as American patriotism, capitalism, liberalism, conservatism, vegetarianism, avid gardening, or attachment parenting.

Good, Bad, and Complicated

Precisely because the human person is bodily, emotional, intellectual, and volitional, communal narratives and rituals that address all of these aspects of the person have profound constructive power. They can form us to be kind, loving, and just in the world. Yet communal rituals often are used to construct persons in ways that are deeply harmful. Performances teach us to accept violence, expect inequities, tolerate suffering, and accept our given roles within hierarchies of domination and oppression. Rituals of militarism and empire, of consumerism and complacency, help sustain hegemonies of power and privilege. Clear dividing lines between positive and negative, helpful and harmful forms of social construction are extremely hard to find. Is an outing to see a baseball game a ritual of wholesome recreation, patriotic tradition, and team spirit? Or is it a jingoistic feast, in which spectators ritually consume unhealthy foods while watching a select few players exercise, players from around the world who are paid to perform this quintessentially American pastime? There is probably truth in both descriptions, and many others, as well.

In trying to understand how the liturgical construction of the self that happens in church relates to, and differs from, other forms of social construction, I turn to theater director Augusto Boal and theologian Letty Russell. Each of these authors is critical of the ways in which theater and church, respectively, are used to sustain systems of oppression and domination. At the same time, each author finds resources to resist oppression and enact positive modes of communal formation. Within their writings, both Boal and Russell also engage the concepts I have termed performative anthropology, performative epistemology, and performative hermeneutics.

Cathartic Theater, Cathartic Church?

Augusto Boal was a Brazilian director who believed theater could form people in ways that were oppressive and repressive. In his influential text, *Theatre of the Oppressed*, Boal claims that theater is often used by those in power to sustain the status quo in situations of oppression and to quell revolutionary impulses. He argues, more particularly, that Aristotelian tragedy is a means of social repression. It is one of many tools (including "politics, bureaucracy, habits, customs") used by the elite to encourage passivity among the oppressed.[3] Boal states that Aristotelian tragedy is an "extremely powerful poeti-political system for intimidation of the spectator, for elimination of the 'bad' or illegal tendencies of the audience."[4] He further claims that Aristotle's repressive poetics are still in use in many forms in the modern West, including television, theater, and film.[5] Although Boal does not expand his assessment to include the church, possible parallels are easy to spot.

Central to Boal's work is his interpretation of catharsis in Aristotle's poetics. This term has a particular meaning in this context that is quite different from its connotation in popular culture.[6] In Boal's writing, Aristotelian catharsis is a complex purging of antiestablishment emotional impulses.[7] The production of catharsis begins with empathy, when the spectator is emotionally linked to the character on the stage, primarily through pity and fear.[8] In this relationship, states Boal, "the spectator assumes a passive attitude and delegates the power of action to the character. Since the character resembles us (as Aristotle indicates), we live vicariously all his stage experiences. Without acting, we feel that we are acting. We love and hate when the character loves and hates."[9]

While catharsis can be produced using many plotlines, it will be helpful to look at the example of a classic tragedy. The process depends on a relationship of empathy between the spectator and the likable hero. The hero has a tragic flaw ("hamartia") that, surprisingly, helps bring the hero to "his present state of happiness."[10] Because the flaw is key to the hero's success, the same flaw (a common one) is stimulated and activated within the empathic spectator. Then the plot unfolds, something new develops, and the flaw could result in the hero's downfall. This is "peripeteia, a radical change in the character's destiny."[11] The spectator fears for the hero's fortunes. The hero has a moment of recognition of his flaw—this recognition is called "anagnorisis"—and the empathic spectator likewise sees the flaw in herself. On stage, the character undergoes "catastrophe," the tragic outcome of his hamartia. The spectator escapes catastrophe but vicariously experiences the consequences of her own flaw. She recognizes and rejects, or is emotionally purged of, the common hamartia that has been acted on the stage. This purgation is catharsis.[12]

When Aristotelian catharsis works well, a particular hamartia is empathically stimulated in the spectator, who then passes through the three stages of peripeteia, anagnorisis, and catastrophe with the tragic hero. Through the process, her own tendencies toward the specific flaw in question are purged. She has seen, feared, and even felt the terrible consequences of this flaw; has recognized the flaw in herself; and turns away from it.

This production of catharsis can happen in very similar ways even when the plotlines alter, as long as the spectator goes through the stages of peripeteia, anagnorisis, and catastrophe. Boal gives a typology of five plot forms that differ broadly but each move through this process. One includes two tragic heroes whose flaws are mirror images, excesses in opposing direction, and catharsis urges the spectator toward middle ground. Another presents a hero in negative form; instead of being good with only one flaw, he is wicked with only one virtue. This hero passes through the recognition of his many flaws and moves on toward happiness based on his one virtue, which has an exemplary effect for the spectator.

In Boal's analysis, this process is highly political, as the hamartia involved is an antisocial impulse of some kind. Produced by those with power, the theater is used as a means of coercion to purge the people of antisocial or rebellious impulses. It is a means to align the social ethos of the spectators with the social ethos of the dominant culture, to reaffirm passivity in the face of existing inequalities. This system can only function within "more or less stable societies, ethically defined," since its chief purpose is to conform the people to the status quo, to "bridle the individual, to adjust him to what pre-exists."[13] Boal asserts, "This system functions to diminish, placate, satisfy, eliminate all that can break the balance—all, including the revolutionary, transforming impetus."[14]

Reading Boal, I wonder, does church function the same way? Are there instances in which the performance of church serves to sanctify the status quo? Consider a fictional mainline Protestant congregation. Members of the congregation are generally professionals of some sort, middle class or higher in socioeconomic status, politically liberal, and well educated. As a group, we are antisexist, antiracist, and concerned for the poor, although we, personally, are doing alright in a sexist, racist, poverty-ridden world. On principle, we would want the world to be otherwise, even though its current condition works to our general advantage. Thus we read the newspaper with chagrin, we have "carbon fasts" of environmental conservation during Lent, and we occasionally serve meals at the local homeless shelter.

Near the beginning of Sunday worship, we confess our sins in prayer that often alludes to our complacency, to our tacit acceptance of the injustices from which we benefit. We then receive, in the spoken words of the minister, forgiveness for our sins. We are assured that while our own action or inaction proves us to be sinners, God forgives us. We shake hands while pronouncing "Christ's peace," identifying ourselves, and each other, as those who are bestowed the undeserved peace of God.

Much of the service that follows focuses on the love of God. There are references to Jesus's identification with the marginalized, of his feeding, healing, and teaching the poor. God's justice and mercy are sung in hymns of praise. In various ways, the congregation is called to follow Jesus, commanded to love others, and exhorted to work toward justice in our world.

After the sermon, a member of the congregation describes good work being currently supported by the larger church organization. The story might describe a school being built for poor children in Africa, an eco-friendly farm in Thailand, or a literacy program in Appalachia. On the one hand, we Christians sitting in the pews on Sunday morning are not, by and large, dedicating our lives to such admirable causes. On the other hand, as members of the organization that supports such programs, we are identified with the doers of such good works. Immediately after this presentation, the morning offering is received. By dropping money in the collection plate, members of the congregation authorize the characters in the stories we have heard to act on our behalf. Through this ritual, we are assured that we are accomplishing good works throughout the world while seated comfortably in the pew. Furthermore, our monetary identification with the mission workers' stories cements our empathic connection with the characters in the biblical stories read earlier in the service.

In Boal's description of how Aristotelian tragedy generates catharsis, the impulses of the audience that might challenge the status quo are vicariously punished in the catastrophe that befalls the protagonist. In the situation I am describing in a congregation, the possible challenge to the status quo takes the form of concrete concern for equality and justice. These "antisocial" impulses are not punished, but rather discharged through rituals performed by ministers who act on our behalf. We do not need to act ourselves, as we are empathically identified with those actors (Jesus, missionaries, etc.) whose work we collectively admire. Thus members of the congregation can leave the service feeling confident that we are antiracist, antisexist, and concerned for the poor. We have identified ourselves, and each other, as part of the solution rather than the problem. We can return to our lives without further ado, reaping the rewards of an unjust system that we combat only ritually.

Of course such a description does not capture all that happens in Christian worship. It is a very negative, one-sided view. And yet, we recall the doubleness of church. We are not what we are called to be. If this Boalian reading of church seems remotely recognizable, if it appears as one possible way in which church is performed, then we should take heed. How do we prevent such performances?

Liberating Theater

Observing that theater has been such a tool in service of the status quo does not lead Boal to abandon theater, but rather to search for a way to harness its power for revolutionary purposes. His own work "seek[s] another

poetics," in which theater does not prevent revolutionary action but provides its training ground.[15] In Boal's poetics of the oppressed,

> the spectator delegates no power to the character (or actor) either to
> act or to think in his place; on the contrary, he himself assumes the
> protagonic role, changes the dramatic action, tries out solutions,
> discusses plans for change—in short, trains himself for real action.
> In this case, perhaps the theater is not revolutionary in itself, but it
> is surely a rehearsal for the revolution.[16]

The primary goal of Boalian poetics is to transform the spectators into
"spect-actors"—that is, people who both see the situation and are agents
within it.[17] Given this aim, Boal was not satisfied with teaching theatrical
texts and modes of production in an oppressed community, or with staging plays that he thought would speak to a given situation. Instead, Boal
wanted to enable the people to make their own theater. Acknowledging
the Marxist influence in his work, Boal desired to "transfer to the people
the means of production in the theater so that the people themselves may
utilize them."[18]

Boal traces this impulse in his work to a pivotal moment in the 1960s
when he was involved in agit-prop theater (agitation and propaganda) in
Brazil, exhorting the oppressed to rise up in violent revolution. At the end
of one such production, the actors sang a spirited anthem saying "let us
spill our blood" for freedom.[19] One of the peasants, Virgilio, was deeply
moved and invited the actors to join with the peasants in armed revolt.
Boal and his players then explained that their guns were not real, that they
were not really peasants, that they were actors unwilling to fight. This
incident convinced Boal that his role was not to persuade the oppressed
groups with which he worked how they ought to respond to a given situation, especially if he was unwilling to take on the risks of such a response.[20]
He writes, "I have never again written plays that give advice, nor have
I ever sent 'messages' again. Except on occasions when I was running the
same risks as everyone else."[21] The theatrical techniques that Boal then
develops are aimed at allowing the group to explore their own solutions to
their own problems.[22] He later writes,

> The Theatre of the Oppressed has two fundamental linked princi-
> ples: it aims (a) to help the spect-actor transform himself into a
> protagonist of the dramatic action and rehearse alternatives for his

situation, so that he may then be able (b) to extrapolate into his real life the actions he has rehearsed in the practice of theatre.[23]

Boal's approach, now broadly known as Theater of the Oppressed, or TO, used theatrical techniques to encourage community members to see themselves as protagonists in ways that would affect their lives beyond the theater.

While developing TO, Boal worked primarily in situations of communal oppression with peasants, workers, and villagers who suffered under the same unjust policies or economic inequity. With these groups, Boal would go through a lengthy, four-stage process to help make this transformation into spect-actors. Each stage of the process includes games, exercises, or "gamesercises." These embodied, communal exercises are pedagogical tools that engage the whole person—and the larger group—in the learning process.

The first stage is designed to help the participant come to know his or her own body. In particular, the exercises help a person recognize how her work shapes her posture, musculature, and physical demeanor. The range of motion of a factory worker, who spends her days lifting heavy parts, will differ from that of a seamstress, who sits over needle and thread all day long. Each person occupies several social roles that shape his body and his way of being in the world: "The combination of roles that a person must perform imposes on him a 'mask' of behavior."[24] Boal states, "Each one of us, in real life, exhibits a type of pre-established, mechanized behavior. We create habits of thought, of language, of profession. All our relations in daily life are patterned."[25]

One exercise in this first stage might be a slow motion race, which forces the participants to think about bodily movements. Such a simple event can serve as a sophisticated pedagogical tool, as it fosters embodied analysis of the self and of society. The exercise encourages a high level of self-awareness, both bodily and intellectually, and contains a latent analysis of the worker's body as a tool within the system of production. Scholar Philip Auslander comments on Boal's technique, "Because the mechanisms of oppression shape the body, it is through the body and its habits that those mechanisms can be exposed."[26]

The second stage comprises games that require participants to express themselves bodily. Imagine a game in which each person is given a piece of paper with the name and sex of an animal, such as "male hummingbird." For ten minutes each person in the group imitates his or her animal bodily, trying to communicate to the others what kind of animal he or she is without making any sound. Then each person tries to find his or her animal mate.[27]

The third stage includes various activities in which the spectators of a scene intervene in its performance. Someone proposes a situation that is acted out to the point where the conflict is to be addressed. People from the audience then suggest different methods of resolution, each of which is improvised on the spot. For example, a woman finds her husband has been unfaithful and wants revenge. How should she avenge herself? The audience offers options to act out.[28] Another activity in this third stage is "image theater," in which a person is asked to communicate her feelings on a particular subject by sculpting the bodies of the other participants into a scene that conveys her views. She engages in conversation with the others present to develop an image of the situation as it actually is; an image of the situation in an improved, ideal state; and then a transitional image that communicates something of how the movement from actual to ideal could take place.[29]

Another exercise within this third stage is one of the most influential elements of Boal's work: forum theater. A brief skit is developed by the participants to portray a social or political problem that they face, along with a possible solution. After the first performance, the skit is enacted again. This time, anyone can stop the action, replace an actor, and enact a new solution to the conflict. It is vital that the person proposing an alternative path for the drama actually acts it out, bodily, within the performance. Boal writes,

> The participants who choose to intervene must continue the physical actions of the replaced actors; they are not allowed to come on the stage and talk, talk, talk: they must carry out the same type of work or activities performed by the actors who were in their place. The theatrical activity must go on in the same way, on the stage. Anyone may propose any solution, but it must be done on the stage, working, acting, doing things, and not from the comfort of his seat.[30]

The technique of forum theater enables a community to examine different possible responses to a particular conflict or problem. When the participants act out the solutions on stage, they are rehearsing these actions for their own lives. It is this acting out that prevents forum theater from having any cathartic effect. Instead of identifying with the actions of another, the participant performs them herself; instead of purging impulses, forum theater rehearses them.[31] Boal asserts, "the rehearsal stimulates the practice of the act in reality…[Forum theater] creates a sort of uneasy sense of incompleteness that seeks fulfillment through real action."[32]

   In the fourth stage, the participants create scenes in order to generate dialogue on an issue or to rehearse certain actions. One exercise in the fourth stage is invisible theater, in which participants enact a scene in a public place to start a discussion. For example, two men start an argument about wages in a local café. The other diners join in, a debate is started in the community, and only the actors know that theater took place.[33] Another exercise involves a participant remembering and reenacting a moment when she was repressed, when she did not resist oppression; and then she acts it out again, this time with resistance.[34] Because the participant is acting out a new response to the repression, this exercise does not produce catharsis but rather prepares her to resist in future situations.[35] In this fourth stage, the participant has become a spect-actor. She sees her situation and acts within it.

   Boal develops Theater of the Oppressed as a liberating form of theater in contrast to Aristotelian poetics. Through the four stages of TO, participants use physical exercises to understand their own experiences, analyze communal circumstances, envision new possibilities, and ready themselves for action beyond the stage.

Liberating Church

Although Boal was not explicitly concerned with church, the goals of Theater of the Oppressed bear significant similarity to the ecclesiology put forth in the writings and life of liberation theologian Letty Russell. Like Boal, Russell was deeply formed by her work with communities of struggle. She served the East Harlem Protestant Parish in New York City from 1952–1968, first as a Christian educator and then, for ten years, as pastor of the Presbyterian Church of the Ascension. This decade of ministry was an enormous influence on Russell's theology, described in her first book, *Christian Education in Mission*, and referred to repeatedly in later writings.[36]

   Russell, a white woman of privilege, did not want to come into a multiracial congregation struggling with poverty and impose her own authority. She recognized the many ways in which ecclesial institutions mirrored, rather than countered, hierarchical structures that privileged the few over the many. She was also aware of the dangers of reproducing race and class privilege within efforts for social justice. Russell emphasized themes of partnership and hospitality in order to create an alternative model for ministry. The Reformed tradition, of which Russell is a part, has long affirmed the value of shared leadership, based on the theological affirmation that all baptized Christians are called to ministry in some form.[37] In her theological writings, Russell uses these principles to argue that hierarchical distinctions between clergy and laity uncritically repeat the oppressive structures of society, when church should offer a prophetic alternative vision.[38] She sought means for the members of the community to take up their own roles as ministers to one another, and to create a performance of church that extended beyond the sanctuary into community life.

The process by which she prepared sermons exemplifies her broader approach. She began with the Bible. For nine years, she wrote *Daily Bible Readings*, a kind of lectionary Bible study resource specifically for the community in East Harlem. These were illustrated by an artist in the parish, Joseph Papin, and published by and for the congregation.[39] Each week, churchgoers of all ages were encouraged to read the daily verses and focus on a particular text. Several Bible study groups met in people's houses during the week. The leaders of these groups would meet with Russell and the other members of the church staff, in part so the reflections of the community members could inform and shape the Sunday morning sermon. Russell wrote, "the same text is studied by staff and Bible study leaders on Monday, by all the House Bible Study groups on Wednesday, by the children and youth on Sunday, and is the basis for the sermon."[40] This is an example of the kind of communal leadership that Russell later wrote about in her theological texts. Throughout her career, the degree to which Russell garnered and nurtured the ministerial gifts of others is remarkable. In East Harlem, the church secretary became increasingly active in educational programs. The janitor became a lay evangelist, teaching and preaching in Spanish.[41]

In addition to the *Daily Bible Readings*, Russell wrote another text during her time in East Harlem, the *Christian Education Handbook*. She called this text a "do-it-yourself kit," since it was designed as a guide to help other church communities develop their own resources for ministry, specific to their own church contexts and congregational settings.[42] Within this *Handbook*, Russell encourages "teachers to see themselves as learners, and pupils as the teachers."[43]

Russell's work in East Harlem exemplifies her commitment to "praxis," an ongoing process of action, reflection, and action.[44] In her writings, Russell develops a theological methodology that includes four steps. One is "commitment to the task of raising up signs of God's new household with those who are struggling for justice and full humanity." This commitment is not merely internal assent to theoretical principles, but rather embodied, enacted participation in the struggle of a particular community. Another is "sharing experiences" of such commitment and struggle within specific contexts. Communities can see their circumstances more clearly together. A third step is "critical analysis" of those specific contexts, including social and historical analysis. A fourth step is questioning biblical and church tradition regarding the experiences they have shared together and the contexts they have analyzed communally.[45] Through this process, church members share their struggles and interpret them in light of Scripture, while also interpreting Scripture in light of their own struggles. The tradition, while flawed, is also rife with concepts and conversation partners that can help in current circumstances.

With the steps listed in this way, it is easy to imagine that this is a single, linear process with a clear beginning and end. However, Russell refers to this as a spiral to emphasize that it is ongoing. One can enter the spiral at any point—start with any step—and going through all four will lead one to begin anew, rather than arrive satisfied. In classes, Russell often distributed a handout—usually printed on hot-pink paper—with these four steps arranged visually in a spiral.[46] This ought not be seen as a circle, Russell states, because "the movement of action and reflection" does not lead back to the same place each time, but rather to "new clues and questions in a continuing spiral that never comes out in exactly the same place."[47] This spiral methodology maps Russell's theological writings, her pastoral ministry, and her activism, for each of these elements of her career was interwoven with the others, part and parcel of the same praxis.

Boal and Russell seek to restructure theater and church, respectively, to guard against inculcating passivity. Russell is not working against a system of Aristotelian catharsis, exactly, but rather against a hierarchical church structure in which the ordained clergy are active authorities while the laity are disempowered.[48] They both develop concrete methodologies to make the most of their traditions. Putting the two authors in conversation, as I do here, highlights techniques that are useful in both arenas. These include attention to embodied action, shared leadership, and—perhaps most vitally—the importance of inhabiting multiple roles.

Role Switching

Boal and Russell seek to break down divisions between actor and audience, clergy and congregation. To do this, they advocate role switching. This starts quite early on in Boal's exercises. Even the first stage of his process, the early exercises in which participants become aware of how their work shapes their bodies, has role switching as a goal. He writes that these exercises are intended to "disjoint" or "'undo' the muscular structures of the participants...to take them apart, to study and analyze them...to raise them to the level of consciousness."[49] If these structures can be thoroughly analyzed, Boal argues, then the participant will be able to "assemble structures characteristic of other professions and social classes; that is, one will be able to physically 'interpret' characters different from oneself."[50]

Boal describes the value of role switching by recalling his work on a project aimed at developing human rights in prisons in São Paulo.[51] The prisoners considered the guards to be the powerful oppressors, while the guards viewed themselves as oppressed, working long hours in dangerous conditions for low pay.[52] Boal's method involved the guards putting on one piece of theater and the prisoners another, together at a shared performance. Some of the guards, presenting a piece about their own working conditions, portrayed prisoners, donning "the uniforms of the sentenced men, as well as adopting their physical stances—the head lowered, the hand on the shoulder of the man in front."[53] For their part, the prisoners' performances revealed that they were more than convicts; they were fathers, mothers, and artists. Boal proudly relates that one of the outcomes of this project was an increase in respect between guards and prisoners as they began to see each other not as enemies, but as persons.[54] I suspect many elements of the project contributed to this outcome, since Theater of the Oppressed is a complex process. However, Boal's depiction of the events highlights the importance of playing multiple roles—the guard plays the role of prisoner, the inmate of father, the father of actor, and so forth.

It is not just watching the prisoners perform that opens the eyes of the guards regarding the humanity of their fellows; it is wearing the uniform and lowering their heads, as prisoners were expected to do. In part, this is merely an extension of the importance of multiple perspectives, understood in an embodied and performative way. To understand something in a new way, it helps to stand—physically—in someone else's shoes.

Auslander sees Boal's emphasis on multiple roles as a technique to foster critical distance from all socially constructed roles. He writes, "the point is for the spect-actor to be able to move from one mask to another while retaining a critical distance from all masks."[55] Boal does not imagine, Auslander argues, that a subject can really divest herself from all socially and ideologically constructed roles. Instead, Boal hopes that by physically inhabiting multiple roles on the stage, the spect-actor gains enough critical distance regarding such roles to engage her own agency in choosing what roles she plays. Auslander asserts, "The spect-actor is a postmodern subject, divided in itself, fully aware that it cannot escape ideology, that its only choice is amongst different ideological masks... [but] even if the only choice we have is a choice of masks, some masks are better than others."[56]

The new perspectives gained by role switching are even more important if we accept Boal's position that acting in theater can change how one acts in life. Boal wanted theater to be rehearsal for revolution; he believed acting as protagonists onstage would help people engage their own agency offstage. In many ways, the goal of Theater of the Oppressed is to encourage and develop the agency of community members in order to address shared problems in their own contexts. To accomplish this goal, Boal designed an approach to theater in which leadership was shared among various members of the community and strong divisions between roles and functions (such as actor, director, and audience) were blurred.

At different points in his career, Boal tinkered with the dividing lines between almost all the roles in theater. The work of the playwright and the director was shared by the community in forum theater. Boal also constructed a complex "Joker" system of producing a play as a means to allow multiple actors to act out multiple characters within the same performance.[57] The Joker system was designed to help the community tell and interpret its own story for itself.[58] The fluidity of roles was key to enabling shared leadership and preventing hierarchical power relations.

Similarly, Russell's theology articulates a vision of shared leadership as vital to church. She writes of "authority in community" and "leadership in the round" as nonhierarchical ways of thinking about leadership such that each person's gifts are welcomed.[59] She writes, "A feminist leader is one who inspires others to be leaders, especially those on the margins of church and society who do not think they are 'somebody.'"[60] Russell understood the experience of one's own agency as vital to human flourishing. To be able to participate in shaping our own unfolding stories, in community with others, is "to live as subjects of worth and not objects of manipulation."[61] She writes, "When circumstances are such that we have no perception that we can share in making even a small difference in our future, an important part of human life is denied."[62] Part of what it is to know oneself as "somebody" is to act in the hope of shaping the future of one's community, even in small ways.[63] Stepping into a leadership role can have a profound effect on a person's sense of self and sense of possibility.

Shared Context, Distinct Strengths

Some of the similarities between Boal and Russell regarding leadership and community can be traced to the cultural moment they shared and to the particular work of Paulo Freire. Boal, Russell, and Freire were part of a cultural shift that took place from the 1960s to the 1990s in the Western hemisphere. It was a time of hope in the possibilities of political activism, desire for freedom and justice, and a sense of the necessity and potential for structural change.

One aspect of this movement that was particularly vital for Russell was the emergence of liberation theology. This is a broad theological movement that began to coalesce at a conference of Latin American Roman Catholic Bishops in Medellín.[64] What makes liberation theology distinctive is not so much its content but its methodology. It takes place within communal struggles for justice. It is praxis—an ongoing process of action and reflection, of seeing and acting. Liberation theology requires the risk of self-involvement in communal movement toward justice and can only be done within such a context.

To my knowledge, Boal was not directly involved in liberation theology, yet he was familiar with the movement.[65] There are obvious similarities between Boal's methodology and the commitment to praxis found in liberation theology. Recall Boal's encounter with Virgilio and his subsequent decision never again to tell a community to do something without taking on the risk of being part of the action. Also recall that within forum theater, no one is permitted merely to say what the actors should do. If someone wants a voice in how the drama unfolds, she must take the stage and join the action. While Boal was not directly involved in liberation theology, he was nurtured by the same broader movements and concerns in which liberation theology emerged.

Boal and Russell were both directly influenced by Paulo Freire's text on education, *Pedagogy of the Oppressed*.[66] Freire and Boal became friends;

both Russell and Freire were involved with the World Council of Churches.[67] Some of the methodological choices made by Boal and Russell clearly echo Freire's work, including the importance of critical reflection on experience, analysis of social contexts, and communal interpretation of texts. Yet these close connections ought not be seen as simply linear. While Boal and Russell both drew on Freire's texts and claimed his influence, it is not the case that all of these ideas originated with Freire and were later taken up by readers of his work. Russell was already enacting part of this methodology in East Harlem in the 1960s, before *Pedagogy of the Oppressed* was published. Boal was already developing Brazilian theater in São Paulo in ways that were politically critical and contextually focused. There is more happening in the relations between Boal, Russell, and Freire than straightforward textual influence. All three authors were nurtured by a broader cultural trend that was committed to grassroots social change.

Within their overlapping contexts, Boal and Russell developed somewhat parallel strategies to guard against oppressive social construction through theater and church and to foster liberating structures. They were also markedly different. Although she was profoundly aware of the ways in which Christian traditions have perpetrated harm, Russell remained committed to Christian ecclesiastical organizations. Her own work was guided and shaped by traditional resources, including creeds and confessions. Most important, Scripture was Russell's script. In comparison, Boal was less committed to remaining within a set theatrical community or convention. More radical than Russell in many regards, Boal was a revolutionary figure, open to possibilities in which scripts were rewritten or disregarded altogether, in which roles were shared, switched, or destroyed.

Even when Boal's and Russell's strategies are most similar, they have different roots. Boal's theatrical techniques are grounded in a broad understanding of how people know. He has a performative anthropology and a performative epistemology, which together fund TO. Put simply, it is because of who we are and how we know that doing particular physical activities can have liberating effects. Boal states, "Scientists have demonstrated that one's physical and psychic apparatuses are completely inseparable. Stanislavski's work on physical action also tends to the same conclusion, i.e. that ideas, emotions and sensations are all indissolubly interwoven."[68] He states simply, "the whole body thinks—not just the brain."[69]

The active and embodied elements of Boal's epistemology have proven useful in diverse educational settings around the globe. His techniques continue to influence educational theory and pedagogical practices. Suzanne

Burgoyne states, "Augusto Boal's interactive Theatre of the Oppressed (TO) provides embodied learning experiences that engage the senses, emotions, and imagination as well as the intellect."[70] Thus it is a form of "active learning," which has been shown to "develop critical thinking."[71] In a similar vein, Jacqueline D. Burleson asserts that "Boal's interactive performance techniques" help students understand course materials in a way that develops and activates "a critical consciousness."[72]

Boal explains how people know in wide-reaching terms, offering a general epistemology that is applicable to many different kinds of knowledge. His performative epistemology is rooted in a view of the human person in which intellect, embodiment, emotion, and volition are intricately interwoven. We think in the body, and some things can only be known through the embodied language of theater.

In contrast, the primary reasons for the connections between acting and knowing in Russell's work are theological. Russell's methodology springs not from a general theory of knowledge, but from the specific context of knowing the God of Jesus Christ. Theological knowledge requires action because of who God is. In Jesus Christ, "word and deed" are fully integrated in the incarnation. Part of why we know God in whole-personed ways is because God gives Godself to be known in the person of Jesus. Therefore it is in "the integration of thought and action [that Christians] attempt to find out more fully the nature of the incarnation and of true humanity."[73]

Throughout the Bible, particularly in narratives of the Exodus and stories of Jesus, God is portrayed as present with and caring for those who suffer, moving toward justice and desiring the salvation of all.[74] The God of Jesus is the God of justice and hospitality, the God who chooses to partner with humanity in the mending of creation.[75] For this reason, Christians must act to know God, and the kind of action necessary is communal struggle for liberation. For Russell, the importance of action for knowledge is not due to generically accessible characteristics of humanity (body, mind, emotion, and intellect together), but rather due to the characteristics of God (just, partnering, hospitable) and how God acts in history, as seen in Jesus Christ.[76]

The framework for all of Russell's work is God's love for creation. Church is a postscript, a footnote to "God's love affair with the world."[77] Church must be understood within this context, which focuses on God's activity rather than a static view of the nature of church itself.[78] The category of mission is central to Russell's understanding of church.[79] From her days as a pastor throughout her scholarship, Russell offered a vision of mission that focuses on God's love for the world, into which we are welcomed. In *Church in the Round,* her mature ecclesiology, Russell writes, "the church does not have a mission; rather, it participates in God's Mission in the redemption of humanity and the restoration of all creation." We are invited "to take part through acts of justice and peace."[80] This is in keeping with her work from the early 1960s, when she described Christian education as "participation in Christ's invitation to join God's Mission of restoring us to true humanity."[81]

This unswerving faith in God's Mission is the context in which Russell's own life's work flourished. God's Mission is the ground of our hope and our struggle.[82] Russell states clearly that "our own puny efforts" bear fruit not of themselves, but because they participate in God's Mission.[83] It is "the promised intention of God," the vision of a mended creation and a restored humanity, that gives us the hope and assurance necessary to risk our own actions for justice.[84] This larger framework of God's love and God's Mission is quite different from anything I have found in Boal's writings. In his texts, communal struggles for justice appear to be motivated by the combination of sheer need and human dignity, moving forward into an unknown future, sustained by an admirable—if unaccountable—determination.[85] For Russell, we know something of the future toward which we are moving. It is "God's future of new creation."[86]

Russell has an unabashedly eschatological focus. Over and over again, she commends thinking from "the other end." She suggests that we "begin from the point of view of New Creation and of what God intends us to become in Jesus Christ."[87] She defines the "eschatological future" as "the goal or purpose of life that is prefigured in the coming of Christ and opened up by the promise and actions of God."[88] This future of who we are called to be is who we most truly are. Furthermore, this eschatological future is not passively waiting for us at the end of time; rather, "God's future comes toward us, breaking into our lives."[89] We are called to live toward the future that is coming toward us, to proleptically anticipate the New Creation, to live as if it were already fully present.[90] Insofar as churches do this, they become "enclave[s] of the future," suffering from "Advent shock" in their maladjustment to present realities that contradict the intended future of God.[91]

Christian faith offers Russell more than a vague affirmation that the future is God's; it also offers "clues" as to what that future looks like.[92] Christians know something of what God's intended future looks like because it has broken into our lives in God's activity, particularly in Jesus Christ. Russell describes this in two ways that are suggestive for a performative ecclesiology. In one text, she refers to the Bible as script:

> One place to begin discussing clues for new creation is with God's initiative in becoming a partner with humanity as seen in the Biblical story. The Bible is both Scripture and script. As Scripture it is a record of what God has done and is doing in and through the lives of people and their history. We study the Bible to understand how God acts so that we can participate in those actions on behalf of humanity. Our participation as Christians makes the Bible a script that begins with Jesus Christ and stretches back through the whole story of God's dealing with Israel to creation. It stretches forward into our own life stories and beyond, as we join together with others in the continuing struggle toward a new creation in which God will make all things new![93]

More commonly, Russell refers to the biblical accounts of God's love for humanity as a "memory of the future."[94] Creation in the image of God and the incarnation of Jesus Christ are aspects of this memory that give us clues as to God's intended future.[95] She writes,

> In Jesus Christ, God has chosen to be partner with us in our world and lives. That choice is known to us in a "memory of the future." We remember the story of God's love and live out that story, moving with hope in the promised future of New Creation. The other end of the story draws us into God's future and illuminates our present journey.[96]

There is a pattern to Christian action: remembering God's love in the past, reflecting on this as the basis of the future, and anticipating this future in the present. In her words, "Because we remember the past and live with it as the promise of the future, we have a memory of the future which God is bringing toward us. It is this memory of the future which makes us 'prisoners of hope' (Zech. 9:12)."[97]

Russell's account resonates with more general descriptions of performance as moving between past, present, and future. Always a present event, performance repeats the past and rehearses the future. Yet the lines of causality are not simply from past to present to future. The future to which we aspire affects our present performance and our interpretation of the past.[98] Given his revolutionary hopes, Boal might well agree with Schechner's words on this topic:

> Although restored behavior seems to be founded on past events...the past is recreated in terms not simply of a present...but of a future. This future is the performance being rehearsed, the "finished thing" to be made graceful through editing, repetition, and invention. Restored behavior is both teleological and eschatological...It is a model of destiny.[99]

For Russell, this performative pattern is quite specific. Christian memory of the future is known in and through Scripture and tradition, as they are interpreted within the community of faith and struggle, aided by the Holy Spirit. Scripture was vitally important to Russell's faith and theology. Even though she was not a Bible scholar, she edited two books on biblical interpretation.[100] She understood tradition as being quite related to God's Mission. Tradition with a capital "T" refers to God's "handing over" Jesus Christ to all people.[101] Within this framework it is possible to distinguish "tradition" as the "witness of scripture and church doctrine," "traditions" as the particular patterns of church life within particular groups, and "traditioning" as the ongoing process by which Christians participate in God's "sending" or "handing over" of Jesus Christ.[102] This active form, "traditioning," is key for Russell, as it marks our participation in God's Mission through the ongoing process of "handing over" Jesus to other persons and to future generations.[103]

In her description of traditioning and her approach to biblical interpretation, Russell engages in performative hermeneutics. Scripture and doctrine are vital, yet their contemporary meaning comes to be within the "situation-variable" realities of particular communities, in the praxis of action and reflection. Russell's emphasis on situation variability does not indicate that the reality of God changes from place to place and time to time.[104] Rather, it is rooted in her conviction that God is relentlessly loving and just, an incurable optimist in regards to humanity, who continually calls us to faithfulness and righteousness.[105] She writes of the Bible:

> The Word of God is living and liberating to those who hear with faith and live it out in faith. The Biblical message becomes good news to each successive generation as the power of the Holy Spirit conveys this message through the study and action of Christian communities. Because the gospel speaks in ever-new ways to chang-

ing situations, we have nothing to fear from listening to it afresh as our consciousness and experience change.[106]

Note how Russell's language includes action as part of how Christians interpret tradition and Scripture. Because God partners with us for the mending of creation, we know God in the work of mending, as our efforts participate in God's Mission. Russell emphasizes the performative element of this hermeneutic: "The Coming One is already present with us as we live out his story. It is *living out that story* in order to give an account of the hope that is in us that helps us to discover the meaning of that story."[107] Her hermeneutic is performative because of who she understands God to be: active, incarnate, inviting us to participate in God's own Mission. Also, the conjunction of metaphors is provocative. Russell describes the Bible as script and as conveying memory. It helps us to see the future to which we are called. When we live out the story in the script, when we act out the memory in our own variable situations, we are already participating in God's future.

Russell portrays Jesus as living and dying on the margins of society, such that Christians are also called to struggle in solidarity with the marginalized. It is little wonder, then, that she advocates for a biblical hermeneutic in which texts are interpreted through the eyes of the marginalized. This includes reading with and listening to those who are marginalized in the contemporary world. It also includes identifying with those who are marginalized within the biblical stories. We must read from the margins. Sometimes this means identifying with the oppressed in the story, which pushes us to question assumptions. For example, Russell urges reading stories traditionally associated with Abraham from the perspective of either Sarah or Hagar. This provides perspective on the patriarchal assumptions in the text and casts new light on God's activity.[108] Alternatively, reading from the margins sometimes means resisting the impulse to quickly identify with the poor, recognizing our own complicity and privilege within contemporary social structures. Luke 4 recounts Jesus reading from the book of Isaiah in the temple at Nazareth. He reads:

> The Spirit of the Lord is upon me,
> Because he has anointed me to bring good news to the poor.
> He has sent me to proclaim release to the captives and recovery of
>   sight to the blind,
> To let the oppressed go free,
> To proclaim the year of the Lord's favor.
>
> (Luke 4:18–19)

Although the townspeople in Nazareth are initially impressed, when they realize that the good news might threaten, rather than improve, their social status, they attack Jesus and attempt to harm him (Luke 4:22–30). In relation to this text, Russell writes, "Often Christian congregations don't hear this word of judgment because they identify with the wrong persons in the story. In Luke 4 they hear only the comforting words about Jesus' call to ministry of service and identify with Jesus...it is possible that the word of judgment might come home more sharply if we were to identify with the townspeople of Nazareth."[109] Readers who are privileged by contemporary society could read this text from the margins by recognizing their own comfort and hearing the call to work in solidarity for justice.

Russell advocates a kind of hermeneutical agility in reading the text while identifying with different people in the story. If Scripture is the script for our community, and in enacting it we come to participate in the future we remember, then Russell is, again, reminding us that it is important to change roles. This is theologically grounded in Jesus's life and ministry. He identifies with those on the margins of society, bringing them back into community (the lepers are healed and sent to the priests to be re-admitted into society) (Luke 17:11–19). He challenges those in the center of society to move to the edges (the rich man is to give up all he owns) (Mark 10:21).

Jesus teaches role switching as a discipline and incorporates this into the form of his teaching, as well. Consider the parables. Often the hearer or reader is invited into a situation that seems familiar, or at least accessible, only to have her initial identification with a particular character thrown into question. She is challenged to empathize with a different person, to see the scene from another perspective. Reading the parables in identification with various characters provides nearly endless possibilities for preachers and teachers of Scripture. The parable of the Good Samaritan turns on the revelation that it is one of the despised Samaritans who embodies the virtues to which Jesus's Jewish hearers aspired. It was a direct contradiction of assumed roles. Our own roles are unsettled, as well. We can read and regret those moments when we have walked to the other side of the road, give thanks for the good neighbors who have helped us in the past, and be challenged to stop and assist another. Through all of this we are provoked to question: Who fills the role of despised Samaritan in our society? Who casts the roles, and why? The structure of parables makes them particularly apt for the role-switching discipline.[110]

Revisiting Church

With Boal and Russell in mind, church can be seen as the performance in which we become spect-actors, people who learn—in a whole-personed way—to see the situation and act within it. Although there are many contexts in which one can become a spect-actor, including theater, church is unique among them because it is in church that we learn to see the world in the light of God's activity and to act in the world in relationship with Jesus Christ. Like some other contexts, in church we gather to interpret our situations and ourselves in communal and embodied ways. However, in church this interpretation takes place within the ongoing retelling and reenacting of God's love for the world. Some of this is captured in the traditional Christian language of witness. To witness is both to see and to act. In the words of theologian M. Shawn Copeland, "A witness can never be a spectator."[111]

In differing ways, both Boal and Russell emphasize the transformation of persons into spect-actors, into people who both see and act in their particular situation. They also both reject any unidirectional rendering of this transformative process. It is not always the case that people first see, then act; nor is it always the case that people act, then see. Rather, the dynamic between seeing and acting is multidirectional and ongoing.

This dynamic is related to another, namely, the boundaries of performance. For Boal, theater does not start when the curtain rises and end when it falls. Any given production of a play is one part of a larger process that includes the preparatory gamesercises, the rehearsals, the production itself, and the societal changes toward which it moves. Each of these events can be seen as performance, and indeed the demarcations between these elements are not hard and fast, nor are they severed from performances in everyday life. Games and rehearsals help the community to analyze social situations. The play itself is rehearsal for revolution. Similarly, for Russell, church does not happen only and discretely during Sunday morning worship. Bible study moves toward liturgy, which moves toward advocacy, which is part of how we understand the Bible. What happens in the hour of Sunday worship is one performance within a larger lineage of performances that includes choir practice, Sunday school, committee meetings, and clean-up crews. It includes the work of the whole community, throughout their life together and their life in the broader world. Every performance is also a rehearsal; every rehearsal is also a performance; every exit is an entrance somewhere else. Strict demarcations between formation, liturgy, and Christian life are inadequate.

In this light, church is, among other things, an advanced program of role switching in which participants identify with multiple persons within the Bible and the ongoing Christian community. Focusing on various texts of the Bible over a period of time, we collectively identify with Adam and Eve, the murmuring Israelites, the befuddled disciples, and Zaccheus in his tree. Through readings, homilies, and songs, over time I have identified with Miriam and Mary and Martha, with Judas and Barrabas, with Peter and Paul. Furthermore, every week we liturgically occupy multiple theological positions. I am, with every other baptized Christian, a minister in the church, responsible for both leading and being led. When it works well, this role switching trains Christians to interpret Scripture and social reality in ways that attend to various perspectives. At its very best, it trains Christians to interpret ourselves in complex ways that instill deep humility and Spirit-gifted agency.

Earlier in this chapter, I offered a Boalian interpretation of a mainline Protestant congregation. I read the liturgy as a cathartic process in which the impulses for justice that might threaten the status quo are activated only to be relieved, ritually discharged by a congregation that remains passive. Surely there are moments when church is like this. Yet Boal and Russell offer strategies to resist this and resources for more liberating performances. Shared leadership and attention to embodied learning are vital. Likewise, understanding the performance of church as extending beyond Sunday morning worship is an important shift in limiting Aristotelian possibilities. Finally, we must switch roles. Many of these strategies are already in use in Christian congregations. Boal and Russell can help us notice them. Attuned by Boal and Russell, we can read the same church service in a new way. We can understand church as a communal performance of multiple roles that trains us to see the world through many perspectives and rehearses us in acting for justice. Taking our place within the narratives we reenact, we affirm a vision of the world in the uncompromising light of the fierce, demanding love of God. The performance of church is an event where past, present, and future come together—where the memory of Jesus Christ calls us toward God's future. Through word and deed, song and prayer, we bring our lives before God, in relationship with Jesus as he is known in Scripture. Impulses toward justice that threaten the status quo are not dispelled by the service. Rather, they are generated and nurtured by the particularity of Jesus Christ and by the whole-personed affirmation of the advent of God's future. In this way, church is the performance of embodied hope.

4

Changing Scenes

Introduction

In chapter 2 I argued that Christian liturgy trains the person in a pattern of affections. We form a storehouse of Christian affections and a repertoire of physical gestures to which these affections rise. We learn, in a whole-personed way, to feel with Jesus, see with Jesus, hear with Jesus, to weep and cry and hope with Jesus. Our performance of Scripture is thus a performance of relationship with Jesus Christ—disciplined by liturgy and mediated by Scripture—that forms us to the bone. In the previous chapter I drew on the work of Boal and Russell to critique the negative possibilities of formation in church and to point toward structural safeguards that can help church form persons in positive ways disciplined by the life and ministry of Jesus Christ. These safeguards include awareness of embodied learning in liturgy, appreciation of the many ways in which church extends beyond the sanctuary, shared leadership in community, and emphasis on changing roles. Yet this is not enough. The brokenness of church—the particular doubleness between who we are and who we are called to be, who we have been in the past and who we desire to be in the future—runs too deep. The history of harm done by Christian congregations requires further reflection.

In each chapter of this book I have invited two new guests—a theater director and a theologian—to my eclectic dinner party, and I will do so in this chapter as well. Director Bertolt Brecht and theologian Delores Williams will join our conversation. But first, allow me to say a word about why their voices are so needed.

The role switching advocated by Boal and Russell nurtures critical thinking and Spirit-filled agency. It also takes a lot of hard work and threatens many ecclesial institutional structures. Because such role switching reverberates well beyond Sunday morning worship, it challenges hierarchical and static societal structures. And because we are finite and flawed, human and sinful, our church performance does not often attain the desiderata gleaned from Russell and Boal. Instead, our liturgies often allow us to become comfortable in one perspective. Instead of requiring multiple roles that cultivate critical distance from all roles and agency about what roles we choose to inhabit, Christian liturgies sometimes entrench in us a singular perspective and interpretation, sanctified and stabilized by a monovocal theology. Once we are formed in a singular perspective, the fact that it is a perspective—instead of simply the truth—becomes invisible to us. There are two issues intertwined here. The first has to do with the depth of formation in liturgy. The second involves singularity of perspective. The combination is quite dangerous.

The Strength of Social Memory

Sociologist Paul Connerton analyzes how performances of ceremonies and rites form social memories within a given community. In the book *How Societies Remember*, Connerton distinguishes "between three distinct classes of memory claim."[1] Personal memory involves remembering one's own life history. Cognitive memory involves remembering information learned in the past. Habit memory involves, in a somewhat more complex manner, "having the capacity to reproduce a certain performance."[2] Habit memory includes skills like reading or riding a bike. Many times we do not remember precisely when we acquired this knowledge. This is a type of memory wherein "often it is only by the fact of the performance that we are able to recognize and demonstrate to others that we do in fact remember."[3] This type of memory, Connerton claims, is distinctly embodied. It is performative. Connerton argues that performative memory—social habit memory—is a neglected but vital aspect of human life.

More concretely, he explores commemorative events as moments of transfer in which social memories are formed through ritual performances.[4] These social memories include both habit memory and cognitive memory.[5] This means that the bodily practices of commemorative events—which can take place with the unreflective ease of riding a bike—simultaneously reinforce cognitive content. When we engage in communal bodily practices, we in some sense ratify our belief in particular understandings of reality that are stored and transferred in the practices.

Commemorative events—from nationalistic parades to religious rites—retell a historical narrative in such a way as to include present participants in the happenings retold. Connerton writes of a particular commemorative event:

> This narrative was more than a story told…It was a rite fixed and performed. Its story was told not unequivocally in the past tense but in the tense of a metaphysical present. We would underestimate the commemorative hold of the rite, we would minimize its mnemonic power, if we were to say that it *reminded* the participants of mythic events; we should say rather that the sacred event…was *re-presented*; the participants in the rite gave it ceremonially embodied form.[6]

Ceremonies are more than re-narrations because the participants in the rite "assent to [the] meaning" of the event through their embodied actions.[7] They claim continuity with the narration.[8] To participate in a ceremonial event is thus both to learn the story that is told and to place oneself within its horizon. To explain how this is so, Connerton employs the concept of "performative" as developed by J. L. Austin, which was mentioned earlier in this text. Under certain circumstances, to say something is to make it so. Within the context of a wedding ceremony, to say "I do" is to get married. "I do" is thus a performative utterance. Connerton claims that ceremonial events are rife with such performatives, such that participants in the events perform the actions they ceremonially speak. He writes:

> Curses, blessings and oaths, together with other verbs frequently found in ritual language, as for instance 'to ask' or 'to pray' or 'to give thanks', presuppose certain attitudes—of trust and veneration, of submission, contrition and gratitude—which come into effect at the moment when, by virtue of the enunciation of the sentence, the corresponding act takes place. Or better: that act takes place in and through the enunciation.[9]

Connerton's description resonates deeply with much of the material that has already been discussed regarding church as performance. His analysis both confirms and contributes to a rich description of whole-personed knowledge. Saliers defined affections as belief-laden emotions that also involve the will. Drawing on Harak and Ignatius, I argued that affections also include the body and are formed in relationships over time. With Stanislavski as a guide, I further explored the role of memory and argued that these Christian affections can be evoked through bodily gestures.

Connerton's work draws attention to the social nature of performative knowledge, and offers further analysis of how rituals engage the will, shaping what Saliers refers to as how we "intend" the world.[10]

The resonances between what Connerton's description of performative social memory and Christian affections make his cautions trenchant. Connerton argues that social memory stored in performance is harder to critique than memories transmitted through written texts. Performative social memories are rarely brought to specific verbal articulation. A belief transmitted and ratified in performance can elude intellectual scrutiny because it is knowledge that is bodily and emotional, and because the only persons who have access to this knowledge (those who perform it) have been shaped by it themselves. Performances are "not easily susceptible to critical scrutiny and evaluation" by those who perform.[11] Connerton writes, "Both commemorative ceremonies and bodily practices…contain a measure of insurance against the process of cumulative questioning entailed in all discursive practices."[12] Societies, Connerton argues, will entrust their most vital memories and knowledge to communal performances.[13]

Of course this power of performance cuts both ways. Because it is less susceptible to criticism, censorship, and constraint, performance can preserve and transmit communal knowledge more securely than written texts. However, these same strengths make it dangerous. Persons can be formed in ways of knowing that are not brought to self-critical articulation.

Performing a Single Role

What happens when the strength of performative knowledge is combined with a singularity of perspective? Oftentimes the answer is a stubborn invisibility. One perspective can be entrenched in a community, passed on for generations. This perspective is not subject to the kind of intellectual critique that a written declaration could receive. At the same time, the community that performs such knowledge does not gain the critical thinking skills and critical distance that inhabiting multiple roles engenders. If such knowledge is performed often enough, then even when the beliefs are brought to articulation, the community lacks the skills to read them critically. Christian knowing should be whole-personed—involving intellect, body, emotion, and will. Yet when performative knowledge is shaped by a single perspective, the intellectual and volitional aspects of this can be compromised.

Theologian Willie James Jennings provides a heartrending example of this in the book *The Christian Imagination: Theology and the Origins of Race.* Tracing the social construction of race, Jennings looks back to the history of colonialism. He argues that colonialism was supported by British Christians reading Scripture and identifying with Israel. Translations and interpretations of Scripture in that era replaced references to Israel with references to Britain.[14] This remapping of biblical geography was a matter of singular perspective. British Christians placed themselves in the biblical narratives, but only within one role—that of the chosen people of God. Identifying themselves with God's elect, colonialists fashioned a theology in which they had divinely sanctioned claim upon all land and all peoples. The theological justification for conquest, and thus a significant element of the social construction of race, was enabled by Christian resistance to role switching. British Christians identified with Israel in the biblical texts to such an extent that Israel itself fell from view, a mere pre-figuration or precursor to Britain.[15] Thus Jennings argues that a great deal of the devastating legacy of colonialism is tied to Christian supersessionism.[16]

Delores Williams

Jennings is not alone in analyzing the damaging effects of Christians identifying with a singular perspective with Scripture. Womanist theologian Delores Williams provides a powerful model in her groundbreaking text, *Sisters in the Wilderness: The Challenge of Womanist God-Talk.* She critiques white theology, black theology, and feminist theology for their lack of attention to black women's experience.

She counters this exclusion by carefully choosing with whom she will identify within the biblical texts. Like Russell, Williams wants to read Scripture from the margins. However, Williams notes that this is a complicated task for black women, who are doubly or triply oppressed according to race, gender, and economic status. She finds a starting point in a "tradition of African-American biblical appropriation" regarding Hagar, "the African slave of the Hebrew woman Sarah."[17] Williams notes several similarities between Hagar's situation and the historical and contemporary realities of black women in the United States.[18] She writes, "Hagar's predicament involved slavery, poverty, ethnicity, sexual and economic exploitation, surrogacy, rape, domestic violence, homelessness, motherhood, single-parenting and radical encounters with God."[19] Each of these can also be found in the experience of black women.

Many white male Christians over the centuries have identified with Abraham and his heirs. Many black male Christians have identified with "personalities who were involved in liberation struggle," such as Moses, Paul, Daniel, and the Hebrew slaves delivered in the Exodus.[20] Some white feminists identify with Miriam or Sarah. Williams chooses to identify with Hagar.[21]

This identification—this role taken up—profoundly shapes Williams's theology, particularly regarding the salvific work of Jesus Christ. This is evident in two ways. First, Williams notes that God did not liberate Hagar from slavery. Instead, God provided her with resources for survival and aid in developing "an appropriate quality of life."[22] Thus Williams interprets God's saving activity primarily in terms of survival and quality of life. Second, Hagar's story draws attention to surrogacy. As a slave, Hagar was forced into surrogacy. Through socially sanctioned rape, she carried Abram's child at Sarai's command. This child was not intended to be Hagar's, but rather to be Abram and Sarai's heir. Throughout slavery, black women were raped and their children stolen, most often not to be raised as heirs to the household but to be enslaved. Surrogacy can also be interpreted more broadly. Under slavery, black women were subject to "coerced surrogacy," forced "to function in roles that ordinarily would have been filled by someone else."[23] This included everything from raising white children to repairing roads (a task that society would ordinarily have charged to men).[24]

While coerced surrogacy was outlawed by emancipation, social-role surrogacy continued. Economic pressures and societal structures curtail black women's choices to such a degree that many are pressured to voluntarily take up surrogacy roles. Social-role surrogacy encompasses surrogate motherhood as a means of income production, domestic service to white families, and black women stepping into culturally masculine roles such as household provider.[25] Williams identifies many ways in which such social-role surrogacy continues to threaten the survival and quality of life of black American women. She states, "Surrogacy has been a negative force in African-American women's lives. It has been used by both men and women of the ruling class, as well as by some black men, to keep black women in the service of other people's needs and goals."[26]

Given how surrogacy harms black women, Williams questions understandings of Christology in which Jesus saves humanity by dying on the cross in our stead. She writes:

In this sense Jesus represents the ultimate surrogate figure; he stands in the place of someone else: sinful humankind. Surrogacy, attached to this divine personage, thus takes on an aura of the sacred. It is therefore fitting and proper for black women to ask whether the image of a surrogate-God has salvific power for black women or whether this image supports and reinforces the exploitation that has accompanied their experience with surrogacy. If black women accept this idea of redemption, can they not also passively accept the exploitation that surrogacy brings?[27]

Williams does not assert that Christian understandings of the cross cause black women's surrogacy. She does not claim that Jesus on the cross is entirely equivalent to black women's surrogacy.[28] She suggests that if we think the logic of surrogacy is employed by God, we will be slower to reject the logic of surrogacy among humans. If we think of Jesus's surrogate suffering as holy and salvific, we will be less likely to condemn surrogate suffering in our midst.

The "theological yield" of Williams's decision to read through Hagar's eyes includes a nuanced argument for carefully choosing what roles we take up in biblical stories and a call to take up more than one.[29] It includes a focus on survival and quality of life that leads Williams to see Jesus's salvific power in the ministerial vision he embodied in his life.[30] And finally, it includes a powerful rejection of any conceptualization of the cross of Christ as salvific. Williams states:

There is nothing divine in the blood of the cross. God does not intend black women's surrogacy experience. Neither can Christian faith affirm such an idea. Jesus did not come to be a surrogate. Jesus came for life, to show humans a perfect vision of ministerial relations that humans had very little knowledge of. As Christians, black women cannot forget the cross, but neither can they glorify it. To do so is to glorify suffering and to render their exploitation sacred. To do so is to glorify the sin of defilement.[31]

Williams writes with conviction and power, choosing words sure to rile many Christian readers. Her argument is too compelling to be taken lightly; it demands response. Several prominent theologians, including JoAnne Marie Terrell, M. Shawn Copeland, and James H. Cone, acknowledge learning from Williams's Christological critique while ultimately rejecting her dismissal of the cross as salvific.[32] Students are often less measured. Teaching her work in classes over many years, I have come to expect strong reactions. Several students have been offended; many have written angry papers in response. Once I felt physically threatened by a student who clearly felt theologically threatened by Williams's work. For some Christians, Williams's critique of traditional Christology falls like a blow. It shakes deep foundations of belief and forces an unwelcome distance from cherished affections. The longer I live with Williams's wisdom, the more I think that is the point. I have come to understand her work as an example of the alienation effect, a technique developed by director and playwright Bertolt Brecht.

Bertolt Brecht

A German playwright, poet, and director, Bertolt Brecht is one of the giants of modern Western theater. In this chapter, I draw on a very small part of his influential work, while hoping to develop a more sustained conversation between Brecht and theology in the future. Brecht can be placed in relationship to the two directors already at the table, so to speak. Stanislavski sought realism on the stage to counter the mechanized techniques inherited by his generation. Brecht rejected this, for reasons that were later taken up by Boal. Brecht criticized naturalism on the stage for generating an Aristotelian empathy and even identification between spectator and character, which fosters passivity and complacence well beyond the theater. In contrast, Brecht wanted theater to be both instructive and entertaining. He wanted theater to be an arena in which "vital questions [are] freely aired with a view to their solution."[33] He wanted theater to fulfill a social function in which communal realities—especially realities of "hunger, cold and oppression"—could be brought to light and addressed.[34] Stanislavski's realism is an impediment to this, in Brecht's assessment, since "What [Stanislavski] cared about was naturalness, and as a result everything in his theater seemed far too natural for anyone to pause and go into it thoroughly. You don't normally examine your own home or you own feelings…"[35]

Brecht's goals for theater were quite influential on Boal and it is easy to spot similarities. Both men wanted theater to foster critical awareness of oppressive social structures and to contribute toward movements for justice outside the theater. They shared some techniques, including an emphasis on collaboration and a desire to have more active participation among audience members. However, they also developed very different poetics. While Boal focused on embodied practices, Brecht sought to engage the intellect of the audience and demand volitional response.

If audience members simply identify with the protagonist of the play, theater becomes an experience of empathy. (Brecht's discussion of empathy serves as a cornerstone for Boal's later analysis of catharsis.) It produces pleasure, but neither insight into reality nor the will to change it for the better.[36] In this kind of theater, Brecht argues, the spectator "submit[s] to an experience uncritically (and without any practical consequences) by means of simple empathy with the characters in a play."[37] Naturalism contributes to this, allowing the spectator to empathically step into a theatrical world without question. Naturalism and the empathy it fosters can inhibit intellectual engagement with the production. Brecht writes, "When something seems 'the most obvious thing in the world' it means that any attempt to understand the world has been given up."[38]

One of the techniques Brecht develops to counter identification between spectator and character is the alienation effect. The German word *Verfremdungseffekt* refers to making something familiar appear foreign, and is related to the critical distance discussed in chapter 3. Brecht sought to remind the theatergoer that she was, indeed, watching a play, to interrupt her identification with the characters onstage and reengage her critical thinking skills regarding the content of the production. Alienation, Brecht claims, "is necessary to all understanding." He created the alienation effect in many different ways. Instead of staging plays with an invisible "fourth wall" through which the audience observes naturalistic happenings, Brecht staged plays in which the actors spoke directly to the audience. Actors would hold up placards with surprising explanations or commentary. Stage directions would be read aloud and props used for incongruous purposes. Songs would interrupt dialogue.[39] The means of achieving the alienation effect are endless. The point is simply to create critical distance between the audience member and the play, as well as between the audience member and her experience of the play. Brecht used the alienation effect so "that the audience was hindered from simply identifying itself with the characters in the play. Acceptance or rejection of their actions was meant to take place on a conscious plane, instead of, as hitherto, in the audience's subconscious."[40]

The strategy of the alienation effect is to disrupt identification and the empathy upon which it is built. The proximate goal is to engage intellectual evaluation of the production. The ultimate goal is to provoke a conscious, thoughtful, volitional response from the audience member. Only those who are alienated from the social arrangements that seem natural and inviolable are able to imagine improvement. Through "alienating the familiar," theater can stimulate intellectual inquiry into what otherwise attains the invisibility of the commonplace.[41] And by making these familiar arrangements alien, theater demands response. In Brecht's ideal theater, "the spectator, instead of being enabled to have an experience, is forced as it were to cast his vote[. T]hen a change has been launched which goes far beyond formal matters and begins for the first time to affect the theatre's social function."[42]

Alienating Christology

Brecht's development of the alienation technique helps me to understand the unsettling power of Williams's protest against the saving power of the cross. She alienates Christology. Williams interrupts familiar emotional responses to Jesus on the cross, triggers intellectual engagement, and demands ethical response that extends beyond the sanctuary. *Sisters in the Wilderness* is not just good theology; it is also a superb performance of Brechtian alienation.

With the resources accumulated in the preceding chapters, this statement can be fleshed out more fully. Church is a performance that shapes us as whole persons—bodily, emotionally, intellectually, and volitionally— into a pattern of affections that is consonant with Jesus Christ, as known in and through Scripture. Christians, both individually and communally, have deep storehouses of emotion memory that are part and parcel of these affections, and we also have a repertoire of bodily gestures that evoke these memories. These form us deeply, in ways that affect our entire lives. We have, using the terms of Taylor and Connerton, a repertoire of social memory of Jesus Christ. Furthermore, our embodied and communal practices of knowing Jesus in and through Scripture discipline us to occupy multiple roles, and thereby attain critical distance and epistemic humility. This is not merely a happenstance regarding how Christianity has developed over time. It is deeply fitting with Christian theology, in which the logos is incarnate, God is with us in our embodied and communal lives, and Jesus chooses to identify with those on the margins. The performative nature of such knowledge means that it is deeply ingrained and not easily dislodged from a community.

However, church is not what it is called to be. Often we do not take up multiple roles, but rather allow our performative interpretation of

Scripture to be singular, such that we identify with the same character in a story each time we hear it and we each have our own, static role to play. Thus our deeply ingrained knowledge can lack critical distance and become unexamined, seemingly natural, and unavailable to critique. In such instances, the pattern of affections we perform is fundamentally *malformed*. Both the intellectual and volitional aspects of knowledge are compromised. We do not clearly see the narrative in which we place ourselves, the beliefs that we communally ratify with our performance. We are blinded to the possibility that the way things are is not the only possible way they could be. Emotional and bodily patterns continue to store and transfer social memory, but it is not the whole-personed knowledge that it ought to be.

Although Williams does not present her theology using Brechtian terms, I interpret her work as bringing the technique of alienation into such a situation. Theological explications of God's saving activity that are deeply familiar to Western Christians—Christologies of subsitutionary atonement, penal substitution, and sacrifice—are made strange. Our empathy is disrupted by Williams's identification with Hagar, by the connection of Hagar and Jesus through surrogacy, by linking Jesus with black American women suffering oppression. Even if the reader rejects Williams's conclusions, the cross is no longer available in a familiar form that does not require intellectual struggle or volitional choice. This, I believe, is the brilliance of Williams's performance. Christians who read Williams's text and continue to claim salvation through the cross and in the blood of Jesus will do so differently, with distance and alienation, after an intellectual engagement and through volition.

Performing the Cross

Williams's intervention takes place at the level of academic theology. She is critiquing intellectual theories of how salvation works. Reading her work in light of performance raises further questions. If the description of church as performance I have given has merit, then the difficulties of singular perspective, of uninterrupted empathic identification with one point of view, will not be confined to our academic theories. They will permeate our life together. So we must ask, are there ways in which not just our academic theology, but also our Christian performance more generally, is compromised by a singularity of perspective? Are our performances so familiar that aspects of them become invisible?

In *The Cross and the Lynching Tree*, theologian James Cone ponders the silence of Christian preachers and theologians on the subject of lynching. Between 1880 and 1940, roughly five thousand black men, women, and children were lynched in the United States.[43] These were often large, public events where spectators cheered the torture, mutilation, burning, shooting, and hanging of human beings. People bought and sold souvenirs, including picture postcards and bits of the corpse.[44] Lynchings in the United States bore many similarities to the crucifixion of Jesus centuries before. Cone writes:

> As Jesus was an innocent victim of mob hysteria and Roman imperial violence, many African Americans were innocent victims of white mobs, thirsting for blood in the name of God and in defense of segregation, white supremacy, and the purity of the Anglo-Saxon race. Both the cross and the lynching tree were symbols of terror, reserved primarily for slaves, criminals, and insurrectionists—the lowest of the low in society. Both Jesus and blacks were publicly humiliated, subjected to the utmost indignity and cruelty. They were stripped, in order to be deprived of dignity, then paraded, mocked and whipped, pierced, derided and spat upon, tortured for hours in the presence of jeering crowds for popular entertainment. In both cases, the purpose was to strike terror in the subject community. It was to let people know that the same thing would happen to them if they did not stay in their place.[45]

Given the similarities, it is remarkable that so few preachers or theologians of that era drew connections between lynching and crucifixion.[46] Cone examines the work of ethicist Reinhold Niebuhr, who wrote and said many things that were supportive of racial equality. Niebuhr was, to a certain degree, both intellectually attuned to the theological issues of racism as sin and practically involved in advocacy for racial justice. Niebuhr's theology also emphasizes the cross. Yet, Cone points out, Niebuhr was silent on lynching. Cone asks, "How could Niebuhr make the tragedy of the cross the central theme in his theology while ignoring...lynching in the United States?"[47]

In answering this question, Cone repeatedly refers to Niebuhr's limited ability to empathize with black people.[48] Niebuhr had a "limited perspective" and failed to empathize or identify with black people in general and black suffering in particular.[49] Niebuhr's own writings note how difficult it is for members of one human group to see the world from another group's perspective.[50] He himself, Cone concludes, was unable "to step into black people's shoes and 'walk around in them.' "[51] I argued in the previous chapter that church, at its best, involves walking around in the shoes of others, performing various perspectives in order to gain both empathy and critical distance. It did not work that way for Niebuhr. The point here is not that this particular man failed. Rather, I follow Cone in taking Niebuhr as an exemplary specimen of twentieth-century American Christianity. The reality that even Niebuhr did not identify with black Americans reveals the depth and breadth of white Christian communal failure in this regard.

Cone asks how Niebuhr could fail to connect the cross and the lynching tree. He concludes that this was a deficit of empathy on Niebuhr's part. Cone uses Niebuhr as a figure for much of white—especially liberal—theology, and therefore his analysis has larger scope. He implies that white Christians more generally lacked empathy with black Americans. I want to build on this argument in light of my description of church as performance. White Christians lacked the agile empathy that disciplined role switching in church instills, and therefore were ill equipped to empathize with black neighbors. This may well have been due to long practicing of reading and interpreting Scripture while identifying too closely with a single role.

The cross was a common theme in black church performance. Cone writes about the congregation in which he was raised, "There were more songs, sermons, prayers, and testimonies about the cross than any other theme. The cross was the foundation on which their faith was built."[52] He asserts that "Black ministers preached about Jesus' death more than any other theme because they saw in Jesus' suffering and persecution a parallel to their own encounter with slavery, segregation, and the lynching tree."[53] In other words, black Christians identified with Jesus on the cross. Primarily through contrast, Cone intimates that white Christians of the lynching era did not identify with Jesus on the cross in the same way or to the same degree. "'Jesus Keep Me near the Cross,' 'Must Jesus Bear the Cross Alone?' and other white Protestant evangelical hymns did not sound or feel the same when blacks and whites sang them because their life experiences were so different."[54] I want to push this point farther. Perhaps many white Christians performed church such that they identified not with Jesus suffering on the cross but with those saved by Jesus's suffering.

One could, of course, identify with both, and this is what Cone advocates. He both reports and endorses a theology of solidarity, in which Jesus on the cross stands in solidarity with those who suffer and thereby turns it from "a symbol of death and defeat" into "a sign of liberation and new life."[55] That God is present with humanity in our suffering, even to the point of death on a cross, is good news to those who suffer in this life, even as it consistently threatens those who ignore or cause the suffering of others. Cone states, "The cross, as a locus of divine revelation, is not good news for the powerful, for those who are comfortable with the ways things are, or for anyone whose understanding of religion is aligned with power."[56] Yet as Williams ably demonstrates, solidarity is not the only way in which the cross has been understood to have salvific power. For many Christians who hold different views of soteriology, it is not necessary to identify *with* Jesus on the cross in order to identify as *saved by* Jesus on the cross. In various understandings of salvation, as they are performed in Christian communities, the suffering of Jesus is vicarious or surrogate. Jesus suffers not with us, but in our stead, and therefore the role of one who suffers and the role of one who is saved are quite distinct.

What happens when a Christian community performs the role of one who is saved by the suffering of another, without switching roles and gaining critical distance? What if this singular perspective becomes a social memory, performed in repertoire but not brought to critical scrutiny? It seems plausible that when such a community feels threatened, it might well reenact this pattern from within their shared communal narrative.

Cone notes that white communities justified lynching as a means of protecting themselves from threat or harm.[57] Free black Americans put white superiority in peril and racial purity at risk. Black men, in particular, were depicted as a menace, preying on white women and jeopardizing public safety. Feeling themselves to be at hazard, perhaps such white Christian communities reenacted the narrative of salvation as they knew it, crucifying another person to secure their own safety. Lynching, then, would be a performance of crucifixion.

To my knowledge, neither Williams nor Cone argues that white Christianity was a causal factor in lynching.[58] Williams's work—alienating as it is—only goes so far as to suggest that thinking about the cross in a particular manner makes it more difficult to resist patterns of surrogacy in contemporary life. Cone questions how white Christians could participate in or ignore lynching while honoring the cross. He marvels that they "did not see the irony or contradiction in their actions."[59] His terms—"irony" and "contradiction"—mark a clear distinction and opposition between Christianity and lynching. For Cone, Christianity cannot be causally linked to lynching because it is antithetical to it. Anyone who is truly Christian must oppose lynching, therefore those who lynched or stood silent forfeited their claim to Christianity. He states, "White conservative Christianity's blatant endorsement of lynching as a part of its religion, and white liberal Christians' silence about lynching placed both of them outside of Christian identity...There was no way a community could support or ignore lynching in America, while still representing in word and deed the one who was lynched by Rome."[60]

Of course, Cone is right; lynching and racism are antithetically opposed to the Gospel of Jesus Christ. Therefore Christianity at its best, Christianity as it is called to be, is antithetically opposed to lynching. However, we are not what we are called to be. To expel by theological fiat this most offensive aspect of Christian history is another means of turning away from the connections between the cross and the lynching tree. Cone asks, "How could Christians do this?" and answers "they were not really Christians." This might work if he had not, in the intervening pages, so persuasively argued that the cross and the lynching tree are too similar to be dissociated.[61]

Cone refers to the suffering of lynched African Americans as a "re-enactment of Christ's suffering."[62] He states that "[t]he lynching tree is a metaphor for white America's crucifixion of black people."[63] Drawing on the knowledge and experience of black Christians, Cone articulates a theology of the cross as revealing humanity's salvation through solidarity with those who suffer.[64] I write from the context of a different community, namely, that of white Christians in the United States. Cone's work challenges and invites me to identify with the crucified, both in Scripture and in contemporary life.[65] Perhaps, however, there is another important step, which is to reckon with those who crucified. They, too, were formed in the narratives of Scripture through church performance. They, too, claimed Jesus Christ as Lord and Savior. If we are going to take performance seriously and acknowledge the resonances between crucifixion and lynching, then we have to ask the painful question: Could some types of Christian church performance, particularly our social memory of the cross, have contributed to lynching? Did white Christians perform church in such a way that it was a rehearsal for crucifying?

This question is not particularly new. It has roots in Williams's work, in Cone's, and in broader critiques of violence at the heart of Christian narratives and imagery. It has been addressed by theologians such as M. Shawn Copeland and Kelly Brown Douglas.[66] Neither is this question easy to answer, given the historical distance and the difficulties of establishing a causal or contributing relationship. However, the question must be raised if we are to acknowledge the power of embodied and communal performance. The consequences of malformed performance can be dire. Even if we cannot answer this historical question with scholarly precision, the question itself attunes us to the high stakes of our contemporary church performances.

Performing the Eucharist

A converse form of this question is more popular and has been addressed by a number of Christian theologians and ethicists: namely, how can church, particularly liturgy, counter social violence and oppression? There is a rich body of literature about how performing worship well fights social ills. Several authors focus on the Eucharist and point to particular aspects of this performance as politically and spiritually powerful in resisting violence. Three of these aspects that have been addressed already in this study will be taken up again in this light: community, bringing past and future into the present, and taking up a different role. Let us tarry a moment with the power of Eucharistic performance.

Community

Connerton notes that in the context of commemorative events, "we" is a performative utterance. Using "pronouns of solidarity" performatively constitutes the community as a group, as a social body. Connerton claims that when a group repeatedly says "we," "[t]heir speech does not describe what such a community might look like, nor does it express a community constituted before and apart from it; performative utterances are as it were the place in which the community is constituted and recalls to itself the fact of its constitution."[67] This description of performing a social body aligns with the emphasis throughout this text on the communal nature of Christian performance. Claiming that we perform ourselves as a social body does not deny the working of God in constituting the community, as well. It is not an exclusive claim. There is room for the agency of individual Christians, the activity of congregations, the ongoing cultural traditions of Christianity, the initial performance of Jesus Christ at the Last

Supper, and the work of the ever-present Spirit. Indeed, the concept of performativity constantly highlights the multidirectional flows through which identity is formed.

In his book *Torture and the Eucharist*, William T. Cavanaugh argues that Christian church performance is politically powerful because it is the performance of a social body that is not fully bound by the state. The primary allegiance of the social body constituted in church performance is to the God of Jesus Christ. Cavanaugh's claim is set in the context of the use of torture in Chile under the Pinochet regime. He argues that torture functioned not just to damage individual bodies, but also to disintegrate social bodies that could threaten the power of the state. Cavanaugh writes, "modern torture is predicated on invisibility"—on secret police and the disappearance of tortured bodies—and thrives on the incommunicability of pain. Individuals suffer in isolation and the apparatus that sustains such suffering is kept invisible.[68] In sharp contrast, the Eucharist constitutes the social body of the Christian community, making visible the body of Christ. "Christians" Cavanaugh states, "…make the bizarre claim that pain *can* be shared, precisely because people can be knitted together into one body."[69] In its very being, the social body constituted in Eucharistic performance is a countercultural political body. Thus Cavanaugh argues that the performance of church, in and of itself, works against social and political forces of injustice and harm.

Past, Present, and Future

Another aspect of Eucharistic performance that can counter violence and oppression is the way that it brings together past, present, and future. This resonates with the reflections on time and eschatology in chapter 3.[70] Indeed, the phrase "memory of the future" is one way of understanding the anamnesis that takes place in Christian liturgy, when the remembrance of past events in the life, death, and resurrection of Jesus highlights the presence of God and points toward the future of Jesus's second advent, the coming of the New Creation.[71] Johann Baptist Metz refers to this as "anticipatory memory."[72] It is a memory of the past that makes claims upon us in the present as we are drawn into an eschatological future. Bruce T. Morrill, drawing upon Metz and others, emphasizes that Christian anamnesis is a form of knowledge that is both practical and imitative.[73] He writes,

> In the Eucharist Christians perform with praise and thanksgiving the remembrance of the crucified and risen Christ whom they

encounter in liturgical word and gesture and, moreover, anticipate joining in the heavenly banquet. The anticipatory memory of Christ in the Eucharist nurtures their own lives now as his followers, who imitate him in kenotic service in the Church and to the world.[74]

In reenacting the Last Supper, Christians are re-presenting the past, making it present again and taking up roles within it.[75] At the same time, Christians are participating in the eschatological future. The Eucharist is the inbreaking of God's future into the present.[76] In the Eucharist, Christians proclaim that "Christ has died. Christ is risen. Christ will come again." The ritual re-presentation of the death of Jesus in the past is also a re-presentation of his resurrection and the eschatological vision of his return in glory. Cavanaugh writes, "The secular imagination of time is overcome in the Eucharist by embodying the three temporalizations implicit in I Cor. 11:26: 'For as often as you eat this bread and drink the cup, you proclaim the Lord's death until he comes.'"[77]

Eucharistic performance is political because it reorients Christians in time. We are not beholden to modern optimism based on ongoing strategies of cause and effect with calculations of acceptable compromise and necessary losses. We are not moving forward on a temporal line in which past is left behind and future is an accomplishment to be attained. Instead, as Christians we are oriented within a more radical, less linear sense of time. The future is God's eschatological consummation, in which the past participates.

Metz argues that it is only faith in the future of God—"resurrection faith"—that affords us the courage to face the memory of those who have suffered and died. Because we believe that the fullness of God's future is coming, but has not yet fully arrived, we can affirm that "those already vanquished and forgotten, have a meaning that is as yet unrealized."[78] The content of Christian hope is far bolder than modern optimism, which holds promise only for those in the future. Christians hope even for those who have gone before. Because Jesus's death was not the end of his story, so too do the stories of those who have died remain open to new meaning in eschatological fullness.

In the Eucharist, past, present, and future come together, not in a linear pattern of progress but in a multidirectional pattern of redemption. We look to the past to see the future, and this vision of the future shapes our present life in embodied hope for its fulfillment. This means that Eucharistic performance, in and of itself, challenges oppressive sociopolitical structures under which those in the past have suffered, and those in the present do suffer, in the vain expectation of benefit to the victors of a linear history.

Multiple Roles

Eucharistic performance is also political because it is a remembrance of *Jesus Christ*, a man who was tortured, suffered, and died. In the remembrance of this man, Christians are united with the body of someone who suffered, we are identified with the tortured, and we are aligned with the afflicted. It requires that we empathize and identify with all who have suffered and died. Metz writes, "It forces us to look at the public *theatrum mundi* not merely from the standpoint of the successful and the established, but from that of the conquered and the victims."[79] The memory of Jesus is "dangerous and subversive" because it counters narrations of history that hide the casualties of injustice and cruelty, that inure us to human pain cast as acceptable, unavoidable, necessary, or unworthy of notice.[80] Christian anamnesis holds the dangerous potential of generating solidarity between Christians today—who communicate their pain to one another—and all those who suffer, even those who have already died.[81] This questions and condemns social realities that make the suffering of others palatable.

The Eucharistic liturgy performatively constitutes a social body of solidarity with those who suffer. This stands in direct contrast to the "anti-liturgy" of torture in Chile under Pinochet.[82] It stands in opposition to the "antiliturgy" performed by racism in the United States, according to M. Shawn Copeland, and indeed to any "intentionally divisive segregation of bodies on the specious grounds of preference for race or gender or sexual orientation or culture."[83] Copeland writes, "Eucharistic solidarity orients us to the cross of the lynched Jesus of Nazareth, where we grasp the enormity of suffering, affliction, and oppression as well as apprehend our complicity in the suffering, affliction, and oppression of others."[84]

Metz, Copeland, Cavanaugh, and Morrill argue that Christian liturgy has profoundly liberating power. They offer normative visions of what the Eucharist ought to be and do in Christian liturgy. Where my question about Christian performance contributing to lynching points to the worst of what church can be, these authors hold up the power of Christian performance at its best. They portray the ideal that Christians strive to be in our performance. While I learn much from their work, I also question: Does Christian liturgical performance always, necessarily, work to such good effect? If we recognize the power of Christian performance to be a force for good in the world, should we not also recognize its power to do ill? History is replete with examples of Christians who worshipped on Sunday and committed atrocities the rest of the week, often without perceiving any discrepancy between the two. These authors are not naïve about these issues, yet their work presents Christian liturgy as it ought to be, rather than as it often is.

Shifting away from a view of church as a stable entity toward a view of church as performance can help us recognize and wrestle with the varied consequences of Christian liturgy. Church is a performance, and therefore is event, interaction, and doubleness. This doubleness means we cannot simply point to the ideal we are striving for as the true measure of our identity. Our performance is a repetition of the past and a rehearsal for the future. We are not the ideal we strive to be, yet we are also not not that ideal. We perform in the space between the negative and the double negative. Neither side of this doubleness can be dismissed.

Theologian Siobhán Garrigan sees a need for greater clarity about whether our accounts of the Eucharist are normative or descriptive.[85] She writes, "because so much is written about what 'should be,' it can blinker the interpretation of what 'is.' "[86] Garrigan's groundbreaking work begins with what is, using case studies of ritual practices in actual congregations. In *The Real Peace Process: Worship, Politics and the End of Sectarianism*, she closely examines the role of Christian liturgy in violent political strife in Ireland. Instead of constructing an ideal vision of how the Eucharist can heal divides, Garrigan investigates what takes place in both Protestant and Roman Catholic worship services.[87] She discovers that many congregations are enacting sectarianism in ways they do not recognize. From how visitors are greeted to how the Eucharist is presented, the embodied performances of several congregations implicitly support and reaffirm sectarian divisions. Because this is happening performatively, in embodied and communal ways that form those who participate, the people involved often do not realize what is happening. The memories and beliefs that are stored and transmitted in performance are not brought into verbal articulation and therefore escape scrutiny. Garrigan's scholarship brings the social memories and communal beliefs being performed into words, into intellectual articulation. This allows church members and worship leaders to engage their own practices intellectually and to make conscious choices about how to perform in the future.

Throughout this book I have argued that church performance ought to be communal and whole-personed: bodily, emotional, intellectual, and volitional. To counter the emphasis placed on archive (inscribed texts) over repertoire (performed knowledge) in modern theology, I have emphasized the importance of embodiment and emotion, particularly in Christian formation. However, honoring body and emotion should not entail neglect of intellect and volition. When communal knowledge and social memory are not subject to intellectual scrutiny, the possibility of harmful performances increases. We can do harm unawares.

Sometimes we need our emotional and bodily patterns to be jolted and our intellects to be reengaged, so that we can choose more carefully. One model for this is Garrigan's careful analysis of church practices. Another is the provocative work of Williams. Both serve to alienate us, in Brechtian fashion, and make the familiar strange. Such alienation is, I believe, one vital way in which we prevent our performances from becoming harmful to ourselves and others. It is not a perfect answer. Even our most thoughtful and considered performances will be those of sinful, finite humans. Yet our unreflective performances are surely worse.

Furthermore, the spiritual and political power of liturgy, including the Eucharist, to resist violence and oppression is not automatic. I believe that our best performances are whole-personed—that is, that they incorporate body, emotion, intellect, and will. We perform better when we understand, and choose, the import of our actions. By engaging our intellect and will, alienation can be an important resource in enabling our church performances to more closely approximate what they ought to be. We come closer to our politically and spiritually powerful ideals when we perform them with our whole selves.

Alienated by the Cross

Alienation is particularly fitting in regard to the cross, because the cross generates alienation. Several aspects of the biblical narratives read so much like Brecht's own practices that it seems he may have used the Passion as a prompt book. Expectations are thwarted, roles are reversed, and patterns of identification and empathy repeatedly disrupted. Jesus, the Messiah, is executed as a common criminal. The male disciples—likely candidates for our identification—scatter and betray, while a thief and a centurion prove faithful. Jesus's crown is made of thorns and a placard is placed at the head of a dying man, proclaiming the despised to be "The King of the Jews." It is not simply that there are examples of alienation in the passion narratives. When we see the cross as revealing the depth of God's love, alienation is pervasive. The cross alienates us from the rest of the world. It makes the familiar strange, the hierarchies and values of society—so often deemed natural—unacceptable. Yet for us to be alienated *by* the cross, we first need to be alienated *from* the cross. We need to have our long-performed patterns interrupted, so that we engage them intellectually and carefully. This is the work of pastors and theologians, of Sunday School teachers and church organists, and of every baptized Christian. In the Gospel of Mark, Jesus recounts the great commandment: "you shall love the Lord your God with all your heart, and with all your soul, and with all your mind, and with all your strength"(Mark 12: 30). The rigorous workings of our minds are required if we are to perform our worship well.

While Williams and Garrigan alienate within scholarly writing, it is also possible for alienation to be performed liturgically. Consider, for example, the Stations of the Cross. These are fourteen moments within the narrative of Christ's passion, which traditionally are rendered and displayed in painting, sculpture, or some other artistic medium. Christians walk from station to station, cultivating empathy and identification with Jesus in his sufferings as he carried the cross. This is often done during Lent, particularly Good Friday. However, some contemporary versions of this—particularly potent among wealthy congregations—do not use artwork displayed in the sanctuary. Instead, participants walk through the city they live in, stopping at "stations" associated with suffering today. The store selling cheap clothes stitched in maquiladoras. The payday lender. The food bank. Such observance of the Stations of the Cross invites participants to ask how their own way of life causes suffering today.

Another example is a Good Friday service in the Anglican tradition. Normally, at a time in the rite called the Veneration of the Cross, a large cross would be carried down the center aisle and either held or propped at the front of the sanctuary. Members of the congregation would then come forward and pay homage, kneeling or bowing before the cross, touching or kissing it. Yet imagine that in this particular service, the participants were invited not to kneel or kiss the cross, but instead to hammer nails into the rough-hewn wood.

At the end of Lent, culminating a season of repentance, the performers of this Good Friday service might identify themselves as those in need of salvation by the cross. They might identify with Jesus, suffering on the cross. The liturgy itself, however, asks them to identify—briefly—with those who crucified. Ironically, such an alienating performance might help us guard against performing church in ways that rehearse crucifixion.

5

Striking the Set

WHILE THERE ARE many opportunities for alienation within Christian liturgy, it can be difficult to actually implement them. Even the smallest change in worship practice can be met with fierce resistance from parishioners who find comfort and security in familiar patterns. On a deeper level, many Christians fear that if we perform worship differently, we will necessarily be doing it wrong. Here we have much to learn from theater practitioners. At the end of every production, theater companies strike the set. The cast and crew literally tear the set apart, down to the bare floor and walls of the theater. This is not a repudiation of their own hard work, but rather an honoring of its nature as an event—not an object—and an enactment of trust that more inspiration and creativity will follow. Striking the set does not mean that all traditions are destroyed. The scripts, conventions of the theater, theater building, community, and so forth all remain. As most theaters are not well funded, every salvageable scrap of the set is saved. Even the unbent nails are collected for use in the next production. At the same time, room is made for something new, in the sturdy hope that inspiration will come again.

Is our Christian hope that sturdy? Sometimes it seems as if our worship is guided by competing fears. On one hand, we worry that if we do not perform church in the same way we always have, God might stay away on Sunday. On the other hand, we are scared that if we do not perform church in the same way we always have, God might show up!

I have argued that church is a performance of embodied hope. In this chapter, I describe this as hope in the Holy Spirit, and argue that one vital way in which this hope is performed is in a discipline of emptiness.

Early in this text I suggested that my method for bringing authors to these pages is akin to inviting guests to a dinner party, gathering people with enough similarity and difference for stimulating conversation. This final pairing begins with Karl Barth, who might well decline the invitation.[1] Yet he must be reckoned with as a powerful challenge to the view of church I am developing in these pages: to my view of church as the disciplined performance of relationship with Jesus Christ, mediated by Scripture, in hope of the Holy Spirit. Barth, in conversation with director Peter Brook, brings to the table an emphasis on emptiness, in which we await and expect the presence of the Spirit of God.

Karl Barth

Karl Barth was a Swiss Reformed theologian and pastor who lived from 1886–1968. He is one of the most influential theologians of the twentieth century. A prolific writer, Barth produced an enormous amount of published theological work, of which I will highlight three examples. First, as a young man Barth wrote, published, then greatly revised a commentary on Paul's letter to the Romans. The second edition of this commentary was published in 1922, overturning the current assumptions of Protestant theology and changing its trajectory for decades to come. Second, in 1934, Barth was the primary author of the Barmen Declaration. This is a statement of the Confessing Church in Germany, an organization that resisted the cooptation of Christianity by Nazism. The brief document does not detail all of the many reasons why Christians might find the Nazi ideology objectionable, but rather "affirms the sovereignty of the Word of God in Jesus Christ over against all idolatrous political ideologies."[2] It is arranged in six articles, and the first article includes the following: "We reject the false doctrine that the church could or should recognize as a source of its proclamation, beyond and besides this one Word of God, yet other events, powers, historic figures, and truths as God's revelation."[3] While the Barmen Declaration has been criticized for all that it does not say and do, it remains a powerful witness to those Christians who resisted the Nazis when so many complied, and to the fierce faith that enabled them to do so. Third, Barth wrote *Church Dogmatics*, a multivolume, unfinished, doctrinal theology that spans thousands of pages and was published in parts over four decades. Immense, complex, and brilliant, this work affected generations of scholars, both Protestant and Roman Catholic. In the pages that follow, I cannot do justice to all of these three works, much less to his other publications and sermons. I will, however, engage some of the major points of his work as they relate to performance ecclesiology.

There is ample reason to believe Barth would have serious reservations about my entire project. From the second edition of Romans on, Barth was consistently critical of the tendency of liberal Protestant theology to both start with and focus upon the human. He argued that this reverses the proper order of theology by making God a predicate of our knowledge or experience. At best we create a false god amenable to our own self-understanding. At worst we have no norm by which to reject divine pretensions, in ourselves or others. Either way we are not addressing the reality of the God of Jesus Christ, God who is subject and not object, God who is "wholly other" than human beings.[4]

Barth connects beginning with humanity and natural theology as it was promoted by liberal Protestantism. He contends that many theologians, such as Friedrich Schleiermacher and Emil Brunner, falsely imagine there is a natural point of contact between God and humanity. Such a point would allow humans to know something of God on our own steam, or at the very least would enable us to discriminate among various revelatory sources. This is a form of arrogance that breeds idolatry and denies the "infinite qualitative distinction" between God and humanity.[5] In other words, it nearly guarantees that we will invent gods to support our own ideas and comforts, rather than being confronted by the God of Jesus Christ who overwhelms and masters us.

Barth's conviction that theology should be about God and not a discourse about the human person is maintained in his treatment of ecclesiology not as a separate doctrinal locus, but rather within discussions of the Holy Spirit and Jesus Christ.[6] He describes church as constituted by God, not as constituted by human persons or traditions. While it is surely possible to offer analysis of church employing the methods of anthropology, sociology, or ritual studies, such analysis of church as human community misses the true constitutive element of church, which is divine action.[7] Since God is the "true and primary acting Subject,"[8] in church as elsewhere, ecclesiology should be addressed within pneumatology and Christology. Treating ecclesiology as a separate doctrine enhances the risk of focusing on the human, once again.

Barth offers a challenge to my ecclesiology regarding both method and content. My inquiry begins with the activity of humans, engages in dialogue with other disciplines (performance and theater studies), and argues that our activity is theologically significant and constitutive of church. Given the scope of the disagreement, it seems wise to look closely at the rationale behind Barth's position. At the same time, I find in Barth a compelling theology of emptiness.

Romans

Barth's commentary on Paul's letter to the Romans was written for readers familiar with war. In the Preface to the English Edition, Barth writes,

"When I first wrote it...it required only a little imagination for me to hear the sound of the guns booming away in the north."[9] Within the context of the mass carnage of World War I, Barth wrote of the grace and revelation of God using deeply unsettling military imagery. He compares the life of Jesus Christ with "the crater made at the percussion point of an exploding shell, the void by which the point on the line of intersection makes itself known in the concrete world of history."[10]

In his definition of the Gospel, Barth undercuts many traditional ways of speaking about the church in service of God or world. He offers, instead, a disturbing vision of the community living in the aftermath of an explosion.

> [T]he activity of the community is related to the Gospel only in so far as it is no more than a crater formed by the explosion of a shell and seeks to be no more than a void in which the Gospel reveals itself. The people of Christ, His community, know that no sacred word or work or thing exists in its own right: they know only those words and works and things which by their negation are sign-posts to the Holy One. If anything Christian (!) be unrelated to the Gospel, it is a human by-product, a dangerous religious survival, a regrettable misunderstanding. For in this case content would be substituted for a void, convex for concave, positive for negative, and the characteristic marks of Christianity would be possession and self-sufficiency rather than deprivation and hope.[11]

Church must remain empty in response to the grace of God and in recognition that grace comes from God alone and not from human efforts. Both divine revelation and human faith are gifts of God. Barth focuses on the activity of God to such a degree that obedient human activity is rendered in negative terms. Being faithful includes the readiness "to accept the void" and "tarry in negation."[12] He writes, "Depth of feeling, strength of conviction, advance in perception and in moral behavior...are not positive factors, but negations of other positive factors, stages in the work of clearance by which room is made in this world for that which is beyond it."[13]

When human efforts to know and relate to God are rated highly and understood as efficacious, there emerges what Barth terms "the criminal arrogance of religion."[14] Whenever we presume to possess knowledge of God, whenever we assume that God needs something from us, or whenever we assign to God the most exalted place within our human-centered framework, we are creating a "No-God."[15] This is not the God of Jesus Christ, the God whose explosive grace undoes our human possibilities. When we view ourselves in such near proximity to God, our worship becomes a form of self-adulation. Barth writes,

> Secretly we are ourselves the masters in this relationship. We are not concerned with God, but with our own requirements, to which God must adjust Himself. Our arrogance demands that, in addition to everything else, some super-world should also be known and accessible to us. Our conduct calls for some deeper sanction, some approbation and remuneration from another world. Our well-regulated, pleasurable life longs for some hours of devotion, some prolongation into infinity. And so, when we set God upon the throne of the world, we mean by God ourselves. In 'believing' on Him, we justify, enjoy, and adore ourselves.[16]

Barth rails against all the ways in which churches substitute a visible God of their own creation (No-God) for the incomprehensible, invisible God of Jesus Christ. He writes, "The invisibility of God seems to us less tolerable than the questionable visibility of what we like to call 'God.'"[17] Church communities are set up for this structurally, for they attempt to make God visible and comprehensible, "attempt to humanize the divine."[18] This always fails. Either the failure is straightforward or it appears successful by partaking of idolatry, trading a visible No-God for the invisible God of Jesus Christ.

When it fails honestly, Barth claims, religion is the highest human possibility.[19] "Religion compels us to the perception that God is not to be found in religion."[20] This is not, for Barth, an excuse to abandon religion and sleep in on Sundays, for religion is not a consumer good to be chosen or rejected in aisle 7. He states, "Religion is not a thing to be desired or extolled: it is a misfortune which takes fatal hold upon some men, and is by them passed on to others."[21]

This low evaluation of religion and church in Barth's text is an important element of his rejection of natural theology as well as an admonition of triumphalist views of church. Pleasant pictures of the role of church congregations go hand in hand with optimism about human efforts to reach God. Barth critiques them both. In doing so, he outlines a vital role for religion: as religion acknowledges its own failure, it rejects natural theology and triumphalism. While Barth repeatedly emphasizes that God is the only one who can cross the immeasurable distance between God and humanity, we have some small part to play in the work of clearance, in recognizing that we cannot reach God on our own. Barth says "the Church is constituted" by the Word of God, for which we must wait. He relies, again, on wartime imagery to describe its power.

> The Word is nigh unto us. Wherever we cast our eye, the dynamite is prepared and ready to explode. But if there is no explosion, or if something less final takes place, can we not take just the smallest risk which is, in fact the greatest? Are we always to prefer a thousand other days to one day in the outer courts of the Lord? Shall we never permit our hands to be empty, that we may grasp what only empty hands can grasp?... So in like manner is it with the Word of God. But here we must not forget to reckon with impossibility. For impossibility is, as such, nigh at hand, ready at our elbow, possible. Impossibility presses upon us, breaks over us, is indeed already present. Impossibility is more possible than everything which we hold to be possible. The light shineth in the darkness.[22]

There is a positive note about emptiness here, an affirmation of its value. Declaring the futility of human action in accessing God on nearly every page, Barth still affirms that emptiness, and our awareness of it, can play a role as we await the Word of God. This is most clear, perhaps, in Barth's description of the apostle Paul. He writes,

> A man may be of value to another man, not because he wishes to be important, not because he possesses some inner wealth of soul, not because of something he is, but because of what he is—not. His importance may consist in his poverty, in his hopes and fears, in his waiting and hurrying, in the direction of his whole being towards what lies beyond his horizon and beyond his power. The importance of an apostle is negative rather than positive. In him a void becomes visible.[23]

Church Dogmatics

Barth's writing on church in *Romans* has been described by scholar James Buckley as "an apophatic or negative ecclesiology and sacramentology in contrast to the kataphatic or positive ecclesiology and sacramentology

Barth would later develop."[24] While *Romans* presents church as an empty crater, *Church Dogmatics* offers a more substantive account. However, certain aspects of his thinking appear with remarkable consistency in various places.

First, Barth's view of church is profoundly Christological. James Livingston writes, "[a]fter 1935 Barth's entire theology is focused on Christology."[25] This is clear in Barth's ecclesiology, where he takes up the Pauline image of the church as the Body of God.[26] Barth makes this claim as more than a metaphor. He writes, "The community is the earthly-historical form of existence of Jesus Christ Himself."[27] The community is not the Body of Christ because of its own character or of its own accord, but rather becomes the Body of Christ through the "awakening power" of the Holy Spirit, which continually "refound[s]" the church.[28] This refounding and awakening that constitutes the community as the Body of Christ is an "event."[29] Barth writes, "To describe [church] we must abandon the usual distinctions between being and act, status and dynamic, essence and existence. Its act is its being, its status its dynamic, its essence its existence."[30] Thus Barth presents a series of statements in the form of "the Church *is* when…"[31] The event that is church is the act of the Holy Spirit; the acting subject of church is God.[32] This is not, on Barth's part, a simple denial of human subjectivity in church. Of course there are many ways in which the human participants are "the obvious subjects" of the activities of church. Yet what constitutes church as church—that is, as the Body of Christ—is the event of the Holy Spirit awakening persons to faith, the event of the Holy Spirit gathering the community.[33]

Interestingly, Barth draws upon the relation between visible and invisible in his account of the relation between human and divine activity in the church, using the terms rather differently than he did in *Romans*. He begins by describing Christian communities as having a "third dimension." This third dimension is the "hidden," "spiritual character" of church, namely, that it is Body of Christ.[34] It is possible and tempting to understand such communities entirely as human groups and activities, in only two dimensions. This is done by sociologists, anthropologists, and—in Barth's view—Schleiermacher.[35] Yet such studies always miss the point because their disciplinary tools do not allow them to apprehend the third dimension: the awakening by the Holy Spirit, which is definitive of the identity of church. No matter how hard one looks at the visible church, the invisible third dimension cannot be ascertained by human effort or intellectual study. It is perceived by faith. Thus even the visible church has a "special visibility," meaning that its true identity can only be seen by those who believe.[36]

Barth rejects the notion that the true church is an invisible reality.[37] From the beginning, church involved the invisible becoming visible. He asserts: "the work of the Holy Spirit as the awakening power of Jesus Christ would not take place at all if the invisible did not become visible."[38] He also rejects any notion that there are two churches.[39] The visible and the invisible in their unity "are the body...of the one living Lord Jesus Christ." Within this unity, "[t]he visible lives wholly by the invisible," while the invisible is "represented and to be sought out in the visible."[40]

Christians, those people who are part of the visible church, are the fortunate ones who can see the special visibility of church, due to the awakening power of the Spirit. They are the ones who know what God has done for us all in Jesus Christ. Time and again, Barth refers to the benefits of church in epistemological terms.[41]

Barth's distinctive ecclesiology—and particularly his low estimation of theological significance of human activity in church—has garnered criticism even among scholars who appreciate his work. Three questions come up regularly in the large magnitude of scholarship on Barth's work. First, is church necessary? Barth affirms the historical reality of church as how God actually does go about God's business. In that sense, of course there is, always has been, and always will be church. However, church does not play a role in God's salvific activity in Jesus Christ. Church witnesses and attests to Jesus's reconciliation, but does not help it along in any way. Implied throughout, this point is fairly clearly stated by Barth in *Church Dogmatics*, where he writes, "the world would not necessarily be lost if there were no church."[42] For many theologians, this is a drawback to Barth's work.

A second question follows quickly after. What is the role of human agency in church? By defining church in terms of God's action, Barth limits the role and importance of human agency in church. This is exacerbated by the anti-sacramental bent of his later writings.[43] Joseph Mangina notes that Barth's "sharp cleavage between divine and human action is problematic from the perspective of an ecclesial ethics."[44] That church exists is important for Barth—or, at least, a fully recognized given. However, what we do in church is less theologically significant. Theologian Nicholas Healy writes of Barth's ecclesiology, "*What* people do, as such, is not a constituent element of the church's identity."[45]

The third question follows logically close upon the heels of the second. In distinguishing so sharply between what God does in church (the awakening power of the Holy Spirit that constitutes the church as the Body of God) and what we do in church (witness and attest to this), has Barth split the church in two? Mangina refers to this as "an odd hiatus,"[46] Healy calls it "the bifurcation of the church,"[47] and James Buckley refers to the problem as "ecclesiological 'Nestorianism.'"[48] They agree that Barth's attempt to hold the visible and invisible together is not entirely successful.

Healy points out that in describing the invisible church as the event of God's activity, Barth presents a true church that is sinless. This is a bit hard to square with church as we know it. Healy writes, "[W]hen the 'church' sins it cannot be the action of the Body of Christ. It must therefore be something else that sins, some other entity, namely the 'false' church. At such times, the true church must be understood either as non-existent or else perhaps existent in another place."[49] I suspect that this aspect of Barth's theology might be one influence on Cone's assertion that white churchgoers who did not fight against lynching are simply not Christian. Such white congregations are simply not church. There is a deep presumption in Barth's ecclesiology that it is possible to clearly distinguish the saving activity of God (that can be discussed in theological terms) from the mundane activities of humanity (that can be discussed in sociological or psychological terms). However, this provides little room for the messy permeability between the two, for the ways in which the saving work of the incarnate God happens in the midst of human society and the thick of human frailty.[50]

All three of these questions are related, rooted in Barth's rejection of a human-centered view of church and his embrace of church as an event of God's action. The possible cost of his opening gambit is that the church he describes is hard to recognize as the place I try to go on Sundays. As Mangina puts it, "The problem is that the term 'church' itself has been stripped of its ordinary, denotative reference. Rather than referring to a perceptible community existing across time, the subject of its own actions, the church in Barth's scheme is sheerly a predicate of the divine action. The human communities, institutional structures, sacramental and moral actions etc. that we call 'church' are only potentially such."[51]

I have clearly taken a different tack from Barth's, beginning with human performance. However, Barth does describe church as event.[52] Could he be offering a different performative view of church?[53] Consider the three characteristics of performance outlined in the first chapter of this text: event, interaction, and doubling. Church is certainly an event for

Barth, to a degree that leaves him open to criticism that it has no abiding presence and could be episodic or intermittent. Church is also interaction, for Barth, on a number of levels. In church, the Holy Spirit awakens the faith of humanity and gathers the community. The faith thus awakened takes place in relation to Christian community and simply does not exist without it.[54] There is also interaction between the Holy Spirit and Jesus Christ, as well as the interaction of Jesus witnessing to Himself in the world.[55] There is plenty of interaction in Barth's church. Finally, is there doubling? Recall that doubling refers to the gap between a remembered, imagined, or ideal action and the action of the performance itself. Prime examples of doubleness include fulfilling social roles and striving for superior athletic performance. Doubleness is also described by the phrase "restored behavior," which indicates behavior we have been taught or have learned, either intentionally or unaware, from particular teachers or through the unarticulated norms of culture. It seems like there ought to be plenty of doubleness in Barth's ecclesiology, given all the talk about the invisible and visible church, about the earthly historical form of existence of Jesus Christ and the heavenly historical form of existence of Jesus Christ.[56] Yet the dialectics present in the text are not doubleness in the technical, performance theory sense of the word.

We must recall that, for Barth, the one who acts in church—the acting subject—is God. Is this action of God a performance? I do not think so, precisely because the acts of God do not have the characteristic of doubleness. God's behavior is not restored; God is not repeating an act God has learned from someone else or been taught by society. Creation is a divine original! God is not trying to meet an ideal or attempting to fulfill a social role. Barth would surely reject the idea that God strives in vain to embody something—God fully embodies Godself, magnificently succeeding in God's salvific act of love in Jesus Christ![57] That the God who acts to create, redeem, and consummate is Triune does not mean that doubleness is a characteristic of these acts.

My stance on this issue stems from my engagement with performance theory. If performance is strictly used as an analogy, then it is not problematic to assert that God performs. However, if performance is used in an analytical mode, drawing on the resources of performance theory, then the characteristics of performance are more specific. James Fodor and Stanley Hauerwas, in an essay titled "Performing Faith: The Peaceable Rhetoric of God's Church," use the language of performance and improvisation to emphasize elements of Christian life that are obscured by the language of narrative and story alone. These elements include time, repetition, and embodiment.[58] In this essay, Fodor and Hauerwas refer to God as performing, stating, "Christians worship a God who is pure act, an eternally performing God."[59] The authors recognize that God's performing would have to be quite different from human performing.[60] However, this appears to be based on an analogical approach, rather than an analytical one, without full exploration of the distinctions between acting and performing. Referencing John Webster, the authors state, "It may be that the Christian faith is 'primarily an account of divine action' and 'only secondarily an account of the believing subject,' and then go on to claim "our God is a performing God who has invited us to join in the performance that is God's life."[61]

The language is a bit difficult here, since we use the term "act" to mean both "do" and "perform on stage." However, there is a distinction between doing something and performing it. Performance is marked by doubleness in a way that doing is not. God certainly acts. God *does*. Jesus of Nazareth performs, as do all human beings. He followed the conventions of daily interaction in his culture, restoring bits of behavior, with his own improvisations.[62] Furthermore, some of the words of God are performative utterances.[63] When God said, "Let there be light!" there was light. However, to speak of God performing makes no sense if we consider God's acts to be *sui generis* and recognize that performance is marked by doubleness. God's creating, redeeming, and consummating are unique and fully successful.[64]

While Barth's rendering of church as event and his emphasis on God's act provide a strong temptation to performance language, ultimately such language does not fit his ecclesiology. God acts, but does not perform. We perform, but our actions are not constitutive of church. Thus Barth's ecclesiology is not easily amenable to performative interpretations.[65]

For Barth, God reveals Godself to humanity. Given the magnificence and mystery of God, such revelation does not become knowledge that humanity possesses. Often we would prefer a smaller god, more amenable to our own agendas and less likely to spark transformation, more comprehensible and therefore less frightening. One danger of religion is to begin worshiping a No-God of our own creation, who sanctifies our own views and strivings, who becomes visible at our command. Barth stands guard against such a No-God, a vigilant gatekeeper against human pretensions. He demands emptiness in which God's revelation can be both perceived and hoped for.[66] Barth reiterates that human effort contributes nothing to the event of God's revelation, that our subjective agency is passive and receptive. However, he also indicates that there is value in the work of clearance, in which religion exposes the visible No-God as a fraud.

There is an appreciation for emptiness here, and suggestions that Christian life together might at least point to its own emptiness in a work of clearance. At the very least, we can be critical of our own arrogance and idolatry. This is a vital word for Christian communities, everlastingly timely.

Barth does not offer a model of performative ecclesiology but rather some valuable insights and important cautions. The insights include a strong realism regarding God and the identification of the work of the Holy Spirit in church. For Barth, the movement of the Spirit is definitive of church. I differ significantly on this, as I begin with the human and define church as human performance. However, the difference is not absolute. Why do we perform? In hope of the Spirit.

Furthermore, it is vital to remember that our performance cannot be equated with the Spirit's movement or the value of church. We cannot achieve inspiration or force the Spirit's hand. Rather, our performance, at best, is a work of clearance. Our performance should be a self-critical reminder of our own limitations, a check on our pretensions, and a curb to the arrogance of religion. Given his larger theological framework and commitments, Barth cannot further develop what a discipline of emptiness in church might look like. For that, we turn to Peter Brook.

Peter Brook

An English theater director, Brook does develop a discipline of emptiness. Brook's work has been enormously influential on modern theater in Europe and America, bringing an emphasis on experimentation and a sense of spiritual seeking.[67] This sense of seeking led Brook—particularly in the middle of his career—to engage various cultures and religious traditions in ways more fitting a seeking artist than an academic scholar. However, a number of theologians and ethicists have engaged his first book, a theater classic entitled *The Empty Space*.[68]

Brook notes that "[t]he word theatre has many sloppy meanings. In most of the world, the theatre has no exact place in society, no clear purpose, it only exists in fragments: one theatre chases money, another chases glory, another chases emotion, another chases politics, another chases fun."[69] So he questions, "Why theatre at all? What for? Is it an anachronism, a superannuated oddity, surviving like an old monument or a quaint custom? Why do we applaud, and what? Has the stage a real place in our lives?"[70] Brook begins to answer his question with a typology of theater, in which he repeatedly employs religious language of holiness, ritual, and even incarnation.

Holy Theater

One type of theater that Brook describes is Holy Theater, which is "The Theatre of the Invisible-Made-Visible." To communicate what he means by this, Brook offers an assortment of images and stories, from which he then draws a few markers for identifying theater that is holy. The first image is that of the conductor of an orchestra (and a biblical reference, as well).

> We hear that trumpets destroyed the walls of Jericho, we recognize that a magical thing called music can come from men in white ties and tails, blowing, waving, thumping and scraping away. Despite the absurd means that produce it, through the concrete in music we recognize the abstract, we understand that ordinary men and their clumsy instruments are transformed by an art of possession. We may make a personality cult of the conductor, but we are aware that he is not really making the music, it is making him—if he is relaxed, open and attuned, then the invisible will take possession of him; through him, it will reach us.[71]

Brook takes it as given that his readers will know what he means, that this invisible will be familiar. He states, "many audiences all over the world will answer positively from their own experience that they have seen the face of the invisible through an experience on the stage that transcended their experience in life."[72] This assumption—that we will recognize what he is talking about—is vital to Brook's argument in *The Empty Space*. He does not provide a philosophical argument for why theater is important or what vital role it plays. Neither does he provide sociological or anthropological accounts of the role of theater in particular cultures. Instead, Brook gives a theological rendering of theater based on the assumption that his readers will recognize what he is talking about based on their own past experience.

Furthermore, Brook's own experience apparently leads him to believe that seeing the invisible-made-visible is more likely to occur in a theater or at a musical performance than in a traditional Christian church setting. He does not attack church, but rather seems to take it as a depressing yet valid cultural given that church no longer functions well. At one point, Brook describes the theater led by Polish director Jerzy Grotowski, writing that his "theatre is holy because its purpose is holy; it has a clearly defined place in the community and it responds to a need the churches can no longer fill."[73] More often Brook suggests that theater and art have their origins in sacred ritual, and that theater now participates in the ongoing deterioration of the same.[74] Theater and church, which have often worked together, are now floundering haplessly together. He writes:

> In Coventry, for instance, a new cathedral has been built, according to the best recipe for achieving a noble result. Honest, sincere artists, the 'best', have been grouped together to make a civilized stab at celebrating God and Man and Culture and Life through a collective act. So there is a new building, fine ideas, beautiful glasswork—only the ritual is threadbare. Those Ancient and Modern hymns, charming perhaps in a little country church, those numbers on the wall, those dog-collars and the lessons, are sadly inadequate here. The new place cries out for a new ceremony, but of course it is the new ceremony that should have come first—it is the ceremony in all its meanings that should have dictated the shape for the place, as it did when all the great mosques and cathedrals and temples were built. Goodwill, sincerity, reverence, belief in culture are not quite enough...[75]

We still need true rituals, Brook asserts, and we often look to artists to create them. Artists draw on the "outer form" of various ceremonies or rituals "and the result is rarely convincing. And after years and years of weaker and waterier imitations we now find ourselves rejecting the very notion of a holy stage. It is not the fault of the holy that it has become a middle-class weapon to keep children good."[76]

Published in 1968, *The Empty Space* articulates a cultural moment of longing and disillusionment in regard to both art and Christianity. Brook writes, "more than ever, we crave for an experience that is beyond the humdrum. Some look for it in jazz, classical music, in marijuana and in LSD. In the theatre we shy away from the holy because we don't know what this could be—we only know that what is called the holy has let us down."[77] He assumes his readers will agree with him that "all the forms of sacred art have certainly been destroyed by bourgeois values" and yet he tries to convince them not to give up on holiness—or the theater—altogether.[78] He still hopes for more moments of invisible-made-visible, and so he tries to remind his readers what they look like. The most poignant images come from Europe after World War II, a time when, Brook says, "the theatre of a battered Europe…[was] reaching back towards a memory of lost grace."[79]

Holy Theater, Brook claims, responds to a hunger. He is clear that the hunger to which it responds is not a hunger for simply "the missing things of life, a hunger, in fact for buffers against reality."[80] Rather, it responds to "a hunger for the invisible, a hunger for a reality deeper than the fullest form of everyday life."[81]

With an admirable level of theological nuance, and drawing upon what he terms "religious teaching," Brook states that the invisible is always visible. However, it cannot be seen "automatically," but only under "certain conditions." Holy Theater, then, "not only presents the invisible but also offers conditions that make its perception possible."[82]

Discerned from memories and images, drawing on religious language and teaching, in conversation with other directors and in the context of a culture of disillusionment, Brook offers a picture of Holy Theater that looks something like this: There is a reality deeper than what we commonly apprehend in daily life. Sometimes this invisible is made visible in theater. When this happens, it is not the achievement of the players involved, for it happens by a sort of possession. (The conductor does not make the music; the music makes the conductor.) At the same time, the work of the company and the audience is vital, as it contributes to the conditions in which the invisible—which is always in the visible—can actually be perceived.

Deadly Theater

This picture of Holy Theater, however, is not Brook's ideal of what theater ought to be. Indeed, he is very clear that attempting to create a purely Holy Theater does not work. One reason for this is quite practical. When we aim solely for the holy, we quickly become concerned with the gravity of our own work and the importance of our own traditions. This easily devolves into what Brook calls the Deadly Theater. Imagine a professional production of one of Shakespeare's plays. The actors are in period costume; the sets are elaborate; the diction is elevated. Couples in fancy dress arrive in time to see their neighbors and, perhaps more importantly, be seen by them as well. The audience knows what Shakespeare is supposed to look like. To the extent that the production fulfills their expectations, they are bored; to the extent that it varies from their expectations, they are disappointed.[83] This is Deadly Theater.

It is easy to speculate how it gets started, particularly from a theological perspective. People glimpse the invisible-made-visible during a play. They want to see it again, aim to learn from past experience, re-create the techniques that once served so well. When they do not catch a glimpse, they strive harder, hold more tightly to tradition, and inwardly begin to suspect that the holy has let them down. Soon adherence to tradition becomes the goal, sanctified by a community unconvinced that there was ever something more.

This movement from an ideal of Holy Theater to a reality of Deadly Theater can be seen often in productions of Shakespeare.[84] Yet Shakespeare's writing also provides a clue for Brook regarding how to avoid this movement. He writes that Shakespeare's "aim continually is holy, metaphysical, yet he never makes the mistake of staying too long on the highest plane. He knew how hard it is for us to keep company with the absolute—so he continually bumps us down to earth...We have to accept that we can never see all of the invisible. So after straining towards it, we have to face defeat, drop down to earth, then start up again."[85]

Rough Theater

Bumping back down to earth is the work of the Rough Theater. This is the theater of dirt and profanity, the popular theater that happens in a barroom or an attic, the theater created on the cheap and enjoyed by the locals. Brook writes, "of course, it is most of all dirt that gives the roughness its edge; filth and vulgarity are natural, obscenity is joyous: with these the spectacle takes on its socially liberating role, for by nature the popular theatre is anti-authoritarian, anti-traditional, anti-pomp, anti-pretence."[86] The energy of the Rough Theater is the energy of liberation, both the liberation of laughter and political liberation.[87] It is the "energy that produces rebellion and opposition."[88] It is powered by "the wish to change society."[89]

In many ways the Holy and the Rough are truly antagonistic to one another. Brook writes, "If the holy makes a world in which a prayer is more real than a belch, in the rough theatre, it is the other way round. The belching then, is real and prayer would be considered comic."[90] While the

Holy Theater "deals with the invisible," the Rough Theater "deals with men's actions."[91] The Rough Theater also has its temptations to excess: "The defiant popular theatre man can be so down-to-earth that he forbids his material to fly. He can even deny flight as a possibility, or the heavens as a suitable place to wander."[92]

Brook's ideal is a theater that brings Rough and Holy together.[93] This is shown by his repeated remarks that Shakespeare—Brook's admitted model[94]—combined Rough and Holy in illuminating juxtaposition. Brook examines Shakespeare's mingling of Rough and Holy in *Measure for Measure*, signaled clearly by the use of prose and verse, respectively: "If we follow the movement in *Measure for Measure* between the Rough and the Holy we will discover a play about justice, mercy, honesty, forgiveness, virtue, virginity, sex and death: kaleidoscopically one section of the play mirrors the other, it is in accepting the prism as a whole that its meanings emerge."[95] Brook regularly uses the term "incarnation" to describe what he hopes for on the stage.[96] He does not explain precisely what he means by this, but I believe it indicates an ideal in which the holy and the human are known together, in all their uncompromised distinction.

While Brook does not fully articulate the connections he is making between Holy and Rough, there are some indications to follow. For example, he writes admiringly about the work of playwright Samuel Beckett, which many people find quite grim. "Beckett's dark plays are plays of light," Brook says, "where the desperate object created is witness of the ferocity of the wish to bear witness to the truth."[97] He continues contemplating the power of Beckett's tragic imagery:

> There are two ways of speaking about the human condition: there is the process of inspiration—by which all the positive elements of life can be revealed, and there is the process of honest vision—by which the artist bears witness to whatever it is that he has seen. The first process depends on revelation; it can't be brought about by holy wishes. The second one depends on honesty, and it mustn't be clouded over by holy wishes.[98]

This honesty—this witness so painful it is a thing to be borne—is also part of the task of theater. Beckett's bearing witness is, in Brook's account, an act of hope. Not optimism, which can make hope harder to find, but real hope.[99]

From my admittedly theological viewpoint, I offer this interpretation of the vital connection between Holy and Rough Theater: glimpsing the deeper reality of the invisible-made-visible changes how one sees everything else. To speak honestly about "everything else" is also part of what theater ought to be, and that is the work of Rough Theater. Humanity looks different in holy light, and acceptable social arrangements suddenly become less acceptable. Indeed, if glimpsing the invisible-made-visible does not change our views of the world around us, then we were mistaken in our assessment and it was not the holy after all. Holiness demands new honesty about roughness. Brook never writes this directly, but it is there in his accounts of Beckett, Shakespeare, and Brecht. It is present, as well, in his own longing, as he writes, "we need desperately to experience magic in so direct a way that our very notion of what is substantial could be changed."[100] This sentence demonstrates both a desire to see the invisible, and a desire to see the visible in new ways.

Empty Space

If we accept the ideal of a Holy/Rough Theater, how do we go about it? What is needed? The opening lines of *The Empty Space* set the stage for this question: "I can take any empty space and call it a bare stage. A man walks across this empty space whilst someone else is watching him, and this is all that is needed for an act of theatre to be engaged."[101] These lines have been called "the commandments on which modern theatre was built."[102] All that is needed is an empty stage, Brook begins, but it turns out an empty stage is rather hard to come by. The rest of the book is, in a sense, an extended essay about how to keep the stage empty, during which it becomes clear that Brook is referring to a particular, metaphorical type of emptiness. Recall the conductor in Brook's anecdote about Holy Theater. "[I]f he is relaxed, open and attuned, then the invisible will take possession of him."[103] Effort on the part of the players cannot force the invisible to become visible.[104] That is a moment of inspiration. However, the work of the theater company is still vital. The conductor must be "relaxed, open and attuned." The musicians must be highly skilled, the players must know their lines and staging, the audience must be amenable to the possibility of holiness. This is all part of the emptiness needed for theater, emptiness that is part of the conditions that make the perception of invisible-made-visible possible. Of course, even the relaxation of the conductor could be "God-sent" or "god-given," but this relaxation—this small element of emptiness—can also be "brought about by work."[105]

 Emptiness is difficult. My dining room table, for example, steadily accumulates school newsletters, returned homework, and half-finished art projects. The mantle in the living room is a haven for special stones and pretty leaves my children collect while walking through the neighborhood. My own dresser overflows with receipts that will never be needed, coupons that will never be used, and church bulletins I will never find when I want them. I try to beat back the encroaching chaos and clear the surfaces to bare wood, but my success is always temporary, as the detritus of daily life continues to accrue. Emptiness escapes me.

Science fiction author Philip K. Dick describes such flotsam and jetsam—candy wrappers and ticket stubs—as kipple, and he claims that it reproduces when we aren't looking.[106] Although we must always fight the ongoing kipplezation of the universe, he says, the best we can hope for is a detente—a stasis where the kipple is kept in check through constant vigilance. That is a pretty good description of what happens with my dining room table. And my desk, and my inbox, and much of my life.

Brook identifies obstacles to keeping the theater empty that are more than loose papers and unopened e-mails. He writes about emptiness metaphorically, addressing more existential kipple. The theater gets filled up well before the play begins, with such things as the expectations of the audience. Perhaps we come to the theater expecting high culture and the experience of something "nobler-than-life,"[107] expecting red velvet, elaborate costumes, and perfect enunciation. Perhaps we come to the theater expecting—even hoping—to be disappointed, since the production is simply an opportunity for us to secure our own status as cultural insiders through the witty critique we offer friends during intermission. The expectations of the audience are one form of metaphorical kipple that clutters the stage. Among these expectations must also be counted the conviction that holiness does not show anymore, that there is no deeper reality, that any glimpse of magic must be a play of the light.

Another, related form of kipple is tradition. Theater companies have patterns of how they do things, how they were taught, how their heroes acted, long-standing traditions of what good theater ought to be. Those traditions can fill up the theater, with everyone so invested on abiding by tradition that tradition itself takes center stage. Yet another form of theatrical kipple is repetition. A stage can be filled with the effort to repeat yesterday's performance, or with the dead weight of rote memorization.

These three things—expectation, tradition, and repetition—fill the stage and prevent the emptiness that Brook desires. They are also all related to Brook's assumption that we remember seeing the invisible-made-visible. Recall that Brook does not rely on philosophy or anthropology to promote the vital role of theater in culture. He does not ground his discussion of Holy Theatre on an external discipline. Instead, he starts with memory. He assumes that his readers have glimpsed the invisible-made-visible in artistic performance, and therefore his task is to remind us, to articulate and theorize this in a way that we can recognize. That dynamic—"you have glimpsed the holy here before, let us be ready to see it again"—involves a movement from past to present to future, from memory to expectation, expectation to repetition to tradition. Brook's own work relies on expectation, repetition, and tradition. Indeed, theater itself requires each of these. These three categories, which I have playfully labeled kipple, are also the stuff of doubleness. They have been described throughout this text using language such as restored behavior, strips of activity, remembered originals, imagined ideals, social roles, and cultural contexts. Performance cannot happen without doubleness; theater cannot happen without expectation, repetition, and tradition.

If the audience truly had no expectations, they might enter the theater and sit on the stage, jump up and join the fight scene, or at the very least answer rhetorical questions. Expectations about what theater is and what our roles are within it are necessary. Likewise, tradition is what allows theater to grow and develop, to be something more than "hey kids, let's put on a show!" Tradition grants depth and richness to theater, pushing us beyond the childish impulse to strut our stuff, toward the higher ground of literature and art. Finally, repetition is a basic building block of theater; it is necessary for remembering lines, rehearsing scenes, and reenacting events on stage. In Brook's analysis then, some of the basic structural elements of theater can also become kipple, cluttering the stage. They are necessary and cannot simply be pitched. Yet they must not be allowed to become kipple. That fine line marks the difficult work of keeping the stage empty.

Brook offers no manual or handbook for emptiness; to do so would be a contradiction. Setting things in stone or believing we know how theater ought to be done is a source of Deadly Theater, antithetical to the emptiness Brook desires.[108] Instead of a handbook, he offers an ad hoc, autobiographical collection of approaches and techniques, to be used as a starting point. He writes,

The director will find that all the time new means are needed: he will discover that any rehearsal technique has its use, that no technique is all-embracing. He will follow the natural principle of rotation of crops: he will see that explanation, logic, improvisation, inspiration, are methods that rapidly run dry and he will move from one to the other. He will know that thought, emotion, and body can't be separated—but he will see that a pretended separation must often take place. Some actors do not respond to explanation, while others do. This differs in each situation, and one day it is unexpectedly the non-intellectual actor who responds to a word from the director, while the intellectual understands all from a gesture.[109]

Brook names this section of his text the Immediate Theater. It is his description of the best he has managed in creating the emptiness needed for Holy/Rough Theater. Here Brook offers suggestions for how to resist the deadly effects of the oh-so-necessary expectation, tradition, and repetition.

He writes of repetition, "It is as though in one word we see the essential contradiction in the theatre form."[110] It is necessary for development and change. Every athlete, actor, musician, or performer of any kind knows that the discipline of repetition "is the only way certain actions become possible, and anyone who refuses the challenge of repetition knows that certain regions of expression are automatically barred to him."[111] The way forward cannot be to avoid repetition, and may, indeed, include even more. Brook writes of the actor Lawrence Olivier, who "repeat[ed] lines of dialogue to himself again and again until he condition[ed] his tongue muscles to a point of absolute obedience—and so gain[ed] total freedom."[112] Olivier no longer had to think about remembering the lines, and therefore he could think about their meaning again, in new and changing ways.

This is part of what Brook calls representation. In representation, something from the past is made present again. An actor saying a line is no longer merely repeating past rehearsals, but rather participating in immediate meaning making in the present. The actor cannot do this on his own. Assistance is needed. Brook says the audience must participate in creating the conditions for this immediate meaning to occur.[113]

For the audience to assist, it must have expectations of more than a night out in fancy dress. If we come to the theater expecting only high culture, there is little room to notice the invisible-made-visible. The conditions

for perceiving the invisible-made-visible are lacking. If we come to the theater with rigid expectations of how the play should be performed, the stage
is not empty. For the audience to assist, it must have some sense that theater can be a space in which the invisible is made visible.[114] The work of
emptiness, then, includes the difficult task of fostering that sense. Brook
says that theater should create "works that evoke in audiences an undeni-
able hunger and thirst."[115] This metaphor is imprecise for here Brook is not
imagining that theater generates the hunger for a deeper reality, but rather
that good theater—Holy/Rough Theater in which this hunger for deeper
reality is met by the invisible-made-visible—teaches people to expect that
this can happen in theater. It enlivens them to the possibility that theater
can be a place where their hunger for a deeper reality is met. If the hunger
of the audience is met in the theater, then they will start to bring their
hunger to the theater, and eventually get hungry when they walk through
the door.

What helps repetition become representation is the work of an expectant audience, and creating such an audience is part and parcel of tradition. Brook is wary and critical of tradition, for its normative connection
to the past is a natural ally of the deadly. However, he also recognizes that
tradition does not have to be deadly. He writes with admiration of Noh
actors who communicate meaning from generation to generation,[116] and
he intimates that even the normative role of tradition can be central in the
search for an empty stage. Brook writes,

> [T]he Living Theatre, exemplary in so many ways, has still not yet
> come to grips with its own essential dilemma. Searching for holi-
> ness without tradition, without source, it is compelled to turn to
> many traditions, many sources—yoga, Zen, psychoanalysis, books,
> hearsay, discovery, inspiration—a rich but dangerous eclecticism.
> For the method that leads to what they are seeking cannot be an
> additive one. To subtract, to strip away can only be effected in the
> light of some constant.[117]

While tradition can be the fossilized remains of repetition, and can clutter
and kipple the stage, it is also necessary. The constants and constraints of
tradition focus and train the actor's skills. Beyond being necessary, tradition can also be vital to the distillation of meaning and its communication
over time. Brook notes that Shakespeare wrote the holy parts of *Measure
for Measure* in verse, not prose. "Shakespeare needs verse because he is

trying to say more, to compact together more meaning."[118] Instead of limiting the communication of meaning, the structure and form of verse allows Shakespeare to say more than he could in prose. Tradition—of poetry, liturgy, or theater—can compact meaning and thereby allow us richer communication. Tradition is what permits generations of Noh actors to pass on living meaning through time.

Tradition, Brook argues, must be kept in the present. The danger is to treat a time-honored tradition as a precious antique to be preserved. The minute this happens, the tradition itself becomes kipple, filling up the space.[119] Instead, a tradition should be treated as a well-crafted item intended for everyday use, valuable for its help in creating disciplined actors and expectant audiences who are both attuned to the possibility of the invisible-made-visible, in ever new and surprising ways.

Emptiness is a discipline for Brook. It is hard work that ultimately cannot generate the Holy/Rough Theater he desires. No amount of human work can make the invisible visible. However, the discipline of emptiness still matters. All the rehearsal and repetition, creativity and tradition, expectation and experimentation can help to create the conditions in which we might perceive the invisible-made-visible. Could we perceive this without all the hard work? Nothing is impossible. Sometimes emptiness, like relaxation, is God given. And yet, having glimpsed the invisible-made-visible, Brook hungers and thirsts for more.

Performing Hope

The differences between Barth and Brook are stark. Their similarities are, also. Both men are committed to hope in something beyond themselves. Barth identifies this in Jesus Christ, in Scripture, and in church. For Barth, the event of church is when the Spirit awakens human awareness to God's reconciling and redeeming work in Jesus Christ. Brook is speaking in an entirely different genre, about a different form of event. Yet he claims that in Holy Theater, the invisible becomes visible, under conditions in which it is possible to perceive.[120] Barth and Brook share a strong realism about the source of inspiration, which is beyond human culture and unattainable by human excellence. They are both hoping for the Spirit.[121] Such hope requires emptiness. Barth's emptiness is a vigilant criticism of church and of the pretensions of Christians, including himself. Brook's emptiness is a disciplined openness to that which is new.

The sharpest distinction between the two men is the role of human beings in relation to the Spirit. For Barth, it is arrogant to presume we have a role beyond joyful gratitude. For Brook, the Spirit does not merely awaken us, but also invites us to be part of the action. Yet perhaps even this contrast is not a complete contradiction. Recall Letty Russell's description of mission in chapter 3. The church has no mission, Russell claimed. God has a Mission and has graciously invited us to participate in it. It is possible, I contend, to learn from Barth's self-critical stance—guarding against ecclesial self-importance—without dismissing this invitation to participate—even as a footnote!—in God's love for the world. In chapter 1 I argued for a performative hermeneutic in which the meaning of Scripture comes to be most fully in our performance of it. Likewise, here I argue that God does not just let us see the meaning that God alone creates, but rather invites us into God's own activity, making meaning of us and with us, as well.

Brook's initial metaphor of the orchestra conductor presupposes long hours of training and rehearsal on the part of the musicians. The conductor himself must be "open, attuned, and relaxed" if anything extraordinary is to happen. Brook uses the language of possession—something beyond the conductor steps in. Finally, he notes that the "conductor does not make the music, the music makes him."[122] Brook is neither a theologian nor a philosopher and his words are, appropriately, more evocative than rigorously precise. Yet he points to something subtle and important. The effort of the conductor does not make the invisible visible, but neither is it beside the point. The long hours of rehearsal form the conductor so he can be taken up in such a way. His discipline readies him for possible possession.

While Brook's use of the term "possession" serves to emphasize the otherness of the Invisible he spies in Holy Theater, it might be more precise to speak of partnership, for the agency and efforts of the conductor are not lost but empowered in this event. The conductor does something for which he has trained extensively. The Invisible makes far more of the conductor's actions than they could be on their own. What the conductor does and what the Invisible does are not in conflict or competition. The formation of the conductor readies him for partnership in this particular way. The Invisible does not possess a gymnast and use her to conduct an orchestra, nor possess a conductor to do flips across the stage. It is the whole-personed discipline of the conductor that allows him to be open to the Invisible in his specificity. His intellect grasps the subtleties of the score and the strengths of the musicians, his emotions access the spirit of the music, his will spurs on the discipline in desire for a holy performance, and his body has developed the particular musculature necessary for artful wielding of the baton. All of this does not guarantee a holy performance, but rather serves as welcome to the Invisible. It is the cultivation of an environment amenable to possession, or better still, openness to partnership. Furthermore, this is true not just of the conductor, but of every member of the orchestra.

I would also push Brook's choice of words regarding the phrase "invisible-made-visible." This sight-oriented, cognitive language emphasizes that we perceive what the Invisible is up to in our midst. Yet Brook's example of the conductor implies much more. The conductor not only perceives what the Invisible is doing, he gets to be in on the action. This is not simply a cognitive awareness for the conductor; his whole person is part of the invisible being made visible. Beyond this one metaphor, such participation is implied throughout Brook's text. He is writing for members of the theater company who work in hope that the invisible will become visible precisely in their performances. The company Brook envisions is not hoping to see the invisible, they are hoping to participate in its movement on the stage.

Brook does not attempt to pin down exactly how Holy Theater is possible or define its contours. Instead, he relies on his readers' memory of past experiences. In Christianity, we have a long social memory of interactions with God. Creation itself is funded by God's desire to be in relationship with humanity. The relationship that God intends is not one in which our role as human beings is simply to perceive, see, or know what God is up to. Such a cognitive account would suggest that God's relationship to us does not involve our whole selves—body, intellect, emotions, and will. Yet Scripture overflows with collective memories of ways in which God has invited us not only to see what God is doing, but to be in on the action. We are invited to participate, to partner with God. Of course, it is a wildly unequal partnership, yet it still involves the activity of both parties. They are not inversely proportional. It is not the case that the more God is active, the less we are. Instead, the more God is active, the more empowered our own activity becomes.

Our church performance is, I contend, embodied hope for partnership with God. In church, we learn the stories and language of Scripture and the repertoire of sacraments. We are formed in the arc of biblical narratives, in the pattern of Christian affections, in relationship with Jesus

Christ. This is a whole-personed discipline that forms us as possible part-ners, as fit players who can be taken up and invited into the drama of God's activity in the world.

Deadly Church

Humanity is in the odd position of both longing for a relationship with God and being scared to death of it. Our impulse is to control it. We want it to come at our beck and call, and when it arrives we want it to condone our actions and bless our aspirations. Thus our various performances in both church and theater often invoke the holy in ways that simultaneously secure us against it.

It takes little effort to picture Deadly Church. It is one where the con-gregation gathers without any real expectation that they might interact with God during worship. Some people come in expectation of fulfilling a societal norm or in hopes of providing a good ethical grounding for their children. Others expect an edifying sermon or entertaining music. One hopes to make friends in a new town, another because she feels guilty if she doesn't. Several come to church to pray, but few expect an answer. Meanwhile, the minister has prepared the service carefully. The theme of the psalm is echoed in the hymns, the bulletin includes a detailed mission statement, the responsive readings are clearly marked for seamless con-gregational participation. The sermon begins with a humorous story, ends on an uplifting note, and includes a bit of sober wisdom in the middle. The entire service is well crafted and there is very little silence. It is almost as if we are saying to God, "don't worry, we've got this covered. Your pres-ence is not needed today." Demonstrating just the right mix of repentance and commitment, we leave little room for God to reveal Godself, for shells to explode in our midst. Such revelation might disrupt our lives far more than we desire, so we secretly prefer a worship service that is boring and predictable.

This illustration assumes a mainline Protestant worship service, but in fact Deadliness can encroach in any church tradition, high or low. Intricate liturgies, rich in tradition and repetition, can seem a particularly easy target. Yet Deadliness can dwell just as comfortably in low-church set-tings. Spontaneous responses can also be scripted, in the sense that there are cultural norms and expected roles to follow. Even the very empty space of a silent Quaker meeting involves a great deal of repetition, tradition, and expectation. These can become static over time, cherished forms of protection from the unruly revelation of God.[123] Any church can become deadly.

Barth and Brook agree that aiming strictly for the Holy produces Deadliness. For Barth, this is because humanity is so finite and so flawed that we can do nothing to move toward Holiness on our own. Indeed, it is only when we realize this that we might be able to be somewhat less deadly in our life together. There is a practical reason for Brook as well, namely, that theater that attempts to be purely Holy starts to ossify. In both cases, the Holy and the Deadly are antagonistic to one another. Barth leaves it at that. The holy church is what God does, when the Spirit awakens, and the deadly church is not really church at all. It is what we do, creating our visible No-God. Brook, however, takes a different path, introducing the Rough Theater.

Rough Church

"The popular theatre always saves the day," says Brook.[124] It is the makeshift, profane, rebellious, and dirty theater that provides Brook a way forward from the Holy/Deadly impasse. In strictly theatrical terms, Rough Theater gives Brook an antiauthoritarian element to fight against the conservative and traditionalist forms of theater that try too hard to be Holy. The theater on the margins—of financial security or cultural norms or social acceptability—is an antidote to the theater that sees itself as the bastion of holy tradition. Bawdy humor gives Shakespeare comic relief from metaphysical aspirations and acknowledges our human limitations in trafficking with the holy. In theological terms, I have argued, Brook's argument goes further. There is an incarnational sensibility to Brook's writing. The Holy and the Rough are incommensurable and the distinction between them cannot be resolved. At the same time, for Brook they belong together. We cannot take the Holy without the Rough; the Rough calls out for the Holy. It is this still-distinct joining, written in poetry and prose, that Brook holds as his ideal of what theater should be.

Within Christian theology, we can take Brook's insights further still. The Holy and the Rough are intertwined because God chooses to be in relation with humanity. This is clearest in the incarnation. In Jesus Christ, fully human and fully divine, God gets dirty. God is present—bodily present—in and to the roughest realities of human life. God belches and bleeds, intimately experiences the harms we can do to one another. The Holy is present in the Rough.[125] In the sending of the Spirit at Pentecost, the founding of church, God invites us into partnership, to be in on the action by performing with the Spirit in consonance with Jesus Christ. The Rough is called to be with the Holy.

In church as in theater, the Rough upsets the Deadliness that results from aiming entirely at the Holy. An honest account of human reality, including our own brokenness, guards against the deadly tendencies of repetition, tradition, and expectation. Repetition is disrupted by current pain expressed. A clear view of the all-too-human realities of tradition—crafted in conflict and susceptible to selfish manipulation—strikes against our pretension. Finally, expectation can be honed by real need. In Rough Church we bring our whole selves—in all our dirt and brokenness, desperation and confusion—into performance of relationship with Jesus Christ. We do not leave parts of ourselves—such as those bodies of which we are not too fond, or those thoughts which we know should be more generous, or those shameful memories and scary emotions—behind. The nerve to do this, to bring our whole selves into the performance, derives from our social memory of God's persistent intent to be in relationship with humanity, from God's Holy/Rough paradigm in Jesus Christ, and from the Spirit's willingness to partner with us.

From this perspective, the lack of the Rough in Barth's ecclesiology seems problematic. Barth's appreciation of the finitude and sinfulness of humanity leads him to a relentless focus on Jesus Christ. Yet can one do justice to Jesus without an appreciation of dirt? Avenues of incarnational thinking are cut off by Barth's refusal to value the Rough. Paradoxically, Barth's Holy-only attempt at a profoundly Christological view of church prevents his ecclesiology from fully appreciating the incarnation, which is so vital to Barth in other moments within his theology.[126]

Within the framework of Barth's theology, assigning any significant import to the work of the people—liturgy—risks imagining that God is at humanity's disposal, to be summoned by our effort and at our whim. Max Harris, a theologian deeply influenced by Barth and Brook, articulates the difficulty. Having argued that theater and incarnation are deeply connected, Harris writes, "it is one thing to suggest that God chose a 'theatrical' mode of self-revelation and quite another to propose that human art may conjure up an incarnation in the theater."[127] Harris addresses this worry by specifying that the "invisible" that is made visible in theater is not God. "Theater may well bear a likeness to that sensory mode of self-revelation attested in the classic texts of the Christian faith. But, at least for the Christian, the theater will not move beyond likeness to rival, claiming to emulate the

Incarnation by summoning spirit or universal will to inhabit its material signs."[128] Theater might bring hidden insights of the human predicament into "greater clarity," but it cannot make God visible through its own efforts.[129] Harris's text does not address ecclesiology directly, but I infer there are similar limitations upon church. As I understand Harris, it is not the case that theater deals with humanity and church deals with God, such that theater cannot conjure an incarnation but church can. Rather, incarnation does not come about through human efforts, but only through divine grace.

Learning from Barth without being entirely beholden to him, I suggest a different approach to this quandary. Human performance—in sanctuary or on stage—can neither conjure incarnation nor summon God. Perhaps, however, we can foster emptiness. God does not require our efforts in order to become visible. Yet our discipline of emptiness might contribute to the conditions in which the invisible-made-visible could be perceived (by others and by ourselves). We might unclutter the stage a bit, as a work of clearance and an act of invocation. Our performance does not force the Spirit's hand. Rather, as a community, we remember that God has partnered with us in the past and we hope in God's Spirit for the present and future. This hope is an embodied performance, a discipline that prepares us for partnership with God.

Immediate Church

Barth's own action in writing the Barmen Declaration and standing against the Nazis provides a strong example of how churches should act in the world. However, his theological framework makes it very difficult for Barth to actually write about how churches should behave, or what people in church should do. Defining church as an act of the Holy Spirit and soundly disabusing churchgoers of any sense of self-importance in relation to the work of Jesus Christ leaves Barth very little room to work. For the most part, we are to be grateful. In more specifics, he writes about being thankful to God, praising God, and praying for the Spirit.[130]

Brook's words on repetition, tradition, and expectation relate readily to church. In an Immediate Church, we would study Scripture repeatedly, so often that the muscles of our tongues remember words of faithfulness and we have the freedom to engage it fully. Through repeated study, we could know the Bible so well that it goes past being familiar and seems always new. Likewise, we would learn Christian traditions well and regard them not as precious heirlooms from the past but useful instruments for the present.[131] Finally, in the Immediate Church we would come to church services expecting to get caught up in the reality of God. I do not mean the kind of commodified expectation that pervades our culture: "I expect to get what I paid for!" In this attitude, any mediocre sermon or too-long service could generate disappointment and frustration. Rather, I mean openness to the surprising newness of God. The God of Jesus Christ is constantly thwarting our sensibilities about where God ought to be. Look for Jesus in the palace and he's in the manger; look for him with the poor and he's with the tax collectors; look for him with the Pharisees and he's with the prostitutes. God is surprising. *Reliably* so. It is possible to cultivate an expectation of having our expectations undone. The theological term for this is humility, and it is a virtue that requires practice.

The part of Brook's discussion of Immediate Theater that does not correlate easily with church is about assistance. For Brook, the assistance that enables theater to move away from the Deadly and toward his Holy/Rough ideal comes from the audience. Since I have drawn on the insights of directors, there is a clear analogy between the members of any given church and a company of players. Yet even within this, the conversation partners at my table have emphasized the importance of breaking down barriers between actor, audience, and director. They have advocated switching roles among the players and preventing identification with a single role. They suggest that overcoming strict divisions between actors and audience is key to theater that is liberating rather than oppressive.[132] Similarly, close theological reading of liturgical practices suggests that Christians move between and among various roles during any given worship service and throughout the liturgical year. We are all actors, audience, and stage crew. We are each repentant sinner, beloved child, believer, doubter, recipient of grace, and minister to others. To assign someone— the congregation, the larger world, even God—the role of audience would contradict all that has come before.[133]

We are left with the question, "whence cometh our help"? The assistance needed by church comes from the Holy Spirit. The Holy Spirit empowers and enables our performance from its earliest beginnings. It is the Spirit who grants us the first pangs of hunger and the Spirit who guides our practices of formation. It is the Spirit who encourages us to stand in multiple roles and the Spirit who calls us up short to challenge our identification with a singular role. Finally, it is the action of the Spirit into which we hope to get caught up. Our performance is disciplined in order to help us become sensitive to the workings of the Spirit in a whole-personed way, to get in on the action and participate in what the Spirit is doing in the world.

The Holy Spirit is always and everywhere present, active in the world. Most of the time, we do not notice. The discipline of church performance does not guarantee that we will be aware of the Spirit, but it is a performance of hope that we might be. Our performance is embodied hope *for* the Spirit and *in* the Spirit—hope that our whole-personed selves will be taken up in the movement of the Spirit of God.

Our performance of hope should be a performance of emptiness, expecting the Spirit. It should be concave, not convex. It should make a void visible. Sometimes, this might mean we have to strike the set. Lash describes faith as "inherently *iconoclastic* its steadfast refusal to identify 'truth' with its particular expressions and achievements."[134] He does not mean iconoclastic in the literal sense of destroying icons, and I am not calling for the destruction of artwork or ecclesial property. Instead, I am suggesting that we hold our ecclesial traditions with an open hand. Instead of grasping tightly to our familiar practices, we could recognize that all of our performances are profoundly provisional. To do this, we would have to trust that the Spirit will come again. If we believe that the Spirit is abundant and will move in our midst again, we do not have to cling to the remnants and reminders of how the Spirit has moved in the past. Like the theater company, we could take apart the structures of one performance and use them to build anew.

For over one hundred years, scholars and clergy have been lamenting the decline of mainline Protestant churches in Europe and America. The church is empty, they declare.[135] With Brook and Barth in mind, I can't help thinking, "I hope so! We're trying!" In our best moments we know that our task is not to keep the pews full but to keep the altar empty, in hope of the Holy Spirit. The Church of the Risen Christ began in an empty tomb, and at our best, we are still there.[136] Like Mary and Mary and Salome, we come with expectations, repeating actions called for by our traditions. These expectations, repetitions, and traditions are what bring us to the moment when all three are overwhelmed and upended by the surprising newness of God.

The Gospel of Mark tells us that "[w]hen the Sabbath was over, Mary Magdalene, and Mary the mother of James, and Salome brought spices" and went to where the crucified Jesus had been laid in a tomb (Mk 16:1–2). The body was not there. Instead, the grace of God appeared in an unexpected way, with a young man telling them that Jesus had been raised. The women who went to the tomb that morning handed down that emptiness to us. In a kind of indirect discourse that would make Kierkegaard green with envy, they told their tale in such a way that we hear they were too afraid to speak it, and when they did no one believed them. They handed over to us not the record of their eloquent success, but the emptiness in which the grace of God appeared.

There is a discipline to emptiness. Barth the theologian and Brook the director speak about this in intersecting ways. Never known for his optimism about human discipline, Barth questions, "Shall we never permit our hands to be empty, that we may grasp what only empty hands can grasp?"[137] Brook says simply, we must. To create a space awaiting holiness, rather than a space of human striving, we have to. "We must open our empty hands and show that really there is nothing up our sleeves. Only then can we begin."[138]

Conclusion

I BEGAN THIS work with a simple question, "why church?" In the pages that followed I built a description of church as a disciplined performance of relationship with Jesus Christ, mediated by Scripture, in hope of the Holy Spirit. Chapter 1 introduced the concept of performance, characterized as event, interaction, and doubleness. Here I also outlined a performative anthropology (human identity is formed in multidirectional interactions that include biology, culture, and relationships over time), a performative epistemology (we know in our whole selves, including body, emotion, intellect, and will), and a performative hermeneutic (Christians interpret Scripture in and through performance, in which its fullest meaning comes to be).

In chapter 2 I looked closely at how we are shaped in church through performing Scripture in various ways, which ultimately forms us in relationship to Jesus Christ. We are shaped in a pattern of Christian affections. Together, we develop a storehouse of emotion memories and a repertoire of physical actions that evoke those memories appropriately. Who we are, what we know, and how we act are all profoundly shaped by performing church. As a Christian, I see a baptism in every cloudburst; every potluck looks like loaves and fishes. When confusion and grief leave me unable to think of anything to say, the muscles in my mouth form the words of the psalms. My body bends at the knees under pressure. My emotions rise and arc to a pattern of redemptive grace.

Chapter 3 acknowledged that performing church can also shape us in harmful ways. Shared leadership in community, attention to embodied knowledge, and an expansive view of church extending beyond the sanctuary are all important safeguards to this. Most important, however, is the discipline of changing roles, a discipline based on the life and ministry of Jesus Christ. The performance of relationship with *this* person Jesus mediated by *this* Scripture leads us straight into the struggle for justice. We are not permitted to remain in comfortable roles. We stand in the role of the prodigal son, the jealous elder brother, and the father who loves them

both. Such role switching, both in liturgy and in struggle for justice, cultivates critical distance and Spirit-led agency.

Finite and flawed, we resist this role switching. Often church rehearses
us in a singular perspective, such that the intellectual and volitional
aspects of our knowing are compromised. Then we need a prophetic
voice, a productive alienation, to startle us out of well-worn patterns of belief and practice. We need to see the world made strange, as it was on
Calvary when God hung lifeless on the cross.

We do all of this in hope of the Spirit. Our performances cannot control the Spirit, but rather help us to be open and attuned to the Spirit's
presence and movement. Through a discipline of emptiness, we clear
away the No-Gods of our own creation, repent of our arrogance, and hope
for something far more than our own strivings. We hope to be taken up,
to be allowed in on the action, to participate in the movement of the Spirit.

At the beginning of this text, I argued that Christians are shaped and
formed in consonance with the narratives of Jesus Christ. This text is
shaped likewise, beginning with incarnation (chapter 2), moving to life
and ministry (chapter 3), the cross (chapter 4), and the empty tomb (chapter 5). It is fitting, then, to look back and read the whole in the light of
resurrection.

The moments in my life when I have been aware of the Spirit in a
whole-personed way are, quite simply, the best of what I know in this
world. I go to church in the hope of more. In this way, my answer to "why
church?" is quite self-interested. I want to be moved by the Spirit of Jesus
Christ. Of course, I cannot make that happen. I can, however, hope for it
with my whole self. I can go to where I have glimpsed the Spirit before:
in Scripture, in liturgy, in struggle for justice, and in Christian community.
I can perform in ways that train my intellect, will, body, and emotions to
be open to the movement of the Spirit that I desire.

In Western theater, the theater building itself is never allowed to go
completely dark. A light is left burning through the night. When the
actors and the crew leave the building, someone turns on the "ghost
light." Often this is a bare bulb, on a plain stand that can be easily rolled
onto the stage. There are many explanations for this tradition, ranging
from safety precaution to pure superstition. But when it was explained to
me, decades ago, I was told that it represents inspiration. Turning on the
ghost light is a way of asking for the source of inspiration to never leave
the theater. Anne Ebersman, then an actress and now a rabbi, connected
the ghost light to biblical traditions of leaving a light burning in the temple.

There are some churches that do something similar, with the church going completely dark only at the end of Maundy Thursday services. Perhaps all of our performing is analogous to this. We are simply turning on the ghost light, asking and hoping for the Spirit to remain, to move again in our midst.

Notes

1. J. L. Austin, *How to Do Things with Words*, 2nd ed., eds. J. O. Urmson and Marina Sbisà. (Cambridge, MA: Harvard University Press, 1962).

CHAPTER I SETTING THE STAGE

* Portions of this chapter have been published in "Command Performance: Rethinking Performance Interpretation in the Context of *Divine Discourse*," *Modern Theology*, 16:4 (2000): 475–494; and "Theology as Performance," *The Ecumenist*, 45:2 (2008): 6–10.

1. In his theological treatise, "Consensus Genevensis," reformer John Calvin explains, "[God] made the whole world for the very end that it might be a stupendous theatre whereon to manifest His own glory," in *Reformed Confessions of the 16th and 17th Centuries in English Translation*, vol. 1, comp. James T. Dennison Jr. (Grand Rapids, MI: Reformation Heritage Books, 2008), 744. Reformed theologian Karl Barth suggests, "the created cosmos including man, or man within the created cosmos, is this theatre of the great acts of God in grace and salvation," in *Church Dogmatics*, vol. 3, part 3, eds. G. W. Bromiley and T. F. Torrance (Edinburgh: T&T Clark, 1960), 48.

2. Hans Urs von Balthasar, *Theo-drama: Theological Dramatic Theory*, 5 vols. (San Francisco: Ignatius Press, 1988–1998); Francesca Aran Murphy, "Hans Urs von Balthasar: Beauty As a Gateway to Love," in *Theological Aesthetics after von Balthasar*, eds. Oleg V. Bychkov and James Fodor (Burlington, VT: Ashgate Publishing Company, 2008).

3. See also Todd E. Johnson and Dale Savidge, who move from analogy to ontology, stating that theater and theology "are not just similar; rather they share major commonalities at the core of their existences. The essential elements of

theater and the essential elements of Christianity—incarnation, community, and presence—are congruent." They assert, "theatre has theological content: not just the content of the performance but as an art form, theatre uniquely reflects the *imago Dei*, the image of God imbued into humanity," in *Performing the Sacred: Theology and Theatre in Dialogue* (Grand Rapids, MI: Baker Academic, 2009), 11, 16.

4. Nicholas Lash, "Performing the Scriptures," in *Theology on the Way to Emmaus* (London: SCM Press, 1986), 37–46; Frances Young, *The Art of Performance: Towards a Theology of Holy Scripture* (London: Darton, Longman & Todd, 1990). See also Stephen C. Barton, "New Testament Interpretation as Performance," in *Scottish Journal of Theology* 52/2 (1999): 179–208.

5. T. J. Gorringe, *God's Theater: A Theology of Providence* (London: SCM Press, 1991).

6. Max Harris, *Theatre and Incarnation* (London: Macmillan Publishers, 1990).

7. See Kevin J. Vanhoozer, *The Drama of Doctrine: A Canonical Linguistic Approach to Christian Theology* (Louisville, KY: Westminster John Knox Press, 2005), 10–11, 16, 166–167, in which he is critiquing both George Lindbeck and Hans Frei, aiming to create a post-critical view of biblical interpretation.

8. Samuel Wells, *Improvisation: The Drama of Christian Ethics* (Grand Rapids, MI: Brazos Press, 2004).

9. Ibid., 45–46, 49.

10. Marvin Carlson, *Performance: A Critical Introduction*, 2nd ed. (New York: Routledge, 2004), 9–80.

11. Ibid., 13.Many writers on performance studies grant Singer's work, particularly Milton Singer, ed., *Traditional India: Structure and Change* (Philadelphia: American Folklore Society, 1959), an important place in the genealogy of the field.

12. Ronald Grimes, "Performance Theory and the Study of Ritual," in *New Approaches to the Study of Religion*, vol. 2, *Textual, Comparative, Sociological, and Cognitive Approaches*, eds. Peter Antes, Armin W. Geertz, and Randi R. Warne (Berlin: Walter de Gruyter, 2004), 110. See also Carlson, *Performance*, 13.

13. Grimes, "Performance Theory," 110.

14. Singer, *Traditional India*, xiii.

15. Erving Goffman, *The Presentation of Self in Everyday Life* (New York: Anchor Books, 1959).

16. Grimes, "Performance Theory," 112.

17. See Carlson, *Performance*, 38; Goffman, *Presentation of Self*, 15–16; Grimes, "Performance Theory," 112.

18. Other pivotal texts in the development of performance studies include Richard Schechner, *Performance Theory* (New York: Routledge, 1988); Joseph Roach, *Cities of the Dead: Circum-Atlantic Performance* (New York: Columbia University Press, 1996); Victor Turner, *The Anthropology of Performance* (New York: PAJ Publications, 1987).

19. Mary S. Strine, Beverly W. Long, and Mary Frances Hopkins, "Research in Interpretation and Performance Studies: Trends, Issues, Priorities," in *Speech Communication: Essays to Commemorate the 75th Anniversary of the Speech Communication Association*, eds. G. M. Phillips and J. T. Woods (Carbondale: Southern Illinois University Press, 1990), 183. The authors are drawing upon the work of W. B. Gallie, *Philosophy and the Historical Understanding* (New York: Schocken Books, 1968).

20. Strine et al., "Research in Interpretation," 183.

21. There are many other schemas for the characteristics of performance. For example, Richard Bauman describes performance as (1) scheduled, (2) temporally bounded, (3), spatially bounded, (4) programmed, (5) coordinated and public, (6) heightened, and (6) reflexive. Richard Baumann, "Performance," in the *International Encyclopedia of Communication*, ed. Erik Barnouw (New York: Oxford University Press, 1989), 264–265. Jeanette Mathews draws on the work of Bauman and others to describe performance by outlining both themes (self-reflexivity, universality, embodiment, process, reenactment) and features (author and script, actor, audience, setting, and improvisation). Jeanette Mathews, *Performing Habakkuk: Faithful Re-enactment in the Midst of Crisis* (Eugene, OR: Pickwick Publications, 2012), 27–48. For a useful sampling of different approaches to performance, see Henry Bial, ed., *The Performance Studies Reader*, 2nd ed. (New York: Routledge, 2007).

22. Theorist Peggy Phelan states that performance studies is "a discipline based on what disappears." Peggy Phelan and Jill Lane, eds. *The Ends of Performance* (New York: New York University Press, 1998), 8. For Phelan and others, attending to performance—which is fleeting—has the political potential to challenge and subvert social hierarchies that appear to be, or rely upon the appearance of, permanence and stability. See Peggy Phelan, *Unmarked: The Politics of Performance* (New York: Routledge, 1993), 3, 148ff.

23. Peggy Phelan, *Unmarked: The Politics of Performance* (New York: Routledge, 1993), 146.

24. See Richard Schechner, *Performance Studies: An Introduction* (New York: Routledge, 2002), 1, 24.

25. See Carlson, *Performance*, 13.

26. Schechner, *Performance Studies*, 22.

27. Ibid., 28. Schechner's phrase "strip of behavior" emerges in relationship to Erving Goffman's "strip of activity." A description of Goffman's phrase can be found in Erving Goffman, *Frame Analysis: An Essay on the Organization of Experience* (Cambridge, MA: Harvard University Press, 1974), 10. Schechner comments on the distinctions between the two phrases in Richard Schechner, *Between Theater and Anthropology* (Philadelphia: University of Pennsylvania Press, 1985), 115 n. 1.

28. Ibid., 22. John J. MacAloon describes this using the notion that performance is pre-formed. See John J. MacAloon, *Rite, Drama, Festival, Spectacle: Rehearsals*

toward a Theory of Cultural Performance (Philadelphia: Institute for the Study of Human Issues, 1984), 9.

29. Schechner, *Performance Studies*, 23.

30. The fact that performance is not pure and exact repetition of past events is what gives it the potential to create social and political change. Phillip B. Zarrilli writes, "Performance as a mode of cultural action is not a simple reflection of some essentialized, fixed attributes of a static monolithic culture but an arena for the constant process of renegotiating experiences and meanings that constitute culture." Phillip B. Zarrilli, "For Whom Is the King a King? Issues of Intercultural Production, Perception, and Reception in a *Kathakaḷi King Lear,*" in *Critical Theory and Performance,* eds. Janelle G. Reinelt and Joseph R. Roach (Ann Arbor: University of Michigan Press, 2007), 108.

31. For more on how performance moves between past, present, and future, see Richard Schechner, *Between Theater and Anthropology* (Philadelphia: University of Pennsylvania Press, 1985), 39, 79.

32. This appears in various places in Schechner's writings, including Schechner, *Between Theater and Anthropology,* 110, 123.

33. I am grateful to Joshua Edelman for the phrase "productive dialectical tension."

34. Schechner, *Between Theater and Anthropology,* 123.

35. Carlson, *Performance,* 5. Here Carlson is drawing on the work of Richard Bauman in the entry for "Performance," in the *International Encyclopedia of Communication,* ed. Erik Barnouw (New York: Oxford University Press, 1989), 262–266.

36. Carlson, *Performance,* 5. The use of the term "doubleness" brings to mind W. E. B. DuBois's account of the "double-consciousness" of African-Americans. There are clear resonances here, since DuBois is speaking of how African-Americans must act in awareness of how they will be perceived by the audience of white America. At the same time, "double-consciousness" is a different and more specific term than "doubleness" and the two ought not be simply elided. DuBois uses "double-consciousness" to refer to the specific reality of being shaped by two cultures, and particularly to being aware of how one is seen by more powerful others. He writes:

> After the Egyptian and Indian, the Greek and Roman, the Teuton and Mongolian, the Negro is a sort of seventh son, born with a veil, and gifted with second-sight in this American world,—a world which yields him no true self-consciousness, but only lets him see himself through the revelation of the other world. It is a peculiar sensation, this double-consciousness, this sense of always looking at one's self through the eyes of others, of measuring one's soul by the tape of a world that looks on in amused contempt and pity. W. E. B. Du Bois, *The Souls of Black Folk* (New York: Dover Publications, 1994), 2.

There is need for a rich discussion of doubleness, double-consciousness, and social power. I regret that such work is beyond the scope of this project.

37. Schechner, *Performance Studies*, 28.

38. See Carlson, *Performance*, 24, 44–45. See also the work of Jacques Derrida and Judith Butler. Butler's work, especially "Performative Acts and Gender Constitution: An Essay in Phenomenology and Feminist Theory," in *Performing Feminisms: Feminist Critical Theory and Theatre*, ed. Sue-Ellen Case (Baltimore: Johns Hopkins University Press, 1990), 270–282, and *Gender Trouble: Feminism and the Subversion of Identity* (New York: Routledge, 1990), has contributed significantly to the analysis of "performativity." The concept of performativity is often used within contemporary discussions of the social construction of the self. A brief overview of this can be found in D. Soyini Madison and Judith Hamera, "Introduction," in *The Sage Handbook of Performance Studies*, eds. Madison and Hamera (Thousand Oaks, CA: Sage Publications, 2006), xviii–xx. Regarding the performance and political change, see Jeffrey C. Alexander, Bernhard Giesen, and Jason L. Mast, eds. *Social Performance: Symbolic Action, Cultural Pragmatics, and Ritual* (Cambridge: Cambridge University Press, 2006), 14–15.

39. See Schechner, *Performance Studies*, 30.

40. See Schechner, *Performance Studies*, 30, 32. Schechner also notes that in a contemporary society of webcams and reality television, performative understandings of gender and sexuality, and increasing technological mediation of everyday life, the boundaries between what IS performance and what is not are often blurry. See *Performance Studies*, 42.

41. See J. L. Austin, *How to Do Things with Words* (Oxford: Clarendon Press, 1962).

42. Judith Butler, *Gender Trouble*, 25. See also "Performative Acts and Gender Constitution," 519–531.

43. Within the field of theological anthropology, the phrase "stable self" is indicative of an abiding, static identity. In contrast, in the field of psychology, the phrase "stable self" would indicate a level of mental health and personal integration.

44. Richard D. McCall interprets Christian liturgy in conversation with performance theory in a different vein, which includes "being-as-event" and explores Medieval liturgical interpretation. McCall takes Aristotle as a primary source in understanding drama, while two of my primary dialogue partners (Augusto Boal and Bertolt Brecht) position themselves in opposition to Aristotle. Thus our similar interests yield distinct results. See Richard D. McCall, *Do This: Liturgy as Performance* (Notre Dame, IN: University of Notre Dame Press, 2007).

45. Serene Jones, *Feminist Theory and Christian Theology: Cartographies of Grace* (Minneapolis, MN: Augsburg Fortress, 2000), 159.

46. See the work of Philip J. Hefner, especially "The Doctrine of the Church—Focus and Challenges," in *Christian Dogmatics*, eds. Carl Braaten and Robert Jenson, vol. 2 (Philadelphia: Fortress Press, 1984), 198–199.

47. Other academic disciplines, including ritual studies and liturgical studies, are also relevant to the present task. In the challenge of interdisciplinary scholarship, I have chosen to focus on texts in theology and theater studies. However, I commend Tom F. Driver, *Liberating Rites: Understanding the Transformative Power of Ritual* (North Charleston, SC: Booksurge Publishing, 2006); Ronald Grimes, *Deeply into the Bone: Re-Inventing Rites of Passage* (Berkeley: University of California Press, 2002); Roger Grainger, *The Drama of the Rite: Worship, Liturgy and Theatre Performance* (Brighton: Sussex Academic Press, 2009); Mary Douglas, *Purity and Danger* (London: Routledge and Kegan Paul, 1966); Catherine Bell, *Ritual Theory and Ritual Practice* (New York: Oxford University Press, 1992).

48. This argument is made eloquently by Nicholas Lash. He writes, "I would wish to argue that the fundamental form of the Christian interpretation of Scripture is, in the concrete, the life, activity and organization of the Christian community, and that Christian practice consists (by analogy with the practical interpretation of dramatic, legal and musical texts) in the performance or enactment of the biblical text..." Nicholas Lash, *Theology on the Way to Emmaus* (Eugene, OR: Wipf and Stock Publishers, 1986), 90. See also Lash, 45.

49. Lash writes, "It is no more possible for an isolated individual to perform [Scripture] than it is for him to perform a Beethoven quartet or a Shakespeare tragedy." Lash, 43.

50. As I have noted above, theater, like church, is widely diverse. Many could contest this statement regarding the nature of theater. Ellen O'Brien and Jack Zerbe have significantly influenced my own sense of theater.

51. In considering communal interpretation of Scripture on a theatrical analogy, I must acknowledge and commend Max Harris's influential text, *Theater and Incarnation*. Harris compares the transformation of text into performance in theater with the transformation of Word into flesh, that is, with the incarnation of God in Jesus Christ. He writes, "the Christian concept of God's mode of self-revelation is theatrical." This implies, for Harris, that "the sensitive reader of script and Scripture alike will need to engage in a form of theatrical hermeneutics that both animates and interprets text." Max Harris, *Theater and Incarnation* (Grand Rapids, MI: William B. Eerdmans, 1990) 1, 12. While Harris and I both discuss Christian communities as interpreting Scripture in ways analogous to theater companies interpreting scripts, there are also significant differences between our works. In this first chapter, I will footnote places of great similarity. In chapter 5, I will engage some of the differences directly.

52. I am aware that it would be interesting and perhaps quite fruitful to engage the work of Hans-Georg Gadamer, *Truth and Method*, trans. Garrett Barden and

John Cumming (New York: Seabury Press, 1975). However, that is beyond the scope of the present work.

53. Harris uses this example. Harris, 23. See also Harris, 14, regarding multiple possible interpretations.

54. I do not know if Harris would go so far as to say that Scripture is incomplete. However, he describes scripts as incomplete and moves in a very similar direction regarding the importance of full, embodied performance of scriptural texts. See Harris, 1, 13.

55. One of the main contributions of performance theory is an emphasis on knowledge that takes place in performance—precisely in embodied, communal, events and practices. The aim is not to denigrate text-based abstract knowledge, but rather to expand our understanding of human knowing. Theorist Dwight Conquergood states, "Performance studies struggles to open the space between analysis and action, and to pull the pin on the binary opposition between theory and practice. This embrace of different ways of knowing is radical because it cuts to the root of how knowledge is organized in the academy." Dwight Conquergood, "Performance Studies: Interventions and Radical Research," in *The Performance Studies Reader*, 2nd ed., ed. Henry Bial (New York: Routledge, 2007), 369–370. This will be discussed often in the coming chapters, as it is particularly important to Christian theology, which is deeply rooted in liturgy and claims that the Word became flesh.

56. Alexander Schmemann has contributed a great deal to current understandings of the relationship between theology and liturgy. He describes liturgy as the grounding condition of theology and as a privileged form of knowing. See Alexander Schmemann, *Introduction to Liturgical Theology*, trans. Asheleigh E. Moorhouse (Crestwood, NY: St. Vladimir's Seminary Press, 1966, 1986); and Alexander Schmemann, *The Eucharist: Sacrament of the Kingdom*, trans. Paul Kachur (Crestwood, NY: St. Vladimir's Seminary Press, 1987).

57. One of the primary contributions of performance theory to contemporary academic discussions is the acknowledgment of various kinds and ways of knowing. Dwight Conquergood makes a useful distinction between "propositional knowledge" that is "anchored in paradigm and secured in print" and a "way of knowing that is grounded in active, intimate, hands-on participation and personal connection." While print culture and modern academia privilege propositional knowledge, performance theory brings active, participatory knowledge into intellectual discourse. Dwight Conquergood, "Performance Studies: Interventions and Radical Research," in *The Performance Studies Reader*, 2nd ed., ed. Henry Bial (New York: Routledge, 2007), 370. I will continue to detail performance epistemology in the coming pages, particularly chapters 2 and 3.

58. Lash offers an expansive view of Christian performance as interpretation of Scripture that goes well beyond the worship hour. He writes, "the fundamental

form of the *Christian* interpretation of scripture is the life, activity and organization of the believing community." Lash, 42. Emphasis his. "The performance of scripture *is* the life of the church." Lash, 43. Emphasis his.

59. Bruce T. Morrill, *Anamnesis as Dangerous Memory: Political and Liturgical Theology in Dialogue* (Collegeville, MN: Liturgical Press, 2000), 203.

60. For more on Hans W. Frei's concept of *"sensus literalis,"* see my article "Command Performance: Rethinking Performance Interpretation in the Context of *Divine Discourse,"* in *Modern Theology*, vol. 16, no. 4 (Oxford: Blackwell Publishers Ltd., 2000), 477–478. See also Hans W. Frei, "The 'Literal Reading' of Biblical Narrative in the Christian Tradition: Does It Stretch or Will It Break?," in *Theology and Narrative: Selected Essays*, eds. George Hunsinger and William C. Placher (New York: Oxford University Press, 1993), 117–152.

61. See Hans W. Frei, *The Eclipse of Biblical Narrative: A Study in Eighteenth and Nineteenth Century Hermeneutics* (New Haven, CT: Yale University Press, 1974).

62. Frei, *Eclipse of Biblical Narrative*, 280. Lash addresses the same issue, in conversation with authors other than Frei. He writes, "Here we are clearly confronted with the mistaken belief that texts 'have meaning' in somewhat the same way that material objects 'have mass.'" Lash, 85.

63. Frei, "'Literal Reading,'" 118, 144.

64. The many different ways that communities read the Bible are deeply connected to political and social contexts. In the United States, defending particular readings as "literal" has historical connections with the defense of slavery. See James H. Evans, Jr., *We Have Been Believers: An African-American Systematic Theology* (Minneapolis, MN: Augsburg Fortress, 1992). In explaining the historical relationship between the Bible and slavery in the United States, Evans reports, "while the proslavery forces appealed to the literal truth of the Bible, especially the Old Testament, as an infallible authority, the abolitionist forces appealed to the moral thrust of the Bible, especially the New Testament, as a guide to ethical behavior. Thus the disagreement between the proslavery forces and the abolitionist forces was primarily over *how* the Bible should be read," 35.

65. Nicholas Wolterstorff, *Divine Discourse: Philosophical Reflections on the Claim That God Speaks* (Cambridge: Cambridge University Press, 1995), 179–182.

66. Ibid., 181.

67. Ibid.

68. Lash uses a similar metaphor to de-center the work of academic interpreters. Lash, 90.

69. Wells, *Improvisation*, 62.

70. Ibid., 63.

71. Ibid.

72. Ibid.

73. Ibid., 65.

74. Wells's work has been fruitful for several other scholars. See, for example, Peter Goodwin Heltzel, *Resurrection City: A Theology of Improvisation*. (Grand Rapids, MI: William B. Eerdmans, 2012).

75. Ibid., 65.

76. Ibid., 74.

77. Ibid., 75.

78. Ibid.

79. Ibid., 74–75.

80. I am grateful to Ivan P. Khovacs for pointing out the emphasis on rehearsal in my previously published work on this issue. Here I contend that performance interpretation happens not only in rehearsal, but also in the realization of the script in performance. See Ivan P. Khovacs, "A Cautionary Note on the Use of Theatre in Theology," in *Faithful Performances: Enacting Christian Tradition*, eds. Trevor A. Hart and Steven R. Guthrie (Burlington, VT: Ashgate, 2007), 45–47.

81. See Richard Schechner, *Between Theater and Anthropology* (Philadelphia: University of Pennsylvania Press, 1985), 120–121.

82. Tom Stoppard, *Rosencrantz and Guildenstern Are Dead*, (New York: Grove Press, 1967), 28.

83. See Vanhoozer, *Drama of Doctrine*, 10–11; George Lindbeck, *The Nature of Doctrine: Religion and Theology in a Postliberal Age* (Philadelphia: Westminster Press, 1984).

84. See Vanhoozer, *Drama of Doctrine*, 32–33.

85. Ibid., 18.

86. Vanhoozer further states, "theology is first and foremost about understanding the drama of redemption, and only then about our participation in the divine word-deed and deed-words," in *Drama of Doctrine*, 187. For a more thorough engagement with Vanhoozer regarding performance and theology, see Joshua Edelman "Can an Act Be True?: The Possibilities of the Dramatic Metaphor for Theology within a Post-Stanislavskian Theatre," in *Faithful Performances*, 51–72.

87. Lash, 42. Emphasis his. Also: "The practice of Christian faith is not, in the last resort, a matter of interpreting, in our time and place, an ancient text. It is, or seeks to be, the faithful 'rendering' of those events, of those patterns of human action, decision and suffering, to which the texts bear original witness." Lash, 90. See also Lash, 73.

88. Lash, 85.

89. Vanhoozer, *Drama of Doctrine*, 19.

90. Ibid., 17. See also 99.

91. Thus the meaning of the text will be consummately performed eschatologically.

92. See Wolterstorff, *Divine Discourse*, 185.

93. Vanhoozer, 32. See also 33, where Vanhoozer asserts that Christians are called "to render the gospel publicly by leading lives in creative imitation of Christ."

94. Erving Goffman, *The Presentation of Self in Everyday Life* (New York: Doubleday, 1959), 15.

95. Carlson, 5. Emphasis his. Henry Bial's definition of performance includes "a performer (someone doing something) and a spectator (someone observing something)." Henry Bial, ed., *The Performance Studies Reader*, 2nd ed. (New York: Routledge, 2007), 59. Jeanette Mathews states, "An audience is essential in any discussion of performance." Mathews, 42.

96. Goffman, xi.

97. I am grateful to Marilyn McCord Adams for this insight and this language.

CHAPTER 2 TRAINING THE ACTORS

1. Don E. Saliers, *Worship Come to Its Senses* (Nashville, TN: Abingdon Press, 1996), 74.

2. Don E. Saliers, *Worship as Theology: Foretaste of Glory Divine* (Nashville: Abingdon Press, 1994), 176; Don E. Saliers, *The Soul in Paraphrase: Prayer and the Religious Affections* (New York: Seabury Press, 1980), 32–34.

3. Saliers, *Soul in Paraphrase*, 92.

4. See Don Saliers, "Liturgy and Ethics: Some New Beginnings," in *Liturgy and the Moral Self: Humanity at Full Stretch Before God*, eds. E. Byron Anderson and Bruce Morrill, S. J. (Collegeville, MN: Liturgical Press, 1998), 17.

5. Saliers, *Soul in Paraphrase*, 9, 27–28, 77.

6. Ibid., 33.

7. Ibid., 26.

8. Saliers, *Worship As Theology*, 86.

9. Saliers, *Soul in Paraphrase* 28–29, 34.

10. Ibid., 7.

11. Ibid., 7, 11.

12. Ibid., 8, 11.

13. Ibid., 36–37.

14. Ibid., 18, 34.

15. Ibid., 57.

16. Ibid., 95.

17. Ibid., 4–7.

18. Ibid., 58.

19. Ibid. Here Saliers's account of liturgical formation functions normatively rather than simply descriptively. Given the doubleness and sinfulness of the church, surely there are moments when worship services do inculcate despair and hopelessness in some of the members of the congregation. Saliers implies that this ought not happen and suggests that when it does, this is a failure to conform to the biblical story of redemption. Given some of the tales of violence and despair in the Bible, and the way many biblical texts have been used as tools of oppression by churches over the centuries, this is

an arguable position. However, in an effort to focus on constructing an account of how the whole person is formed in liturgy, I am not going to engage Saliers on these issues at this point. Some of these concerns will be taken up in chapter 3.

20. Ibid., 58.

21. Ibid., 29.

22. Ibid., 20, 34.

23. Ibid., 32, 34.

24. Saliers, *Worship Come to Its Senses*, 23–24.

25. Saliers, *Worship as Theology*, 40. Further statements about the importance of the body are found in a book coauthored by Don Saliers and his daughter, Emily Saliers. For example, they state, "Spirituality is not an idea in the brain but rather a disciplined bodily experience that grows deeper with practice." Don Saliers and Emily Saliers, *A Song to Sing, A Life to Live: Reflections on Music as Spiritual Practice* (San Francisco, CA: Jossey-Bass, 2005), 21.

26. Ibid., 163ff.

27. Saliers, *Worship Come to Its Senses*, 86–87.

28. Ibid., 74.

29. Liturgical theologian Todd Johnson also addresses the issue of church as performance and the possibility of the goal becoming entertainment. To my reading, the work of both Saliers and Johnson suggests that a strong distinction between actors and audience can make it easier for worship to slip into spectacle and entertainment. This adds to my hesitancy to assign the role of audience to any particular group. See Todd E. Johnson, "Redeeming Performance," in *Liturgy*, 28:3 (2013): 17–24.

30. Robert W. Gleason, S. J., "Introduction to the Spiritual Exercises," in *Ignatius of Loyola, The Spiritual Exercises of Saint Ignatius*, trans. Anthony Mottola (New York: Image Books Doubleday, 1964), 16. The composition of the Exercises happened over several years. The "literary structure of the Exercises was substantially set" by 1535, although revisions and additions were made until it was first published in 1548. George E. Ganss, S. J., ed., *Ignatius of Loyola: Spiritual Exercises and Selected Works* (New York: Paulist Press, 1991), 37.

31. Gleason, "Introduction to the Spiritual Exercises," 13, 16; Ganss, *Ignatius of Loyola*, 37, 50.

32. This has not been without controversy. See Gleason, "Introduction to the Spiritual Exercises," 24–30.

33. Again noting the controversy here and my emphasis on the formative power of the Exercises, see Gleason, "Introduction to the Spiritual Exercises," 20, 26.

34. *Ignatius of Loyola, The Spiritual Exercises of St. Ignatius*, trans. Anthony Mottola (New York: Image Books Doubleday, 1964), 38.

35. The first two exercises are meditations or contemplations, the third and fourth are repetitions of the first two, and the fifth exercise is "the Application of the Senses." See Philip Endean, "The Ignatian Prayer of the Senses," *Heythrop*

Journal 4 (1990): 391–418. Endean offers further nuance of what is meant by repetition and notes that the Spanish text does not use the term "Application of the Senses," 393. There is a significant history of scholarship regarding the technical differences between contemplation and meditation, as seen in Endean's article. While such scholarship is fascinating, it is beyond the scope of these brief introductory comments on the Exercises.

36. This prelude is not found in the first week, but introduced in the second.
37. Ignatius, *Spiritual Exercises*, 54.
38. Ibid., 54. See also, regarding the importance of place in memory, Marjorie O'Rourke Boyle, *Loyola's Acts: The Rhetoric of Self* (Berkeley: University of California Press, 1997), 9.
39. Ibid., 54.
40. Ibid., 69.
41. Ibid., 56.
42. See Endean, "Ignatian Prayer," 391, 403.
43. Ignatius, *Spiritual Exercises*, 58.
44. Ibid., 58.
45. See note 35 regarding Endean, who notes that the Spanish text does not use the term "Application of the Senses," "Ignatian Prayer," 393.
46. Ignatius, *Spiritual Exercises*, 59.
47. Harris discusses the Exercises in regard to senses, imagination, and theatrical hermeneutics. He suggests that using sensory imagination to interpret Scripture is "an apt response to a 'theatrical' and 'sensual' mode of revelation." Harris, 27–28.
48. Ibid., 54, 55.
49. Ibid., 54, 56.
50. Saliers, *Soul in Paraphrase*, 28–29.
51. Ibid., 34.
52. Ignatius, *Spiritual Exercises*, 61.
53. Ibid., 102–103.
54. Saliers, *Soul in Paraphrase*, 32–33.
55. Ignatius, *Spiritual Exercises*, 61.
56. Ibid., 48.
57. Ibid., 49.
58. G. Simon Harak, S. J., *Virtuous Passions: The Formation of Christian Character* (New York: Paulist Press, 1993), 2.
59. Harak implies that the terms are interchangeable by writing "passions (affections)" in the specific context of a discussion of Hauerwas, *Virtuous Passions*, 47. Harak distinguishes his own views from Saliers's more broadly in *Virtuous Passions*, 41–43.
60. Ibid., 8.
61. Ibid., 14. Harak draws on the work of Karl Pribram regarding the biochemical and neurophysiological foundations of habitual response. See Karl Pribram, "Feelings

As Monitors," in *Feelings and Emotions: The Loyola Symposium*, ed. Magda B. Arnold (New York: Academic Press, 1970), 41–54; *Languages of the Brain: Experimental Paradoxes and Principles in Neuropsychology* (Englewood Cliffs, NJ: Prentice-Hall, 1971); "Emotion: A Neurobehavioral Analysis," in *Approaches to Emotion*, eds. Klaus Scherer and Paul Eckman (Hillsdale, NJ: Lawrence Erlbaum Associates, 1984), 13–38.

62. Harak, *Virtuous Passions*, 14.
63. Ibid., 14. Emphasis his. While Harak refers to controlled studies with monkeys, a less-scientific example can serve to quickly illustrate his point. After reading this sentence, close your eyes, place your hands in your lap, and verbally describe where the letters W, H, M, and U are on a qwerty keyboard. Now, place your hands in front of you on an imaginary keyboard and type those same letters. For many people, the first task is quite difficult, while the second is easy. Consider how quickly a driver can respond when a pedestrian steps into the road. She swerves, brakes, and honks the horn within a fraction of a second. While these examples do not have the scientific credentials of the works that Harak engages, they remind us that although embodied knowledge is often neglected in theology, we rely upon it daily.
64. Ibid., 14–15. Emphasis his.
65. Ibid., 19.
66. Ibid., 16. Harak draws on the work of Nico H. Fijda and Neil McNaughton to reach these conclusions. See Nico H. Frijda, *The Emotions* (Cambridge: Cambridge University Press, 1986), 126ff.; Neil McNaughton, *Biology and Emotion*, vol. 5 of *Problems in Behavioural Sciences*, ed. Jeffrey Gray (Cambridge: Cambridge University Press, 1989), 57ff.
67. Harak, *Virtuous Passions*, 3.
68. Ibid., 39–40.
69. Ibid., 23, emphasis his.
70. Ibid., 14, 23.
71. Ibid., 36.
72. See ibid., 25.
73. Ibid., 21–24.
74. Ibid., 25–26.
75. Ibid., 101, emphasis his.
76. See ibid., 113–114, 106–107.
77. Ibid., 106, 110, 116, 120.
78. Ibid., 113. See also 103, where Harak invokes Ignatius on Jesus as ethical expert.
79. Ibid., 113.
80. For surveys of the field, see Michael L. Anderson, "Embodied Cognition: A Field Guide," *Artificial Intelligence* 149, 1 (2003): 91–130; and Margaret Wilson, "Six Views of Embodied Cognition," *Psychonomic Bulletin and Review* 9, 4 (2002): 625–636.
81. Harris also connects Ignatius and Stanislavski. See Harris, 29.

82. The elision of the System and the Method can be seen in Joshua Logan's foreword to Sonia Moore's *The Stanislavski System: The Professional Training of an Actor, Digested from the Teachings of Konstantin S. Stanislavski*, 2nd ed. (New York: Penguin Publishing, 1976), xii–xvi. Simple distinctions between the two are complicated by the fact that many method actors (who draw more from Stanislavski's earlier writings about emotion memory) see themselves as true heirs of Stanislavski. Others (who draw more from his later writings on the method of physical actions) highlight differences between Stanislavski's work and the Method as taught by Strasberg, particularly in America. While I believe noting the distinction between the System and the Method is appropriate to academic discourse using Stanislavski's work, further exploration of the relation between the two is beyond the scope of this text. See also Moore, 6, regarding reception of Stanislavski.

83. Ibid., xiv.

84. Constantin Stanislavski, *An Actor Prepares*, trans. Elizabeth Reynolds Hapgood (New York: Routledge, 1948), 271.

85. Ibid., 121–124. I believe further exploration of Stanislavski's work on objectives in conversation with J. L. Austin's *How to Do Things with Words* (Oxford: Clarendon Press, 1975) on performative language would be fruitful. I am preparing this study for a different work, but it is beyond the scope of the present text.

86. Stanislavski, *An Actor Prepares*, 276.

87. Ibid., 13.

88. Ibid., 13.

89. Note that Stanislavski's method of writing about the System is also oblique, in a way mirroring his statements on inspiration. Instead of writing his theories about acting directly, he describes a class taught by a director. See Jean Benedetti, *Stanislavski: An Introduction* (New York: Theatre Arts Books, 1982), 54–55.

90. Vanhoozer sees parallels between Stanislavski's System and "the process of sanctification," *The Drama of Doctrine* (Louisville, KY: Westminster John Knox, 2005), 369. Vanhoozer refers to Stanislavski's System as "the Method," eliding two approaches to acting. See note 82 above and Joshua Edelman, "Can an Act Be True? The Possibilities of the Dramatic Metaphor for Theology within a Post-Stanislavskian Theatre," in *Faithful Performances*, eds. Trevor A. Hart and Steven R. Guthrie (Burlington, VT: Ashgate, 2007), 51–72.

91. Stanislavski, *An Actor Prepares*, 168. Stanislavski was influenced by the French psychologist Théodule-Armand Ribot and borrowed his term "affective memory" before later developing his own phrase and conception, "emotional memory," Moore, *Stanislavski System*, 41–42.

92. Stanislavski, *An Actor Prepares*, 168–170.

93. Ibid., 170–171.

94. Ibid., 171.

95. Ibid., 171–172.

96. Ibid., 172.

97. Kostya is the shortened version of Constantin, according to Benedetti, *Stanislavski: An Introduction*, 2nd ed. (New York: Routledge, 1982), 78.
98. Stanislavski, *An Actor Prepares*, 173.
99. Ibid., 176, emphasis his.
100. Ibid., 192.
101. Ibid., 179–180.
102. Moore notes that Ivan Petrovich Pavlov's "teaching about conditioned reflexes became important in the same era as Stanislavski's own teaching," *Stanislavski System*, 9. She emphasizes the biophysical and scientific connections between external stimuli, physical actions, and emotion.
103. See Stanislavski, *An Actor Prepares*, 191, for a lovely section on luring emotion.
104. Quoted in Benedetti, *Stanislavski: An Introduction*, 67.
105. Ibid., 66.
106. Ibid., 67, 71.
107. Ibid., 67.
108. Moore, *Stanislavski System*, 19.
109. Quoted in Benedetti, *Stanislavski: An Introduction*, 69.
110. Moore, *Stanislavski System*, 21.
111. See ibid., 47.
112. See ibid., 44.
113. Quoted in ibid., 45.
114. In my brief summary of Stanislavski's work on emotion memory and physical action, I do not discuss will and volition. However, a foundational element of the System is the identification of the objectives and super-objectives of the character. Thus, will is central to Stanislavski's view. See Stanislavski, *An Actor Prepares*, 111–126, 244–251, 271–280.
115. Moore, *Stanislavski System*, 19.
116. Harak, *Virtuous Passions*, 15. Harak relies on the work of Paul Ekman, "Biological and Cultural Contributions to Body and Facial Movement in the Expression of Emotions," in *Explaining Emotions*, ed. Amélie Rorty (Berkeley: University of California Press, 1980), 73–102; and "Expression and the Nature of Emotion," in Scherer and Ekman, *Approaches to Emotion*, 319–343.
117. Ibid., 18.
118. See ibid., 113.
119. This resonates with the question raised by Don and Emily Saliers concerning music: "Could we say that the music encodes our associations and feelings and gives them back to us again?" Saliers and Saliers, *A Song to Sing, A Life to Live*, 35.
120. Dwight Conquergood, "Performance Studies: Interventions and Radical Research," in *The Performance Studies Reader*, 2nd ed., Henry Bial, ed. (New York: Routledge, 2007), 370.
121. Conquergood, 370.

122. Diana Taylor, *The Archive and the Repertoire: Performing Cultural Memory in the Americas* (Durham, NC: Duke Univeristy Press, 2003), 17.
123. Taylor, 17–18.
124. Dwight Conquergood, "Performance Studies: Interventions and Radical Research," in *The Performance Studies Reader*, 2nd ed., ed. Henry Bial (New York: Routledge, 2007), 371.
125. Taylor, 278.
126. Taylor, 19–20.
127. Conquergood, 376.
128. See Samuel Beckett, *Waiting for Godot: Tragicomedy in 2 Acts* (New York: Grove Press Inc., 1954), 15, for an example of how set and stage directions have been included in the publication and copyrighting of the script.
129. Quoted in Moore, *Stanislavski System*, 8.

CHAPTER 3 CHANGING ROLES

1. Siobhán Garrigan uses this term in conversation and develops the concept in two texts, Siobhán Garrigan, *The Real Peace Process: Worship, Politics, and the End of Sectarianism* (London: Equinox, 2010); Siobhán Garrigan, *Beyond Ritual: Sacramental Theology after Habermas*, Aldershot, Hampshire, England: Ashgate, 2004).
2. I am grateful for John Thatamanil's insight, which he has spoken of and which he is articulating in his current work. He began developing this understanding in John J. Thatamanil, "Comparative Theology After 'Religion,'" in *Planetary Loves: Spivak, Postcoloniality, and Theology*, eds. Stephen D. Moore and Mayra Rivera (Bronx, NY: Fordham University Press, 2010), 238–257.
3. Augusto Boal, *Theatre of the Oppressed*, trans. Charles A. and Maria-Odilia Leal McBride (New York: Theatre Communications Group, 1979), 25. In subsequent citations, *Theatre of the Oppressed* will be abbreviated as TO.
4. Ibid., xiv.
5. Ibid.
6. Boal recognizes different forms of catharsis that might be at work in nontheatrical settings. Michael Taussig and Richard Schechner, "Boal in Brazil, France, the USA: An Interview with Augusto Boal," in *Playing Boal: Theatre, Therapy, Activism*, eds. Mady Schutzman and Jan Cohen-Cruz (London: Routledge, 1994), 27.
7. Ibid., 25. It should be noted that several elements of *Theatre of the Oppressed* can be contested, including his idiosyncratic interpretation of Aristotle, his view of the historical development of theater in the West, and the easy parallels he draws between language and theater. For a fairly critical reading, see Jane Milling and Graham Ley, *Modern Theories of Performance: From Stanislavski to Boal* (New York: Palgrave, 2001), 147–172. A quote indicative of their general analysis of Boal, "The *Theatre of the Oppressed* is very hard to follow because of this process of amalgamation, synthesis, reformulation and ultimately misrepresentation of Aristotle's writings, from which summaries are repeatedly given

without reference to any particular source. The influence of the commentator Butcher is extremely strong, and that of (statements or ideas in) the texts of the *Poetics* is distinctly weak," 152.

8. Ibid., 29.
9. Ibid., 34.
10. Ibid., 36.
11. Ibid.
12. Ibid., 37.
13. Ibid., 46, 47.
14. Ibid., 47.
15. Ibid.
16. Ibid., 122.
17. Ibid.
18. Ibid.
19. Augusto Boal, *The Rainbow of Desire: The Boal Method of Theatre and Therapy*, trans. Adrian Jackson (New York: Routledge, 1995), 1, 2.
20. Boal, *Rainbow*, 2–3.
21. Ibid., 3.
22. Mady Schutzman and Jan Cohen-Cruz, eds., "Introduction," *Playing Boal: Theatre, Therapy, Activism* (London: Routledge, 1994), 2.
23. Boal, *Rainbow*, 40.
24. Ibid., 127. This is similar to Goffman's description of the various roles we play in everyday life.
25. Ibid., 168. This resonates with Schechner's definition of performance as "restored behavior."
26. Philip Auslander, "Boal, Blau, Brecht: The Body," in Schutzman and Cohen-Cruz, *Playing Boal*, 128.
27. Boal, 130.
28. Ibid., 132–134. See also Boal, *Rainbow*, 4–7.
29. Ibid., 135–139.
30. Ibid., 139.
31. Ibid., 141.
32. Ibid., 142.
33. Ibid., 144–146.
34. Ibid., 150.
35. Ibid.
36. Letty Russell, *Christian Education in Mission* (Philadelphia: Westminster Press, 1967); also Letty Russell, *Becoming Human* (Philadelphia: Westminster Press, 1982), 85; Letty Russell, *The Future of Partnership* (Philadelphia: Westminster Press, 1979), 137, 144; Letty Russell, *Church in the Round: Feminist Interpretation of the Church* (Louisville, KY: Westminster John Knox Press, 1993), 184.
37. On all being called, see *Future of Partnership*, 132, 134; *Church in the Round*, 50.

38. *Future of Partnership*, 126ff.; *Church in the Round*, 64.

39. Barbara Anne Keely, "Letty Russell," Talbot School of Theology, accessed January 29, 2013, http://www2.talbot.edu/ce20/educators/view.cfm?n=letty_russell.

40. Letty Russell, *Christian Education Handbook* (New York: East Harlem Protestant Parish, 1966), 7. Quoted in Keely, "Letty Russell," Talbot School of Theology. See also *Church in the Round*, 151.

41. Keely, "Letty Russell," Talbot School of Theology.

42. *Christian Education Handbook*, 4–5. Quoted in Keely, "Letty Russell," Talbot School of Theology.

43. Keely, "Letty Russell," Talbot School of Theology.

44. Letty Russell, *Human Liberation in a Feminist Perspective: A Theology* (Philadelphia: Westminster Press, 1974), 55–56.

45. Russell, *Church in the Round*, 30–31.

46. Text by Letty Russell, graphics by Shannon Clarkson. Originally created for the National Assembly of Women Religious, USA 1994.

47. Russell, *Church in the Round*, 34.

48. See Russell, *Future of Partnership*, 126ff.; Russell, *Church in the Round*, 64.

49. Boal, TO, 128.

50. Ibid. See also Augusto Boal, *Games for Actors and Non-Actors*, 2nd ed., trans. Adrian Jackson (New York: Routledge, 2002), 30.

51. Boal writes about the evolution of TO in *Games*, 9, and about the prisons in *Games*, 4.

52. Ibid., 4, 5.

53. Ibid., 6.

54. Ibid., 7.

55. Auslander, *Playing Boal*, 131.

56. Ibid. In his later work, Boal also offers a psychological account of the human being that includes three elements. The first is the person, which is the potential for all human behavior and which is possessed by all human beings. The second is the personality, which is that small portion of the person that is transformed into acts, controlled and moderated by external social forces and internal moral choices. The third element is personnages, which are various potential characters within the person that the actor can bring to the stage. In the therapeutic development of his work, Boal theorizes that someone can bring out different personnages "in the hope of mixing them into his personality." Boal writes: "Who is the 'I'? The person, the personality, or the personnage? It is very easy for us to decide—in fatalistic fashion—that we are the way we are, full stop, end of story. But we can also imagine—in a more creative fashion—that the playing cards can be redealt." Boal, *Rainbow*, 3–39, 35.

In this context, Boal suggests that acting out a particular personnage can have lasting influence on the personality. This would be another way in which taking up various roles could influence the self. However, I do not bring this into my current project for two reasons. First, it is from a later, quite different stage in Boal's work that reflects more psychological than theatrical influences. Second, I follow Boal's lead in wanting to distance Theater of the Oppressed from psychodrama, a field in which Boal's later work has been put to use. Psychodrama is a form of group psychotherapy in which group members act out situations and/or relationships from an individual's life. It was first developed by Jacob L. Moreno.

> Psychodrama is an active form of group psychotherapy where an individual's life situations are presented on stage with support from group members. As its means of expression, psychodrama makes use of speech and body language. There is no script, but scenes from a person's life are enacted the way he or she has experienced them. The psychodrama stage is a safe place where, in the presence of the group and under the director's guidance, human relations are explored. Moreno thought that action, body movements, and dynamic interrelations of characters on the stage—their mutual closeness or distance as expressed in physical, spatial terms, could tell more about the difficulties in interpersonal relations than speech itself. The action taking place on the stage, spoken words and movements, objects and props, make it possible for the protagonist to complete whatever he or she has been unable to, or has not known how to, or dared not do in reality. This is known as act completion. It is on the psychodrama stage that the person realizes the thoughts and emotions that inhibit him, and also the new patterns of behavior that will help him to express himself freely. Psychodrama not only explores one's unspoken thoughts and feelings, but also the situations that have never really happened but could have, the encounters with those who are really absent, the projections for the future, and different perceptions of the past and present. Everything is possible in psychodrama: to play God, to talk to a deceased person, to ask for a divorce, to steal, to love the one we otherwise are not allowed to, to pour it all out to the boss. This concealed dimension of experience, unrecognized or pushed aside, is called surplus reality—more than reality, an extra dimension of reality. The principle underlying psychodramatic enactment is the concept of "as if." Just as we observe in the spontaneous play of children, working with situations "as if" they are real enables the safe encounter with forbidden, painful and traumatic experiences.
>
> Zoran Đjurić, Jasna Veljković, Miomir Tomić, *Psychodrama: A Beginner's Guide* (London: Jessica Kingsley Publishers 2006), 9.

While Boal denied that psychodrama influenced the development of his methods, and likewise distanced himself from psychodrama in his later practice, there are several similarities between Moreno's work and Boal's work in therapeutic settings. (For examples of such distancing, see *Playing Boal*, 26 and 27.) In an article describing connections between the two thinkers, Daniel

Feldhendler writes, "Boal and Moreno share a fundamental conception of theatre and its healing effects and, even further, of human kind." In "Augusto Boal
and Jacob L. Moreno: Theatre and Therapy," in *Playing Boal*, 89.

Another technique I wish to distinguish clearly from Boal and from my own
work is bibliodrama, which is a form of Bible study that incorporates a great deal
of role playing, dream work, and techniques borrowed from therapeutic settings.

> Most simply described, ***Bibliodrama is a form of role playing in which the roles
> played are taken from biblical texts.*** The roles may be those of characters who
> appear in the Bible, either explicitly and by name (Adam or Eve), or those
> whose presence may be inferred from an imaginative reading of the stories
> (Noah's wife or Abraham's mother). In Bibliodrama, the reservoir of avail-
> able roles or parts may include certain objects or images that can be embod-
> ied in voice and action (the serpent in the Garden or the staff of Moses).
> Places can speak (the Jordan River or Mount Sinai). Or spiritual figures may
> talk (angels, or God, or the Adversary). Then there is a host of characters from
> legendary tradition (Lilith or the five perverted judges of Sodom) who can be
> brought onto the bibliodramatic stage. Finally, as an extension of the process
> in a different direction, there are the figures from history who have com-
> mented on the Bible (Philo, Augustine, Maimonides) whose presence and
> perspectives may be imagined and brought alive by an act of role playing.
>   As I have developed it, then, **"Bibliodrama is a form of interpretive play.
> To honor it with a venerable Hebrew name, Bibliodrama can be called a
> form of *midrash*."**

Peter Pitzele, *Scripture Windows: Toward a Practice of Bibliodrama* (Los
Angeles: Alef Design Group, 1998), 11. Boldface his.

One crucial difference (among several) between psychodrama and bibliodrama, on the one hand, and Boal and Russell on the other, is the amount of
power held by a single, guiding individual. The therapist in psychodrama and
the facilitator in bibliodrama are afforded a significant amount of power in relation to the participants, in ways that I find deeply troubling and open to misuse.

57. In true Marxist form, Boal writes, "[I]t is necessary to eliminate the private
    property of the characters by the individual actors: the 'Joker' System." TO, 119.

58. I am grateful to Joshua Edelman for this clarifying phraseology.

59. Russell, *Church in the Round*, 65, 73.

60. Ibid., 57.

61. Russell, *Future of Partnership*, 35.

62. Russell, *Becoming Human*, 20.

63. See Russell, *Human Liberation*, 64–65.

64. For a clear introduction to this topic, see Phillip Berryman, *Liberation Theology:
    The Essential Facts about the Revolutionary Movement in Latin America and Beyond*
    (New York: Pantheon Books, 1987). Regarding Medellín, see 22ff.

65. Boal remarked in an interview that "in Latin America the fight for liberation brings Marxists and priests together," *Playing Boal*, 31.

66. Paulo Freire, *Pedagogy of the Oppressed* (New York: Continuum, 1970).

67. Boal dedicated *Games for Actors and Non-Actors* to Freire, among others. Freire became a special consultant with the Office of Education at the World Council of Churches in Geneva in 1970. He worked there for nine years. Russell writes about Freire's work in Russell, *Human Liberation*, 32, 35, 66, 128; Russell, *Future of Partnership*, 142, 145–146, and 151. She specifically mentions his work with the World Council of Churches on 145.

68. *Games*, 49.

69. Ibid.

70. Suzanne Burgoyne, "Engaging the Whole Student: Interactive Theatre in the Classroom," *Essays on Teaching Excellence: Towards the Best in the Academy*, vol. 15. no. 5, 2003–2004. *apps.carleton.edu/campus/ltc/assets/Engaging_the_whole_student.htm*, consulted 1/28/2013.

71. Burgoyne writes, "Doing theatre is a form of active learning (Gressler, 2002); and research shows that active learning helps develop critical thinking (Bonwell & Eison, 1991). Using TO techniques, faculty can guide students in exploring ideas through images and enactment, rendering the subject matter memorable and meaningful." Burgoyne, *Engaging the Whole Student*.

72. Jacqueline D. Burleson, *Augusto Boal's Theatre of the Oppressed in the Public Speaking and Interpersonal Communication Classrooms*, Dissertation, Louisiana State University and Agricultural and Mechanical College, Department of Communication Studies, 2003, 18. See also Ross McKeehen Louis, *Critical Performative Pedagogy: Augusto Boal's Theatre of the Oppressed in the English as a Second Language Classroom*, Dissertation, Louisiana State University and Agricultural and Mechanical College, Department of Communication Studies, 2002; Candace Kaye and Giselle Ragusa, "Boal's Mirror: Reflections for Teacher Education" presented at the Annual Meeting of American Educational Research Association, San Diego, CA, April 13, 1998; Peter Duffy and Elinor Vettraino, eds., *Youth and Theatre of the Oppressed* (New York: Palgrave Macmillan, 2010).

73. Russell, *Human Liberation*, 65. Also, Russell draws upon Reformed theology to define faith in a whole-personed way, including knowing, trusting, and acting as joined aspects of faith. See Russell, *Church in the Round*, 23. For Max Harris, God's revelation through incarnation—Word made flesh—invites analogies between church and theater and recommends theatrical hermeneutics to Christians who seek to know God. Harris, 12.

74. See Russell, *Becoming Human*, 57; and Russell, *Church in the Round*, 171.

75. For Russell's further work on justice and hospitality, see Letty Russell, *Just Hospitality: God's Welcome in a World of Difference*, eds. J. Shannon Clarkson and Kate M. Ott (Louisville, KY: Westminster John Knox Press, 2009).

76. See Russell, *Church in the Round*, 171.
77. Russell, *Human Liberation*, 158; Russell, *Future of Partnership*, 74.
78. Russell, *Human Liberation*, 158.
79. She wrote her dissertation on understanding Tradition as Mission: Letty Russell, "Tradition as Mission: Study of a New Current in Theology and Its Implications for Theological Education," Ph.D. Dissertation, Union Theological Seminary in New York, 1969. She married Hans Hoekendijk, a Dutch missiologist. (Russell, *Church in the Round*, 90.) After his death in 1975, Russell dedicated the book *The Future of Partnership* to him, writing, "indeed, he is a coauthor, for his ideas have long since become multiplied with my own." Russell, *Future of Partnership*, 14.
80. Russell, *Church in the Round*, 88. Both Hoekendijk and Russell were influenced by Missio Dei theology, which marked a shift from understanding mission as "church-centric" to understanding mission as "world-centric." In Missio Dei theology, churches do not carry out the mission of God, but rather respond to the mission of God in the world. See. J. C. Hoekendijk, *The Church Inside Out*, eds. L. A. Hoedemaker and Pieter Tijmes, trans. Isaac C. Rottenberg (Philadelpia: Westminster Press, 1966). I am grateful to Peter Heltzel for teaching me about the influence of Missio Dei theology on Russell's work.
81. Russell, *Future of Partnership*, 144, quoting Russell, *Christian Education in Mission*, 25.
82. See Russell, *Church in the Round*, 96; Russell, *Human Liberation*, 59.
83. Russell, *Future of Partnership*, 35.
84. Ibid., 36, 103.
85. My sense that this is unaccountable is only slightly mitigated by attributing to Boal a Marxist sense of history moving toward more just material conditions. Furthermore, this does not mesh easily or well with his later psychological focus in *Rainbow of Desire*. For further considerations of Marx and hope within a framework of performance, see Nicholas Lash, "All Shall Be Well: Christian and Marxist Hope," in *Theology on the Way to Emmaus* (Eugene, OR: Wipf & Stock, 1986), 202–215.
86. Russell, *Future of Partnership*, 159.
87. Ibid., 15. See also 21, 51, 157. See also Russell, *Church in the Round*, 89, 128; Russell, *Becoming Human*, 39, 41.
88. Russell, *Future of Partnership*, 164.
89. Ibid.
90. See Ibid., 21. Russell, *Human Liberation*, 42, 45–47. See also Russell, *Becoming Human*, 42.
91. Russell, *Future of Partnership*, 103, 105. See also Russell, *Becoming Human*, 41.
92. Russell, *Future of Partnership*, 165.
93. Ibid., 22.
94. Ibid., 157. Although this is very specific to Jesus for Russell, the notion of a memory of the future resonates with much of performance theory, in which our improvisations upon patterns of the past are shaped, informed by, and aimed at visions of the future. During the First Annual Performance Studies Conference in 1995, the

performance artist Orlan used the slogan, "Remember the Future." Peggy Phelan and Jill Lane, *The Ends of Performance* (New York: New York University Press, 1998), 6.

95. Ibid., 45, 157. See also Russell, *Becoming Human*, 42; Russell, *Church in the Round*, 38.

96. Russell, *Future of Partnership*, 157.

97. Russell, *Human Liberation*, 72, her emphasis.

98. The resonances between Russell and Schechner are very strong on this point. Russell states that Christians need to search within tradition to find elements of the past that can help them move toward a meaningful future. She calls this a "usable past" and says that history "becomes a usable past through reflection on its meaning and mistakes in such a way that human beings build a common sense of direction toward the future." While a meaningful present and future help identify and shape a usable past, "a usable past helps in the search for a usable future." Russell, *Human Liberation*, 72. Her emphasis removed. Schechner writes, "In a very real way the future—the project coming into existence through the process of rehearsal—determines the past: what will be kept from earlier rehearsals or from the 'source materials.'" Richard Schechner, *Between Theater and Anthropology* (Philadelphia: University of Pennsylvania Press, 1985), 39.

99. Schechner, *Between Theater and Anthropology*, 79.

100. Russell, *Feminist Interpretation of the Bible*; Russell, *The Liberating Word*.

101. Russell, *Human Liberation*, 76–77.

102. Russell, *Church in the Round*, 37–38; Russell, *Human Liberation*, 75–77.

103. Russell, *Church in the Round*, 38.

104. Russell uses the phrase "situation-variable" often. See Russell, *Becoming Human*, 89; Russell, *Church in the Round*, 115, 176; Russell, *Human Liberation*, 26, 52.

105. Russell, *Future of Partnership*, 155.

106. Russell, *Liberating Word*, 14.

107. Russell, *Future of Partnership*, 173, her emphasis.

108. Russell, *Church in the Round*, 29.

109. Ibid., 81.

110. My reading of the parables as a role-switching discipline is informed by Mary Ann Tolbert, *Perspectives on the Parables: An Approach to Multiple Interpretations* (Philadelphia: Fortress Press, 1979); and David Buttrick, *Speaking Parables: A Homiletic Guide* (Louisville, KY: Westminster John Knox Press, 2000). William R. Herzog II specifically links the parables to Paulo Freire's work in *Parables as Subversive Speech: Jesus as Pedagogue of the Oppressed* (Louisville, KY: Westminster John Knox Press, 1994).

111. Notes from M. Shawn Copeland, "Embodying Ethics: Solidarity in Action," Katie Geneva Cannon Lecture, Louisville Presbyterian Theological Seminary, September 23, 2012.

CHAPTER 4 CHANGING SCENES

1. Paul Connerton, *How Societies Remember* (New York: Cambridge University Press, 1989), 21.
2. Ibid., 22.
3. Ibid., 23.
4. Ibid., 39–40.
5. Ibid., 88.
6. Ibid., 43. Emphasis his. Note that Connerton is writing about the Nazi commemorations of the Putsch, an event in 1923 in which sixteen were killed.
7. Ibid., 44.
8. Ibid., 45.
9. Ibid., 58.
10. Don E. Saliers, *The Soul in Paraphrase* (New York: Seabury Press, 1980), 28–29.
11. Paul Connerton, *How Societies Remember*, 102.
12. Ibid.
13. Ibid.
14. Willie James Jennings, *The Christian Imagination: Theology and the Origins of Race.* (New Haven, CT: Yale University Press, 2010), 211–219.
15. Ibid., 257.
16. Ibid.
17. Delores Williams, *Sisters in the Wilderness: The Challenge of Womanist God-Talk* (Maryknoll, NY: Orbis Books, 1993), 2.
18. Ibid., 3.
19. Ibid., 4.
20. Ibid., 2. Williams challenged black male theologians, especially James Cone, on this issue extensively in chapter 6, 144–153. In a statement made even more potent by Jennings's later work, Williams writes of black liberation theologians, "Have they, in the use of the Bible, identified so thoroughly with the theme of Israel's election that they have not seen the oppressed of the oppressed in scripture?," 149.
21. Williams offers a compelling description of careful role choosing that she describes as "a womanist hermeneutic of *identification-ascertainment*," 149ff. Emphasis hers.
22. Ibid., 5.
23. Ibid., 60.
24. Ibid., 60–61.
25. Ibid., 61. Williams discusses how black men and women formulated new familial patterns after emancipation, largely based on white patriarchal models, 71ff.
26. Ibid., 81.
27. Ibid., 162.

28. See Delores Williams, "Black Women's Surrogacy Experience and the Christian Notion of Redemption," in *Cross Examinations: Readings on the Meaning of the Cross Today*, ed. Marit Trelstad (Minneapolis, MN: Fortress Press, 2006), 28, for a brief summary of some the pertinent theological questions regarding Jesus as surrogate.

29. Williams, *Sisters in the Wilderness: The Challenge of Womanist God-Talk*, 143, 151.

30. Ibid., 165.

31. Ibid., 167.

32. JoAnne Marie Terrell, *Power in the Blood?: The Cross in the African American Experience* (Maryknoll, NY: Orbis Books), 1998; M. Shawn Copeland, *Enfleshing Freedom: Body, Race, and Being*, (Minneapolis, MN: Fortress Press, 2010), 174. While this citing mentions Williams directly, Copeland addresses the substance of Williams's critique more fully in "Wading Through Many Sorrows," in Emilie M. Townes, ed., *A Troubling in My Soul: Womanist Perspectives on Evil and Suffering* (Maryknoll, NY: Orbis Books, 1993), 109–129. James H. Cone, *The Cross and the Lynching Tree* (Maryknoll, NY: Orbis Books, 2011), 149, 151. While Cone accepts Williams's critique and rejects the notion that Jesus's suffering is redemptive, he retains a sense that the Cross is salvific through solidarity. For further constructive use made of Williams's work on salvation, see Monica A. Coleman, *Making a Way Out of No Way: A Womanist Theology* (Minneapolis, MN: Fortress Press, 2008). While Wonhee Anne Joh deals more directly with Elisabeth Schüssler Fiorenza, Elizabeth A. Johnson, and Rita Nakashima Brock, she offers an insightful contribution to the Christological conversation in which Williams is involved. See Wonhee Anne Joh, *The Heart of the Cross: A Postcolonial Christology*, (Louisville, KY: Westminster John Knox Press, 2006). See also Arnfríður Guðmundsdóttir, *Meeting God on the Cross: Christ, the Cross, and the Feminist Critique* (Oxford: Oxford University Press, 2010).

33. Brecht, "Theatre for Pleasure or Theatre for Instruction," *Brecht on Theatre: The Development of an Aesthetic*, ed. and trans. John Willett (New York: Hill and Wang, 1957), 76.

34. Ibid., 75.

35. Brecht, "Some of the Things that Can Be Learnt from Stanislavsky," *Brecht on Theatre: The Development of an Aesthetic*, ed. and trans. John Willett (New York: Hill and Wang, 1957), editor's note, p. 237.

36. For an introduction to Brecht's analysis of Aristotelian theater and his critique of it, See Brecht, "A Short Organum for the Theatre," *Brecht on Theatre: The Development of an Aesthetic*, ed. and trans. John Willett (New York: Hill and Wang, 1957), 179–205. Brecht focuses on how empathic theater aims solely for pleasure, and in so doing often presents the current realities of the audience as eternal and unquestionable. This does serve to squelch commitment to change the world for the better, but it appears less as a politically motivated form of social control in

Brecht's work than in Boal's. Both Brecht and Boal are influenced by Marx, and Brecht incorporates a nuanced view of history into his work in two ways. First, he understands human persons as both agents in their own lives and deeply influenced by social forces beyond their control. Thus he writes, "The idea of man as a function of the environment and the environment as a function of man, i.e. the breaking up of the environment into relationships between men, corresponds to a new way of thinking, the historical way." Brecht, "Alienation Effects in Chinese Acting," *Brecht on Theatre: The Development of an Aesthetic*, ed. and trans. John Willett (New York: Hill and Wang, 1957), 97. Second, when historical realities of the present day are presented as eternal or universal, they seem unalterable. This fosters passive acceptance of the status quo. However, if the historical distinctions can be highlighted, the historicity and contingency of our own circumstances come to the fore. Brecht writes, "we must drop our habit of taking the different social structures of past periods, then stripping them of everything that makes them different; so that they all look more or less like our own, which then acquires from this process a certain air of having been there all along, in other words of permanence pure and simple. Instead we must leave them their distinguishing marks and keep their impermanence always before our eyes, so that our own period can be seen to be impermanent, too." Brecht, "A Short Organum for the Theatre," 190.

37. Brecht, "Theatre for Pleasure or Instruction," 71.

38. Ibid.

39. See Brecht, "Alienation Effects in Chinese Acting," 96. For further examples, see "Notes to Die Rundköpfe und Die Spitzköpfe," 101–103.

40. Brecht, "Alienation Effects in Chinese Acting," 91.

41. Brecht, "A Short Organum for the Theatre," 192.

42. Brecht, "The Modern Theatre Is the Epic Theatre," 39.

43. James H. Cone, *The Cross and the Lynching Tree* (Maryknoll, NY: Orbis Books, 2012), 3, 31, 99. For further work on lynching, see Angela D. Sims, *Ethical Complications of Lynching: Ida B. Wells's Interrogation of American Terror* (New York: Palgrave, Macmillan, 2010).

44. Cone, *The Cross and the Lynching Tree*, 9.

45. Ibid., 31.

46. Cone notes Quincy Ewing, Andrew Sledd, and John E. White as exceptions. Cone, *The Cross and the Lynching Tree*, 62–63.

47. Cone, *The Cross and the Lynching Tree*, 63.

48. Ibid., 39, 40, 41, 57.

49. Ibid., 41, 43, 57, 60.

50. Ibid., 40, referencing Niebuhr, *Moral Man and Immoral Society: A Study in Ethics and Politics*.

51. Cone, *The Cross and the Lynching Tree*, 40, using words from Harper Lee's *To Kill a Mockingbird*.

52. Cone, *The Cross and the Lynching Tree*, 21.
53. Ibid., 75.
54. Ibid., 23.
55. Ibid., 156.
56. Ibid., 156.
57. Ibid., 4, 8.
58. Cone does cite Walter White's remark that "It is exceedingly doubtful if lynching could possibly exist under any other religion than Christianity." However, Cone presents White as picking out particular denominations fostering fanaticism as the problem. Thus White's challenge is posed as a historical query based on the fanatical nature of particular Christian groups, rather than as a theological issue. Cone, *The Cross and the Lynching Tree*, 112. Walter White, *Rope and Faggot: A Biography of Judge Lynch* (Notre Dame, IN: University of Notre Dame Press, 2001, orig., 1929), 40.
59. Cone, *The Cross and the Lynching Tree*, 31.
60. Ibid., 132. In an earlier work, Cone states, "Racism is a complete denial of the Incarnation and thus of Christianity. Therefore, the white denominational churches are unchristian." James H. Cone, *Black Theology and Black Power* (Maryknoll, NY: Orbis Books, 1969), 73.
61. I suspect that Cone's reluctance to follow through with the implications of his argument might rest in his indebtedness to Karl Barth, in ways that will be addressed in the coming chapter.
62. Cone, *The Cross and the Lynching Tree*, 161.
63. Ibid., 166.
64. Ibid., 160.
65. Ibid., 160.
66. See M. Shawn Copeland, *Enfleshing Freedom: Body, Race, and Being* (Minneapolis, MN: Fortress Press, 2010), 117–128. Kelly Brown Douglas, *What's Faith Got to Do with It?: Black Bodies/Christian Souls* (Maryknoll, NY: Orbis Books, 2005). Douglas specifically addresses the "heretical tradition" of Christianity that supports racism and oppression (5). She traces the roots of this to a platonized, dualistic view of spirit and matter as binary opposites. Such theology is heretical in its failure to value incarnation, a failure that contributes to the brutalizing of bodies. Feminist theorists, such as Luce Irigaray; and performance theorists, such as Dwight Conquergood, connect a dualism between spirit (or mind) and body with the privileging of abstract, propositional, and text-based forms of knowledge over communal, embodied, performance-based forms of knowledge. This hierarchy supports patterns of domination including colonialism, classism, racism, and sexism. Attending to performance is understood as a challenge to some of the central assumptions that fund oppression.

    For a reflection on the role of redemptive suffering—which includes but is not limited to surrogate suffering—see Rita Nakashima Brock and Rebecca Ann

Parker, *Proverbs of Ashes: Violence, Redemptive Suffering, and The Search for What Saves Us* (Boston, MA: Beacon Press, 2001).

67. Connerton, *How Societies Remember*, 59.

68. William T. Cavanaugh, *Torture and Eucharist: Theology, Politics, and the Body of Christ* (Hoboken, Oxford: Wiley-Blackwell, 1998), 280.

69. Cavanaugh, *Torture and Eucharist*, 280. There is a difference here between Cavanaugh's vision and my own. We are operating with differing definitions of both "church" and "performance." He sees church as a social body, capable of performing, while I understand church as performance, which is performed by a social body that comes to be in the performance itself. Nevertheless, in either view there is a social body constituted in and through the performance of the Eucharist, and Cavanaugh persuasively argues for the political potency of this body.

    Cavanaugh states, "The church does not simply perform the Eucharist; the Eucharist performs the church" (235). If I understand Cavanaugh rightly, we fundamentally agree on the point he is making here—in and through the performance of the Eucharist, the identity of the social body of Christians is formed in ways that surpass our own agency. However, Cavanaugh might well reject my starting point (church as performance) for any number of reasons, including the attendant focus on human activity.

    He emphasizes the performative nature of the Eucharist, but does so along with an emphasis on the church as the Body of Christ. See Cavanaugh, *Torture and Eucharist*, 230.

70. Russell does not focus on the Eucharist as liberating, in part due to feminist critiques of blood sacrifice as aligned with patriarchy. See Russell, *Church in the Round*, 143.

71. See, for example, John Zizioluas, *Being as Communion: Studies in Personhood and the Church* (Crestwood, NY: St. Vladimir's Seminary Press, 1985), 180.

72. Johannes Baptist Metz and Jürgen Moltmann, *Faith and the Future: Essays on Theology, Solidarity, and Modernity* (Maryknoll, NY: Orbis Books, 1995), 15. See also Johann Baptist Metz, *Faith in History and Society: Toward a Practical Fundamental Theology*, trans. David Smith (New York: The Seabury Press, 1980), 100–118.

73. Bruce T. Morrill, *Anamnesis as Dangerous Memory: Political and Liturgical Theology in Dialogue*, (Collegeville, MN: Liturgical Press, 2000), 190–191.

74. Ibid., 193.

75. Cynthia Hess writes powerfully about how such theological and ecclesial retemporalization can be healing for persons who have been traumatized. See Cynthia Hess, *Sites of Violence, Sites of Grace: Christian Nonviolence and the Traumatized Self* (Lanham, MD: Lexington Books, 2009).

76. Cavanaugh, *Torture and Eucharist*, 222.

77. Ibid., 227.

78. Johann Baptist Metz and Jürgen Moltmann, "The Future in the Memory of Suffering," *Faith and the Future: Essays on Theology, Solidarity, and Modernity* (Maryknoll, NY: Orbis Books, 1995), 12.

79. Ibid., 6 and 7.

80. Ibid., 11. Regarding "dangerous memory," see also Johann Baptist Metz, *Faith in History and Society: Toward a Practical Fundamental Theology*, trans. David Smith (New York: Seabury Press, 1980), 185. See also Johann Baptist Metz, "Communicating a Dangerous Memory," *Communicating a Dangerous Memory: Soundings in Political Theology*, ed. Fred Lawrence (Atlanta: Scholars Press, 1987), 53.

81. See Metz and Moltmann on those who have died, "The Future in the Memory of Suffering," 12.

82. Cavanaugh, *Torture and Eucharist*, 30.

83. M. Shawn Copeland, *Enfleshing Freedom: Body, Race, and Being* (Minneapolis, MN: Fortress Press, 127).

84. Ibid., 128.

85. Garrigan diagnoses "the largely unacknowledged difference between the 'is,' the 'can,' and the 'should be' of the assembly gathered at Eucharist (and, by extension, of the church as a whole) in nearly all mainstream writing about Eucharist." Siobhán Garrigan, *Beyond Ritual: Sacramental Theology after Habermas* (Hampshire, England: Ashgate, 2004), 119.

86. Ibid., 21.

87. Garrigan, *The Real Peace Process*. Mary McClintock Fulkerson also engages in theology that begins with what actually happens in Christian liturgy. See Mary McClintock Fulkerson, *Places of Redemption: Theology for a Worldly Church* (New York: Oxford University Press, 2007).

CHAPTER 5   STRIKING THE SET

1. Harris also engages Barth on theology and theater, noting that "there is both reason and mischief" in the choice. Harris, ix.

2. James C. Livingston and Francis Schüssler Fiorenza, *The Twentieth Century, vol. 2, Modern Christian Thought* (Upper Saddle River, NJ: Prentice-Hall, 2000), 100.

3. Arthur C. Cochrane, "Barmen Declaration," in *The Church's Confession under Hitler* (Philadelphia: Westminster, 1962.), 237–242.

4. Barth, Karl, *Epistle to the Romans*, trans. Edwyn C. Hoskyns (London: Oxford, 1933), 10.

5. Barth, *Epistle to the Romans*, 49.

6. Karl Barth, *Doctrine of God*, trans. T.H.L Parker et al., vol. 2.1, *Church Dogmatics* (Edinburgh: T & T Clark, 1957), 1:149. "Anthropological and ecclesiologial assertions arise only as they are borrowed from Christology. That is to say, no anthro-

pological or ecclesiological assertion is true in itself and as such. Its truth subsists in the assertion of Christology, or rather in the reality of Jesus Christ alone."

7. James J. Buckley, "Christian Community, Baptism, and Lord's Supper," in *The Cambridge Companion to Karl Barth*, ed. John Webster (New York: Cambridge, 2000), 205.

8. Karl Barth, *Doctrine of Reconciliation*, eds. G. W. Bromiley and T. F. Torrance, vol. 4.3.1, *Church Dogmatics* (Edinburgh: T &T Clark, 1962), 757. Specifically, Jesus Christ.

9. Karl Barth, *Epistle to the Romans*, v.

10. Ibid., 29.

11. Ibid., 36.

12. Ibid., 42.

13. Ibid., 40.

14. Ibid., 37.

15. Ibid., 44.

16. Ibid., 44.

17. Ibid., 47. Throughout this chapter I will return to the play between visibility and invisibility in the work of Karl Barth and Peter Brook. It would be useful and fun to bring performance theorist Peggy Phelan into this conversation, particularly her work on performance, representation, and visibility within culture. Although I omit such a discussion here in order to maintain focus, I hope to delve into these issues in future work. See Peggy Phelan, *Unmarked: The Politics of Performance* (New York: Routlege, 1993).

18. Ibid., 332.

19. Ibid., 242.

20. Ibid.

21. Ibid., 258.

22. Ibid., 380–381.

23. Ibid., 33.

24. James J. Buckley, "Christian Community, Baptism, and Lord's Supper," in *The Cambridge Companion to Karl Barth*, ed. John Webster (New York: Cambridge, 2000), 200.

25. Livingston and Schüssler Fiorenza, *The Twentieth Century*, 107.

26. Karl Barth, *Doctrine of Reconciliation*, eds. G. W. Bromiley and T. F. Torrance, vol. 4.1, *Church Dogmatics* (Edinburgh: T &T Clark, 1956), 661, 663.

27. Ibid., 661. See also 663.

28. Ibid., 661, 647.

29. Ibid., 652.

30. Ibid., 650.

31. Ibid., 651.

32. Ibid., 694, where he discusses specifically that the subject who gives church its holiness is God.

33. See Barth, *Doctrine of Reconciliation*, 688, where Barth writes, "To be awakened to faith and to be added to the community are one and the same thing."

34. Barth, *Doctrine of Reconciliation*, 660–661.

35. Ibid., 656.

36. Ibid., 654. See also 686.

37. Ibid., 658.

38. Ibid., 653.

39. Ibid., 666.

40. Ibid., 669.

41. See Ibid., 661, 666, 667.

42. Ibid., eds. G. W. Bromiley and T. F. Torrance, vol. 4.3.1, *Church Dogmatics* (Edinburgh: T & T Clark, 1962), 826.

43. See, for example, Ibid., 696.

44. Joseph L. Mangina, "The Stranger as Sacrament: Karl Barth and the Ethics of Ecclesial Practice," *International Journal of Systematic Theology* 1, no. 3 (November 1999), 332.

45. Nicholas M. Healy, "The Logic of Karl Barth's Ecclesiology: Analysis, Assessment and Proposed Modifications," *Modern Theology* 10:3 (July 1994), 260. His emphasis.

46. Mangina, "Bearing the Marks of Jesus: The Church in the Economy of Salvation in Barth and Hauerwas," *Scottish Journal of Theology* 52:3 (August 1999) 270.

47. Healy, "The Logic of Karl Barth's Ecclesiology: Analysis, Assessment and Proposed Modifications," 258.

48. Buckley, "Christian Community, Baptism, and Lord's Supper," 208. Nestorianism refers to a view of Jesus Christ in which his divinity and his humanity are distinguished to such a degree that one can no longer say God did the things that Jesus did, such as eat, walk, and breath. This significantly weakens the doctrine of incarnation, as it cannot be understood in terms of hypostatic union within a Nestorian frame.

49. Healy, "The Logic of Karl Barth's Ecclesiology: Analysis, Assessment and Proposed Modifications," 259. There are similarities here between Barth's view and Cone's comments regarding lynchers being outside Christian identity.

50. See Healy, "The Logic of Karl Barth's Ecclesiology: Analysis, Assessment and Proposed Modifications," 264.

51. Mangina, "Bearing the Marks of Jesus: The Church in the Economy of Salvation in Barth and Hauerwas," 280.

52. Barth's own work implies a metaphorical sense of performance by referring to the "drama of Jesus Christ." See Barth, *Church Dogmatics* III.1, 387.

53. I have mentioned earlier the trend among theologians and ethicists influenced by narrative theology, which is itself influenced by Karl Barth. Perhaps then it

should not be surprising that both Healy and Buckley mention the possibility of improving Barth's ecclesiology by further emphasizing narrative. See Healy, "The Logic of Karl Barth's Ecclesiology: Analysis, Assessment and Proposed Modifications," 258, 266, 268; Buckley, "Christian Community, Baptism, and Lord's Supper," 207; James J. Buckley, "A Field of Living Fire: Karl Barth on the Spirit and the Church," *Modern Theology* 10, no. 1 (January 1994), 89.

54. See Barth, *Doctrine of Reconciliation*, 688.

55. Some scholars see Barth's theology as more biniterian than Trinitarian and might therefore object that the Holy Spirit might not have enough agency for real interaction. See Robert Jenson, "You Wonder Where the Spirit Went," *Pro Ecclesia* II/3 (1993), 296–304. See also Mangina, "Bearing the Marks of Jesus: The Church in the Economy of Salvation in Barth and Hauerwas," who presses for a stronger economy of the Holy Spirit.

56. See Barth, *Doctrine of Reconciliation*, 661.

57. I realize that many theologians influenced by process theology might disagree with this characterization. However, Barth was not a process theologian.

58. James Fodor and Stanley Hauerwas, "Performing Faith: The Peaceable Rhetoric of God's Church," in *Rhetorical Invention and Religious Inquiry*, eds. Walter Jost and Wendy Olmsted (New Haven, CT: Yale University Press, 2000), 394, 403.

59. Fodor and Hauerwas, "Performing Faith,"382. Performance theorists would also find the notion of "eternally" performing quite troubling, given the ephemeral and fleeting nature of performance.

60. Fodor and Hauerwas, "Performing Faith," 382. They hope for the Trinitarian nature of God to allow for performance without self-alienation. However, this still does not address the issue of doubleness.

61. Fodor and Hauerwas, "Performing Faith," 382. Hauerwas also appears to be influenced by Lash, who argues that "divine utterance is 'performative.'" Lash, 91. In a purely Austinian way, this is true: God's speech is generative and creative. However, I am employing the concept of performance as it has been developed in performance studies in the years since Austin wrote.

62. Jesus surely performed by engaging in everyday restored behaviors. He performed the social roles of son, carpenter, teacher, and so forth. However, the concept of performance does not apply to the first or third persons of the Trinity, or to the Godhead. One could perhaps argue that Barth subsumes all activity of God into the "act" of Jesus (drawing on texts such as *Church Dogmatics* III.4, 441) in such a way that it could be seen as performance, but I think this does harm to his doctrine of the Trinity in order to make Barth's theology fit a technical description of performance that did not exist when he wrote.

63. As mentioned above, Lash argues that God's speech is performative, but within a strictly Austinian understanding of the term. Lash, 91.

64. I have written on this issue more extensively elsewhere, in an essay titled, "From Narrative to Performance?"

65. Joseph L. Mangina offers a nuanced reading of select Barthian texts to resource a sacramental ecclesiology and ecclesial ethics. In so doing, he draws upon passages in Barth's work that emphasize divine empowerment of human agency to articulate a more complex picture of the interplay between human and divine activity. It is worth reading on the issue of human and divine subjectivity in Barth and Barthian theology. At the same time, the distinction remains between God's act that constitutes the church and our responsive performance. He writes that "the church is constituted by Word and Sacrament" and then asks, "[f]or who performs these actions if not the members of the community in their ordered life together? And yet in performing them it is not we who constitute ourselves as the church, but the Spirit who constitutes the church as Christ's Body." Mangina, "The Stranger as Sacrament: Karl Barth and the Ethics of Ecclesial Practice," 339.

66. There is a lovely passage on recollection and expectation that the Word of God will give itself to be known in Karl Barth, *Church Dogmatics* I.1, *The Doctrine of the Word of God*, eds. G. W. Bromiley and T. F. Torrance, trans. G. W. Bromiley, G. T. Thomson, and Harold Knight (London: T & T Clark, 2010).

67. While Brook's influence continues, note that this is not the cutting edge of theater theory in 2014.

68. See, for example, Timothy Gorringe, *God's Theatre: Theology of Providence* (London: SCM, 1991); Kevin J. Vanhoozer, *The Drama of Doctrine: A Canonical Linguistic Approach to Christian Theology* (Louisville, KY: Westminster John Knox, 2005); Trevor A. Hart and Steven R. Guthrie, eds., *Faithful Performances: Enacting Christian Tradition* (Burlington, VT: Ashgate, 2007); and Shannon Craigo-Snell and Shawnthea Monroe, *Living Christianity: A Pastoral Theology for Today* (Minneapolis, MN: Fortress Press, 2009).

69. Peter Brook, *The Empty Space* (New York: Atheneum, 1987), 27–28.

70. Ibid., 40.

71. Ibid., 42.

72. Ibid.

73. Ibid., 60.

74. Ibid., 44–45.

75. Ibid., 45.

76. Ibid., 46.

77. Ibid., 48.

78. Ibid.

79. Ibid., 43.

80. Ibid., 44.

81. Ibid., 45.

82. Ibid., 56.

83. Ibid., 10–11, 22.

84. Ibid., 10. "The Deadly Theatre takes easily to Shakespeare."

85. Ibid., 62.
86. Ibid., 68.
87. Ibid., 69, 85.
88. Ibid., 70.
89. Ibid.
90. Ibid., 71.
91. Ibid., 70.
92. Ibid.
93. Here my interpretation differs from other theologians and ethicists who iden-tify Brook's goal as the Immediate Theater. See Vanhoozer, *Drama of Doctrine*, 406; and Joshua Edelman, "Can an Act Be True? The Possibilities of the Dramatic Metaphor for Theology within a Post-Stanislavskian Theatre," in *Faithful Performances: Enacting Christian Tradition*. Eds. Trevor A. Hart and Steven R. Guthrie (Burlington, VT: Ashgate, 2007), 52.
94. Brook, *The Empty Space*, 95.
95. Ibid., 88, 89.
96. Ibid., 71.
97. Ibid., 58.
98. Ibid.
99. Ibid., 59.
100. Ibid., 96.
101. Ibid., 9.
102. Fiachra Gibbons, "The Prayers of Peter Brook," *The Guardian*, Sunday 17 January 2010. Accessed June 14, 2012. http://www.guardian.co.uk/stage/2010/jan/17/peter-brook-eleven-twelve.
103. Brook, *The Empty Space*, 42.
104. This resonates with Stanislavski's comments regarding the conscious and sub-conscious in chapter 2. However, Brook is after inspiration, not natural emo-tion, and thus the source is not located within the subconscious.
105. Brook, *The Empty Space*, 105, 109.
106. Philip K. Dick, *Do Androids Dream of Electric Sheep?* (New York: Del Rey Books, 1968), 64–65.
107. Brook, *The Empty Space*, 10.
108. See Brook 14, "the Deadly Theatre approaches the classics from the viewpoint that somewhere, someone has found out and defined how the play should be done."
109. Brook, *The Empty Space*, 124.
110. Ibid., 138.
111. Ibid.
112. Ibid.
113. Ibid., 139–140.
114. See Ibid., 11.

115. Ibid., 133.
116. Ibid., 12. See also 103.
117. Ibid., 63.
118. Ibid., 89.
119. "To seek to 'hang on to' the past is to lose the past and to betray the future." Lash, 55.
120. Brook does not explain precisely what he means by the Invisible in *The Empty Space*. Max Harris attempts to identify what Brook could mean in a way that would be compatible with Barth's theology in *Theater and Incarnation*, 123.
121. Harris might well contest this claim, or at least find it quite problematic from a Barthian frame. See Harris, 123–128.
122. Brook, *The Empty Space*, 42.
123. See Linda B. Selleck, *Gentle Invaders: Quaker Women Educators and Racial Issues During the Civil War and Reconstruction* (Richmond, IN: Friends United Press, 1995). Selleck notes that during Reconstruction, some white Friends were reluctant to welcome black Christians into meeting, out of fear that they would sing (180).
124. Brook, *The Empty Space*, 65.
125. Harris identifies Brook's ideal of Holy/Rough Theater as incarnational, arguing that its roots lie "in the Christian drama of the Middle Ages." Harris, *Theater and Incarnation*, 101.
126. Harris's *Theater and Incarnation* emphasizes the incarnation within a theological framework deeply influenced by Barth and a theatrical framework deeply influenced by Brook. However, he does not specifically take up Barth's ecclesiology, which defines church as the activity of God in the Holy Spirit, so he does not address the degree to which church is, or ought to be, incarnational.
127. Harris, 112.
128. Ibid., 128.
129. Ibid.
130. See Matthew Boulton, "'We Pray by His Mouth': Karl Barth, Erving Goffman, and a Theology of Invocation," *Modern Theology* 17:1 (January 2001), 68.
131. See Lash, 59. He writes, "fidelity to the past demands that we continually risk change in the present."
132. See chapter 3, especially, concerning Boal and Russell.
133. In this I move in a different direction from Stanley Hauerwas. In *With the Grain of the Universe: The Church's Witness and Natural Theology*, Hauerwas takes up Barth's assertion that the task of church is to witness to God's work in Jesus Christ, and does so in a way that implies audience. Hauerwas presses the degree to which Barth's account of ethics intertwines knowledge of God, witness to God in Christian life, and the truth of the world as "nongodforsaken," that is to say, created and redeemed by God (39). Hauerwas's own argument— which he acknowledges goes further than Barth would—is that "the truthfulness

of theological claims entails the work they do for the shaping of holy lives" (17) The part that might worry Barth in this statement is the implied converse: that holy lives have some part to play in the truthfulness of theological claims. For Barth, God's acts determine truth. If we are fortunate enough to be in the know, we can live in responsive and responsible joy, which Barth calls gratitude. Yet our living does not determine truth. Hauerwas finds this to be an insufficient account of the significance of Christian community. He notes, "Barth, of course, does not deny that the church is constituted by proclamation of the gospel. What he cannot acknowledge is that the community called the church is constitutive of the gospel proclamation" (145). Hauerwas argues, in conversation with the work of Bruce Marshall, that church provides a communal witness to the habitability of a Christian view of the world (214–215). There are also strong resonances with Nicholas Lash's work in Hauerwas's argument. (See Lash, 73). Hauerwas argues that this witness is, itself, part of the gospel proclamation, part of how God cares for the world. Indeed, the care for the world that is the gospel demands that it be comprehensible to the world in some way. Ethicist Ted Smith describes Hauerwas's logic: "Because the Word of God was love incarnate, most itself when it was most for creation, its own nature required that it be comprehensible. For the Word to be the Word, there had to be a bridge across which faith and grace might travel" (Smith 18). This is precisely the kind of thinking Barth rejected in terms of modernist appeals to natural theology. Hauerwas hopes to have a still-Barthian ecclesial ethics by making church the bridge instead of reason, feeling, or some other capacity within the human person. This is, according to Smith, part of the turn to culture that is pervasive in contemporary academics (Smith, 16–18).

The ecclesiology I am proposing here has commonalities with Hauerwas's work. I am influenced by Barth, yet I claim that the specific performances of church matter in important ways, rejecting Barth's refusal to focus on the human activities of church. Further similarities might be seen in Hauerwas's use of performance language and his emphasis on formation in church, which I take up in an essay titled "From Narrative to Performance?" However, I am indebted to both Barth and Brook for an understanding of emptiness that stands in sharp contrast to his view. Church is not what makes God's grace visible in the world. It is, instead, the performance of people hoping to know God in whole-personed ways. It is the performance of people who sometimes are caught up in the action of God's mission in the world, to which the church is a footnote. This is related to the efforts in chapters 3 and 4 to trouble the traditional relationship between actors and audience. Finally, I reject the notion that there is one set audience for church performances, even if that audience is broadly described.

Stanley Hauerwas, *With the Grain of the Universe: The Church's Witness and Natural Theology* (Grand Rapids, MI: Brazos Press, 2001).

Ted A. Smith, *The New Measures: A Theological History of Democratic Practice* (Cambridge: Cambridge University Press, 2007).

134. Lash, 12. Emphasis his.

135. The causes, severity, and implications of this emptiness are much debated. Relevant texts include: Thomas C. Reeves, *The Empty Church: The Suicide of Liberal Christianity* (New York: The Free Press, 1996); Robin Gill, *The "Empty" Church Revisited* (Burlington, VT: Ashgate, 2003); Paul R. Carlson, *The Empty Pew: Why Americans Are Abandoning the Churches* (Denver, CO: Outskirts Press, 2009).

136. Vanhoozer also connects the emptiness Brook speaks of and the emptiness of the tomb. However, he takes this resonance in a different direction, stating, "Doctrine directs the church to fill the empty space with redemptive speech and redemptive action." His emphasis removed. Vanhoozer, *Drama of Doctrine*, 403.

137. Barth, *Epistle to the Romans*, 380–381.

138. Brook, 97

Bibliography

Alexander, Jeffrey C., and Jason L. Mast. "Introduction: Symbolic Action in Theory and Practice: The Cultural Pragmatics of Symbolic Action." In *Social Performance: Symbolic Action, Cultural Pragmatics, and Ritual*. Edited by Jeffrey C. Alexander, Bernhard Giesen, and Jason L. Mast. Cambridge: Cambridge University Press, 2006.

Anderson, Michael L. "Embodied Cognition: A Field Guide." *Artificial Intelligence* 149:1 (2003): 91–130.

Aran Murphy, Francesca. "Hans Urs von Balthasar: Beauty as a Gateway to Love." In *Theological Aesthetics after von Balthasar*. Edited by Oleg V. Bychkov and James Fodor. Burlington, VT: Ashgate Publishing Company, 2008.

Auslander, Philip. "Boal, Blau, Brecht: The Body." In *Playing Boal: Theatre, Therapy, Activism*. Edited by Mady Schutzman and Jan Cohen-Cruz 124–133. London: Routledge, 1994.

Austin, J. L. *How to Do Things with Words*, 2nd ed. Edited by J. O. Urmson and Marina Sbisà. Cambridge, MA: Harvard University Press, 1962.

Barth, Karl. *Church Dogmatics*. Vol. 3, Part 3. Edited by G. W. Bromiley and T. F. Torrance. Edinburgh: T & T Clark, 1960.

Barth, Karl. "Doctrine of God." In *Church Dogmatics*. Vol. 2, Part 1. Translated by T. H. L. Parker et al. Edinburgh: T & T Clark, 1957.

————. "Doctrine of Reconciliation." In *Church Dogmatics*. Vol. 4, Part 1. Edited by G. W. Bromiley and T. F. Torrance. Edinburgh: T & T Clark, 1956.

————. *Epistle to the Romans*. Translated by Edwyn C. Hoskyns. London: Oxford, 1933.

Barton, Stephen C. "New Testament Interpretation as Performance." In *Scottish Journal of Theology* 52, no. 2 (1999): 179–208.

Bauman, Richard. *International Encyclopedia of Communication*, s.v. "Performance." Edited by Erik Barnous. New York: Oxford University Press, 1989.

Beckett, Samuel. *Waiting for Godot: A Tragicomedy in Two Acts*. New York: Grove Press Inc., 1954.

Bell, Catherine. *Ritual Theory and Ritual Practice*. New York: Oxford University Press, 1992.

Benedetti, Jean. *Stanislavski: An Introduction*. New York: Theatre Arts Books, 1982.

Berryman, Phillip. *Liberation Theology: The Essential Facts about the Revolutionary Movement in Latin America and Beyond*. New York: Pantheon Books, 1987.

Bial, Henry, ed. *The Performance Studies Reader*, 2nd ed. New York: Routledge, 2004.

Boal, Augusto. *Games for Actors and Non-Actors*. 2nd ed. Translated by Adrian Jackson. New York: Routledge, 2002.

———. *The Rainbow of Desire: The Boal Method of Theatre and Therapy*. Translated by Adrian Jackson. New York: Routledge, 1995.

———. *Theatre of the Oppressed*. Translated by Charles A. and Maria Odilia Leal McBride. New York: Theatre Communications Group, 1979.

Boulton, Matthew. "'We Pray by His Mouth': Karl Barth, Erving Goffman, and a Theology of Invocation." *Modern Theology* 17, no. 1 (January 2001): 67–83.

Brecht, Bertolt. "Alienation Effects in Chinese Acting." In *Brecht on Theatre: The Development of an Aesthetic*. Edited and Translated by John Willett, 91–99. New York: Hill and Wang, 1957.

———. "The Modern Theatre Is the Epic Theatre." In *Brecht on Theatre: The Development of an Aesthetic*. Edited and Translated by John Willett, 33–42. New York: Hill and Wang, 1957.

———. "A Short Organum for the Theatre." In *Brecht on Theatre: The Development of an Aesthetic*. Edited and Translated by John Willett, 179–208. New York: Hill and Wang, 1957.

———. "Some of the Things That Can Be Learnt from Stanislavsky." In *Brecht on Theatre: The Development of an Aesthetic*. Edited and Translated by John Willett, 236–238. New York: Hill and Wang, 1957.

———. "Theatre for Pleasure or Theatre for Instruction." In *Brecht on Theatre: The Development of an Aesthetic*. Edited and translated by John Willett, 69–76. New York: Hill and Wang, 1957.

Brock, Rita Nakashima and Rebecca Ann Parker. *Proverbs of Ashes: Violence, Redemptive Suffering, and The Search for What Saves Us*. Boston: Beacon Press, 2001.

Brook, Peter. *The Empty Space*. New York: Atheneum, 1987.

Buckley, James J. "Christian Community, Baptism, and Lord's Supper." In *The Cambridge Companion to Karl Barth*. Edited by John Webster, 195–211. New York: Cambridge, 2000.

———. "A Field of Living Fire: Karl Barth on the Spirit and the Church." *Modern Theology* 10, no. 1 (January 1994): 81–102.

Burgoyne, Suzanne. "Engaging the Whole Student: Interactive Theatre in the Classroom." *Essays on Teaching Excellence: Towards the Best in the Academy* 15, no. 5 (2003–2004). Accessed January 28, 2013, apps.carleton.edu/campus/ltc/assets/Engaging_the_whole_student.htm

Burleson, Jacqueline D. *Augusto Boal's Theatre of the Oppressed in the Public Speaking and Interpersonal Communication Classrooms*. Dissertation. Louisiana State University and Agricultural and Mechanical College, Department of Communication Studies, 2003.

Butler, Judith. *Gender Trouble: Feminism and the Subversion of Identity*. New York: Routledge, 1990.

———. "Performative Acts and Gender Constitution: An Essay in Phenomenology and Feminist Theory." In *Performing Feminisms: Feminist Critical Theory and Theater*. Edited by Sue-Ellen Case, 270–282. Baltimore: Johns Hopkins University Press, 1990.

Buttrick, David. *Speaking Parables: A Homiletic Guide*. Louisville, KY: Westminster John Knox Press, 2000.

Calvin, John. "Consensus Genevensis." In *Reformed Confessions of the 16th and 17th Centuries in English Translation*. Vol. 1. Compiled by James T. Dennison Jr. Grand Rapids, MI: Reformation Heritage Books, 2008.

Carlson, Marvin. *Performance: A Critical Introduction*, 2nd ed. New York: Routledge, 2004.

Carlson, Paul R. *The Empty Pew: Why Americans Are Abandoning the Churches*. Denver, CO: Outskirts Press, 2009.

Cavanaugh, William T. *Torture and Eucharist: Theology, Politics, and the Body of Christ*. Hoboken, Oxford: Wiley-Blackwell, 1998.

Cochrane, Arthur C. "Barmen Declaration." In *The Church's Confession Under Hitler*, 237–242. Philadelphia: Westminster, 1962.

Coleman, Monica A. *Making a Way Out of No Way: A Womanist Theology*. Minneapolis, MN: Fortress Press, 2008.

Cone, James H. *Black Theology and Black Power*. Maryknoll, NY: Orbis Books, 1969.

———. *The Cross and the Lynching Tree*. Maryknoll, NY: Orbis Books, 2011.

Connerton, Paul. *How Societies Remember*. Cambridge: Cambridge University Press, 1989.

Conquergood, Dwight. "Performance Studies: Interventions and Radical Research." In *The Performance Studies Reader*, 2nd ed. Edited by Henry Bial. New York: Routledge, 2007.

Copeland, M. Shawn. "Embodying Ethics: Solidarity in Action." Katie Geneva Cannon Lecture. Louisville Presbyterian Theological Seminary. September 23, 2012.

———. *Enfleshing Freedom: Body, Race, and Being*. Minneapolis, MN: Fortress Press, 2010.

Craigo-Snell, Shannon. "Command Performance: Rethinking Performance Interpretation in the Context of *Divine Discourse*." *Modern Theology* 16, no.4. Oxford: Blackwell Publishers Ltd. (2000): 477–478.

———. "Theology as Performance." *The Ecumenist* 16, no. 4 (2008): 6–10.

Craigo-Snell, Shannon, and Shawnthea Monroe. *Living Christianity: A Pastoral Theology for Today*. Minneapolis, MN: Fortress Press, 2009.

Dick, Philip K. *Do Androids Dream of Electric Sheep?* New York: Del Ray Books, 1968.

Djurić, Zoran, Jasna Veljković, and Miomir Tomić. *Psychodrama: A Beginner's Guide*. London: Jessica Kingsley Publishers, 2006.

Douglas, Kelly Brown. *What's Faith Got to Do with It?: Black Bodies/Christian Souls*. Maryknoll, NY: Orbis Books, 2005.

Douglas, Mary. *Purity and Danger*. London: Routledge and Kegan Paul, 1966.

Driver, Tom F. *Liberating Rites: Understanding the Transformative Power of Ritual.* North Charleston, SC: Booksurge Publishing, 2006.

Du Bois, W. E. B. *The Souls of Black Folk.* New York: Dover Publications, 1994.

Duffy, Peter, and Elinor Vettraino, eds. *Youth and Theatre of the Oppressed.* New York: Palgrave Macmillan, 2010.

Dulles, Avery Cardinal. *Models of the Church.* New York: Doubleday, 2002.

Edelman, Joshua. "Can an Act Be True?: The Possibilities of the Dramatic Metaphor for Theology within a Post-Stanislavskian Theatre." In *Faithful Performances: Enacting Christian Tradition.* Edited by Trevor A. Hart and Steven R. Guthrie, 51–72. Burlington, VT: Ashgate, 2007.

Ekman, Paul. "Biological and Cultural Contributions to Body and Facial Movement in the Expression of Emotions." In *Explaining Emotions.* Edited by Amélie Rorty, 73–102. Berkeley: University of California Press, 1980.

———. "Expression and the Nature of Emotion." In *Approaches to Emotion.* Edited by Paul Ekman and Klaus Scherer, 319–343. Hillsdale, NJ: Lawrence Erlbaum Associates Publishers, 1984.

Endean, Philip. "The Ignatian Prayer of the Senses." *Heythrop Journal* 31:4 (1990): 391–418.

Evans, James H. Jr. *We Have Been Believers: An African-American Systematic Theology.* Minneapolis, MN: Augsburg Fortress, 1992.

Feldhendler, Daniel. "Augusto Boal and Jacob L. Moreno: Theatre and Therapy." In *Playing Boal: Theatre, Therapy, Activism.* Edited by Mady Schutzman and Jan Cohen-Cruz, 87–109. London: Routledge, 1994.

Fodor, James, and Stanley Hauerwas. "Performing Faith: The Peaceable Rhetoric of God's Church." In *Christian Existence Today: Essays on Church, World and Living in Between.* Grand Rapids, MI: Baker Books, 1988.

Frei, Hans W. *The Eclipse of Biblical Narrative: A Study in Eighteenth and Nineteenth Century Hermeneutics.* New Haven, CT: Yale University Press, 1974.

———. "The 'Literal Reading' of Biblical Narrative in the Christian Tradition: Does It Stretch or Will It Break?" In *Theology and Narrative: Selected Essays.* Edited by George Hunsinger and William C. Placher, 117–152. New York: Oxford University Press, 1993.

Freire, Paulo. *Pedagogy of the Oppressed.* New York: Continuum, 1970.

Frijda, Nico H. *The Emotions.* Cambridge: Cambridge University Press, 1986.

Gadamer, Hans-Georg. *Truth and Method.* Translated by Garrett Barden and John Cumming. New York: Seabury Press, 1975.

Gallie, W. B. *Philosophy and the Historical Understanding.* New York: Schocken Books, 1968.

Ganss, George E., S. J., ed. *Ignatius Loyola: Spiritual Exercises and Selected Works.* New York: Paulist Press, 1991.

Garrigan, Siobhán. *Beyond Ritual: Sacramental Theology after Habermas.* Aldershot, Hampshire, England: Ashgate, 2004.

————. *The Real Peace Process: Worship, Politics, and the End of Sectarianism.* London: Equinox, 2010.

Gibbons, Fiachra. "The Prayers of Peter Brook." *The Guardian.* Sunday 17 January 2010. Accessed June 14, 2012. http://www.guardian.co.uk/stage/2010/jan/17/peter-brook-eleven-twelve

Gill, Robin. *The "Empty" Church Revisited.* Burlington, VT: Ashgate, 2003.

Gleason, Robert W., S. J. "Introduction to the Spiritual Exercises." In Ignatius Loyal. *The Spiritual Exercises of Saint Ignatius.* Translated by Anthony Mottola, 11–31. New York: Image Books Doubleday, 1964.

Guðmundsdóttir, Arnfríður. *Meeting God on the Cross: Christ, the Cross, and the Feminist Critique.* Oxford: Oxford University Press, 2010.

Goffman, Erving. *Presentation of Self.* New York: Anchor Books, 1959.

Goodwin Heltzel, Peter. *Resurrection City: A Theology of Improvisation.* Grand Rapids, MI: William B. Eerdmans, 2012.

Gorringe, T. J. *God's Theater: A Theology of Providence.* Valley Forge, London: SCM Press, 1991.

Grainger, Roger. *The Drama of the Rite: Worship, Liturgy and Theatre Performance.* Brighton: Sussex Academic Press, 2009.

Grimes, Ronald. *Deeply into the Bone: Re-Inventing Rites of Passage.* Berkeley: University of California Press, 2002.

————. "Performance Theory and the Study of Ritual." In *New Approaches to the Study of Religion: Textual, Comparative, Sociological, and Cognitive Approaches.* Vol. 2. Edited by Peter Antes, Armin W. Geertz, and Randi R. Warne, 109–138. Berlin: Walter de Gruyter, 2004.

Harak, G. Simon, S. J. *Virtuous Passions: The Formation of Christian Character.* New York: Paulist Press, 1993.

Harris, Max. *Theatre and Incarnation.* London: Macmillan Publishers, 1990.

Hart, Trevor A., and Steven R. Guthrie, eds. *Faithful Performances: Enacting Christian Tradition.* Burlington, VT: Ashgate, 2007.

Hauerwas, Stanley. *With the Grain of the Universe: The Church's Witness and Natural Theology.* Grand Rapids, MI: Brazos Press, 2001.

Healy, Nicholas M. "The Logic of Karl Barth's Ecclesiology: Analysis, Assessment and Proposed Modifications." *Modern Theology* 10:3 (July 1994): 253–270.

Hefner, Philip J. "The Doctrine of the Church—Focus and Challenges." In *Christian Dogmatics.* Edited by Carl Braaten and Robert Jenson, 198–199. Vol. 2. Philadelphia: Fortress Press, 1984.

Herzog, William R., II. *Parables as Subversive Speech: Jesus as Pedagogue of the Oppressed.* Louisville, KY: Westminster John Knox Press, 1994.

Hess, Cynthia. *Sites of Violence, Sites of Grace: Christian Nonviolence and the Traumatized Self.* Lanham, MD: Lexington Books, 2009.

Hoekendijk, J. C. *The Church Inside Out.* Edited by L. A. Hoedemaker and Pieter Tijmes. Translated by Isaac C. Rottenberg. Philadelphia: Westminster Press, 1966.

Ignatius of Loyola. *The Spiritual Exercises of St. Ignatius of Loyola*. Translated by Anthony Mottola. New York: Image Books Doubleday, 1964.

Jennings, Willie James. *The Christian Imagination: Theology and the Origins of Race*. New Haven, CT: Yale University Press, 2010.

Jensen, Robert. "You Wonder Where the Spirit Went." *Pro Ecclesia* II/3 (1993): 296–304.

Joh, Wonhee Anee. *The Heart of the Cross: A Postcolonial Christology*. Louisville, KY: Westminster John Knox Press, 2006.

Johnson, Todd E. "Redeeming Performance." *Liturgy*, 28:3 (2013): 17–24.

Johnson, Todd E., and Dale Savidge. *Performing the Sacred: Theology and Theatre in Dialogue*. Grand Rapids, MI: Baker Academic, 2009.Jones, Serene. *Feminist Theory and Christian Theology: Cartographies of Grace*. Minneapolis, MN: Augsburg Fortress, 2000.

Kaye, Candace, and Giselle Ragusa. "Boal's Mirror: Reflections for Teacher Education." Presented at the Annual Meeting of American Educational Research Association. San Diego, CA. April 13, 1998.

Keely, Barbara Anne. "Letty Russell." Talbot School of Theology. Accessed January 29, 2013, http://www2.talbot.edu/ce20/educators/view.cfm?n=letty_russell

Khovacs, Ivan Patricio. "A Cautionary Note on the Use of Theatre in Theology." In *Faithful Performances: Enacting Christian Tradition*. Edited by Trevor A. Hart and Steven R. Guthrie, 45–47. Burlington, VT: Ashgate, 2007.

Lash, Nicholas. "All Shall Be Well: Christian and Marxist Hope." In *Theology on the Way to Emmaus*, 202–215. Eugene, OR: Wipf & Stock, 1986.

———. "Performing the Scriptures." In *Theology on the Way to Emmaus*, 37–46. London: SCM Press, 1986.

———. *Theology on the Way to Emmaus*, 202–215. Eugene, OR: Wipf & Stock, 1986.

Lindbeck, George. *The Nature of Doctrine: Religion and Theology in a Postliberal Age*. Philadelphia: Westminster Press, 1984.

Livingston, James C., and Francis Schüssler Fiorenza. "The Twentieth Century." *Modern Christian Thought*. Vol. 2. 2nd edition. Upper Saddle River, NJ: Prentice-Hall, 2000.

Logan, Joshua. "Forward." In Sonia Moore. *The Stanislavski System: The Professional Training of an Actor*. 2nd ed. xii–xvi. New York: Penguin Publishing, 1976.

MacAloon, John J. *Rite. Drama, Festival, Spectacle: Rehearsals toward a Theory of Cultural Performance*. Philadelphia: Institute for the Study of Human Issues, 1984.

McCall, Richard D. *Do This: Liturgy as Performance*. Notre Dame, IN: University of Notre Dame Press, 2007.

McClintock Fulkerson, Mary. *Places of Redemption: Theology for a Worldly Church*. New York: Oxford University Press, 2007.

McKeehen Louis, Ross. *Critical Performative Pedagogy: Augusto Boal's Theatre of the Oppressed in the English as a Second Language Classroom*. Dissertation. Louisiana State University and Agricultural and Mechanical College, Department of Communication Studies, 2002.

McNaughton, Neil. *Biology and Emotion*. Vol. 5 in *Problems in Behavioural Sciences*. Edited by Jeffrey Gray. Cambridge: Cambridge University Press, 1989.

Madison, D. Soyini, and Judith Hamera. "Introduction." In *The Sage Handbook of Performance Studies*. Edited by Madison and Hamera, xiii–xx. Thousand Oaks, CA: Sage Publications, 2006.

Mangina, Joseph L. "Bearing the Mark of Jesus: The Church in the Economy of Salvation in Barth and Hauerwas." *Scottish Journal of Theology* 52, no. 3 (November 1999): 269–305.

———. "The Stranger as Sacrament: Karl Barth and the Ethics of Ecclesial Practice." *International Journal of Systematic Theology* 1, no. 3 (November 1999): 322–339.

Mathews, Jeanette. *Performing Habakkuk: Faithful Re-enactment in the Midst of Crisis*. Eugene, OR: Pickwick Publications, 2012.

Metz, Johann Baptist. "Communicating a Dangerous Memory." In *Communicating a Dangerous Memory: Soundings in Political Theology*. Edited by Fred Lawrence, 37–54. Atlanta: Scholars Press. 1987.

———. *Faith in History and Society: Toward a Practical Fundamental Theology*. Translated by David Smith. New York: The Seabury Press, 1980.

Metz, Johannes Baptist, and Jürgen Moltmann. *Faith and the Future: Essays on Theology, Solidarity, and Modernity*. Maryknoll, NY: Orbis Books, 1995.

Milling, Jane, and Graham Ley. *Modern Theories of Performance: From Stansilavski to Boal*. New York: Palgrave, 2001.

Moore, Sonia. *The Stanislavski System: The Professional Training of an Actor, Digested from the Teachings of Konstantin Stanislavski*. 2nd ed. New York: Penguin Publishing, 1976.

Morrill, Bruce T. *Anamnesis as Dangerous Memory: Political and Liturgical Theology in Dialogue*. Collegeville, MN: Liturgical Press, 2000.

O'Rourke Boyle, Marjorie. *Loyola's Acts: The Rhetoric of Self*. Berkeley: University of California Press, 1997.

Phelan, Peggy. *Unmarked: The Politics of Performance*. New York: Routledge, 1993.

Phelan, Peggy, and Jill Lane, eds. *The Ends of Performance*. New York: New York University Press, 1998.

Pitzele, Peter. *Scripture Windows: Toward a Practice of Bibliodrama*. Los Angeles: Alef Design Group, 1998.

Pribram, Karl. "Emotion: A Neurobehavioral Analysis." In *Approaches to Emotion*. Edited by Klaus Scherer and Paul Ekman, 13–38. Hillsdale, NJ: Lawrence Erlbaum Associates, 1984.

———. "Feelings as Monitors." In *Feelings and Emotions: The Loyola Symposium*. Edited by Magda B. Arnold, 41–54. New York: Academic Press, 1970.

———. *Language of the Brain: Experimental Paradoxes and Principle in Neuropyschology*. Englewood Cliffs, NJ: Prentice-Hall, 1971.

Reeves, Thomas C. *The Empty Church: The Suicide of Liberal Christianity*. New York: The Free Press, 1996.

Roach, Joseph. *Cities of the Dead: Circum-Atlantic Performance*. New York: Columbia University Press, 1996.

Russell, Letty. *Becoming Human*. Philadelphia: Westminster Press, 1982.

———. *Christian Education Handbook*. New York: East Harlem Protestant Parish, 1966.

———. *Christian Education in Mission*. Philadelphia: Westminster Press, 1967.

———. *Church in the Round: Feminist Interpretation of the Church*. Louisville, KY: Westminster John Knox Press, 1993.

———. *The Future of Partnership*. Philadelphia: Westminster Press, 1979.

———. *Human Liberation in a Feminist Perspective: A Theology*. Philadelphia: Westminster Press, 1974.

———. *Just Hospitality: God's Welcome in a World of Difference*. Edited by J. Shannon Clarkson and Kate M. Ott. Louisville, KY: Westminster John Knox Press, 2009.

———. "Tradition as Mission: Study of a New Current in Theology and Its Implications for Theological Educaiton." Ph.D. Dissertation. Union Theological Seminary in New York, 1969.

Saliers, Don, and Emily Saliers. *A Song to Sing, A Life to Live: Reflections on Music as Spiritual Practice*. San Francisco, CA: Jossey-Bass, 2005.

Saliers, Don E. "Liturgy and Ethics: Some New Beginnings." In *Liturgy and the Moral Self: Humanity at Full Stretch Before God*. Edited by E. Byron Anderson and Bruce Morrill, S. J., 15–38. Collegeville, MN: Liturgical Press, 1998.

———. *The Soul in Paraphrase*. New York: Seabury Press, 1980.

———. *Worship as Theology: Foretaste of Glory Divine*. Nashville, TN: Abingdon Press, 1994.

———. *Worship Come to Its Senses*. Nashville, TN: Abingdon Press, 1996.

Schechner, Richard. *Performance Studies: An Introduction*. New York: Routledge, 2002.

———. *Between Theater and Anthropology*. Philadelphia: University of Pennsylvania Press, 1985.

———. *Performance Theory*. New York: Routledge, 1988.

Schmemann, Alexander. *The Eucharist: Sacrament of the Kingdom*. Translated by Paul Kachur. Crestwood, NY: St. Vladimir's Seminary Press, 1987.

———. *Introduction to Liturgical Theology*. Translated by Asheleigh E. Moorhouse. Crestwood, NY: St. Vladimir's Seminary Press, 1966, 1986.

Schutzman, Mady, and Jan Cohen-Cruz, eds. *Playing Boal: Theatre, Therapy, Activism*. London: Routledge, 1994.

Selleck, Linda B. *Gentle Invaders: Quaker Women Educators and Racial Issues During the Civil War and Reconstruction*. Richmond, IN: Friends United Press, 1995.

Sims, Angela D. *Ethical Complications of Lynching: Ida B. Wells's Interrogation of American Terror*. New York: Palgrave Macmillan, 2010.

Singer, Milton, ed. *Traditional India: Structure and Change*. Philadelphia: American Folklore Society, 1959.

Smith, Ted A. *The New Measures: A Theological History of Democratic Practice*. Cambridge: Cambridge University Press, 2007.

Stanislavski, Constantin. *An Actor Prepares*. Translated by Elizabeth Reynolds Hapgood, New York: Routledge, 1948.

Stoppard, Tom. *Rosencrantz and Guildenstern are Dead*. New York: Grove Press, 1967.

Strine, Mary S., Beverly W. Long, and Mary Francis Hopkins. "Research in Interpretation and Performance Studies: Trends, Issues, Priorities." In *Speech Communication: Essays to Commemorate the 75th Anniversary of the Speech Communication Association*. Edited by G. M. Phillips and J. T. Woods, 181–204. Carbondale: Southern Illinois University Press, 1990.

Taussig, Michael and Richard Schechner. "Boal in Brazil, France, the USA: An Interview with Augusto Boal." In *Playing Boal: Theatre, Therapy, Activism*. Edited by Mady Schutzman and Jan Cohen-Cruz. London: Routledge, 1994.

Taylor, Diana. *The Archive and the Repertoire: Performing Cultural Memory in the Americas*. Durham, NC: Duke University Press, 2003.

Terrell, JoAnne Marie. *Power in the Blood?: The Cross in the African American Experience*. Maryknoll, NY: Orbis Books, 1998.

Thatamanil, John J. "Comparative Theology After 'Religion.'" In *Planetary Loves: Spivak, Postcoloniality, and Theololgy*. Edited by Stephen D. Moore and Mayra Rivera, 238–257. New York: Fordham University Press, 2010.

Tolbert, Mary Ann. *Perspectives on the Parables: An Approach to Multiple Interpretations*. Philadelphia: Fortress Press, 1979.

Townes, Emilie M., ed. *A Troubling in My Soul*. Maryknoll, NY: Orbis Books, 1993.

Turner, Victor. *The Anthropology of Performance*. New York: PAJ Publications, 1987.

Vanhoozer, Kevin J. *The Drama of Doctrine: A Canonical Linguistic Approach to Christian Theology*. Louisville, KY: Westminster John Knox Press, 2005.

von Balthasar, Hans Urs. *Theo-drama: Theological Dramatic Theory*. 5 vols. San Francisco: Ignatius Press, 1988–1998.

Wells, Samuel. *Improvisation: The Drama of Christian Ethics*. Grand Rapids, MI: Brazos Press, 2004.

White, Walter. *Rope and Faggot: A Biography of Judge Lynch*. Notre Dame, IN: University of Notre Dame Press, 2001, orig., 1929.

Williams, Delores. *Sisters in the Wilderness: The Challenge of Womanist God-Talk*. Maryknoll, NY: Orbis Books, 1993.

———. "Black Women's Surrogacy Experience and the Christian Notion of Redemption." In *Cross Examinations: Readings on the Meaning of the Cross Today*. Edited by Marit Trelstad. Minneapolis, MN: Fortress Press, 2006, 19–32.

Wilson, Margaret. "Six Views of Embodied Cognition." *Psychonomic Bulletin and Review* 9, no. 4 (2002): 625–636.

Wolterstorff, Nicholas. *Divine Discourse: Philosophical Reflections on the Claim That God Speaks*. Cambridge: Cambridge University Press, 1995.

Young, Frances. *The Art of Performance: Towards a Theology of Holy Scripture*. London: Darton, Longman & Todd, 1990.

Zarrilli, Phillip B. "For Whom Is the King a King? Issues of Intercultural Production, Perception, and Reception in a *Kathakaḷi King Lear.*" In *Critical Theory and Performance*. Edited by Jannelle G. Reinelt and Joseph R. Roach. Ann Arbor: University of Michigan Press, 2007.

Zizioluas, John. *Being as Communion: Studies in Personhood and the Church.* Crestwood, NY: St. Vladimir's Seminary Press, 1985.

Index of Names

Adams, Marilyn McCord, 158n97
Alexander, Jeffrey C., 153n38
Anderson, E. Byron, 158n5
Anderson, Michael L., 161n80
Antes, Peter, 150n12
Aristotle, 153n44, 164n7, 173–174n36
Arnold, Magda B., 161n61
Augustine, 168n56
Auslander, Philip, 73, 165n26,
  166–168n56, 166n55
Austin, J. L., 5, 18, 92, 149n1, 153n41,
  162n85, 180n61

Barden, Garrett, 154–155n52
Barnouw, Erik, 151n21, 152n35
Barth, Karl, 8–9, 12, 113, 114–124,
  135–144, 149n1, 175n61, 177–178n6,
  177n1, 177nn4–5, 178nn7–24,
  178nn26–31, 179nn32–47, 179nn49–52,
  179–180n53, 180nn54–57, 180n62,
  181nn65–66, 183nn120–121, 183n126,
  183n130, 183–185n133, 185n137
Barton, Stephen C., 150n4
Bauman, Richard, 151n21, 152n35
Beckett, Samuel, 65, 129, 130,
  164n128
Bell, Catherine, 154n47
Benedetti, Jean, 55, 162n89, 162n97,
  163nn104–107, 163n109
Berryman, Phillip, 168n64

Bial, Henry, 151n21, 155n55, 155n57,
  158n95, 163n120, 164n124
Boal, Augusto, 7, 35, 68–75, 78–80, 81,
  85, 88, 153n44, 164nn3–7, 165nn8–21,
  165nn23–35, 166nn49–55, 166–168n56,
  168n57, 168n65, 169nn67–69,
  169n72, 170n85, 174n36, 183n132
Boulton, Matthew, 183n130
Boyle, Marjorie O'Rourke, 160nn38–41
Braaten, Carl, 154n46
Brecht, Bertolt, 4, 8, 90, 97–99, 130,
  153n44, 173nn33–35, 173–174n36,
  174nn37–42
Brock, Rita Nakashima, 173n32,
  175–176n66
Bromiley, G. W., 149n1, 178n8, 178n26,
  179n42, 181n66
Brook, Peter, 4, 8–9, 124–144, 178n17,
  181n67, 181nn69–84, 182nn85–105,
  182nn107–114, 183nn115–118,
  183n120, 183n122, 183nn124–126,
  184n133, 185n136, 185n138
Brunner, Emil, 115
Buckley, James J., 118–119, 121, 178n7,
  178n24, 179n48, 180n53
Burgoyne, Suzanne, 81–82, 169nn70–71
Burleson, Jacqueline D., 82, 169n72
Butler, Judith, 16, 18, 153n38, 153n42
Buttrick, David, 171n110
Bychkov, Oleg V., 149n2

Index

Emptiness, 8–9, 113–144
  Barth and, 114–124
  Brook and, 124–135
  Deadly Church and, 138–139
  Immediate Church and, 141–144
  performing hope and, 135–144
  process for, 130–135
  Rough Church and, 139–141
Eschatology, 83, 107
Eucharist
  as community event, 105–106
  emotion memory and, 62
  multiple roles in, 108–110
  as past, present, and future event,
    106–108
  performance of, 105–110
  political nature of, 107
Event
  in Barth's view of church, 121–122
  as characteristic of performance, 6
  church as, 14, 20–21
  Scripture performance as, 27
Exodus narrative, 95
Expectations of audience, 131–135, 138,
    141–142
Expressivist model of self, 19–20
Exterior penance, 46, 60

Fodor, James, 122
Formation
  Christian, 41–47
  embodiment and, 37
  for performance, 50–58
  performativity and, 31–32
Forum theater, 74–75
Frei, Hans, 26–28, 33
Freire, Paulo, 80–81

Garrigan, Siobhán, 66, 109, 110
Gender identity, 18
Goffman, Erving, 13, 35
Good Friday services, 111

Gorringe, T. J., 12
Grace, 116
Gratefulness, 38
Gratitude, 39
Grimes, Ronald, 13
Grotowski, Jerzy, 4, 126

Habit, 31–32, 47–48, 91
Hagar (biblical), 7–8, 86–87, 94–95
Harak, G. Simon, 37, 47–50, 57, 59,
    60, 92
Harris, Max, 12, 140–141
Hauerwas, Stanley, 122
Healy, Nicholas, 120, 121
Hierarchies of domination and
    oppression, 68
Holy Spirit
  in Barth's view of church, 119, 120,
    122, 124
  church performance and, 5, 145
  Deadly Church and, 135–136
  Immediate Church and, 143
  Rough Church and, 139–140
Holy Theater, 125–127
Hope, 5, 9, 135–144
Hopkins, Mary Frances, 14
Humanism, 114–115
Humility, 142

Identity
  of church, 21
  performance and, 17–18, 19
Ignatius of Loyola, 6–7, 37, 41–47,
    59–60, 61, 92
Image theater, 74
Imagination, 44
Immediate Church, 141–144
Immediate Theater, 133
Improvisation, 12, 30, 32
Incarnation, 8, 129, 141, 183n126
Innovation, 15
Inspiration, 51, 146

CPSIA information can be obtained at www.ICGtesting.com
Printed in the USA
BVOW08s1519130616

451837BV00003B/4/P